T0319429

Appetite
for Innovation

Appetite for Innovation

Creativity and Change at **elBulli**

M. Pilar Opazo

Columbia University Press / New York

Columbia University Press
Publishers Since 1893
New York   Chichester, West Sussex
cup.columbia.edu
Copyright © 2016 Columbia University Press

Library of Congress Cataloging-in-Publication Data

Names: Opazo, M. Pilar (Maria Pilar), author.
Title: Appetite for innovation : creativity and change at elBulli /
    M. Pilar Opazo.
Description: New York : Columbia University Press, 2016. | Includes
    bibliographical references and index.
Identifiers: LCCN 2016006100 | ISBN 9780231176781 (cloth : alk. paper)
Subjects: LCSH: elBulli (Restaurant)—History. | Business incubators. |
    Organizational change. | Creative destruction.
Classification: LCC TX945.5.E44 O63 2016 | DDC 647.95068—dc23
LC record available at http://lccn.loc.gov/2016006100

Printed in the United States of America

c 10 9 8 7 6 5 4 3 2 1

Cover design: Lisa Hamm
Cover image: © Martin Parr / Magnum Photos

To Jose and Amanda
. . . and the little one on his way

❧

Contents

Acknowledgments

J ust as mobilizing newness is not a solitary enterprise, the development of this book was the result of a series of efforts and contributions of many people who helped me move forward. Without their support and advice, this book would simply not have been possible.

My mentors at Columbia University provided great inspiration, encouragement, and advice that shaped my research throughout. I am immensely grateful to my advisor, Peter Bearman, for his great generosity, sharp ideas, and careful guidance. People who visited me at my office were surprised to see three Post-its that I had next to my computer, and which guided my writing: "Have fun," "Pick up flowers," "Think crazy and wild!" Three comments that, in fact, summarized Peter's latest feedback. My conversations with him offered both intellectual stimulation and happiness throughout the entire process of developing this book.

My mentor Diane Vaughan introduced me to the richness of ethnographic work; she encouraged my care for details and the depth of my theoretical analyses. I am deeply indebted to her for her insightful and constructive comments at each step of this process, and for her keen (and often contagious) sense of humor. I am also very thankful to Priscilla Ferguson for her enthusiasm in my project from the very start. Her great knowledge of the sociology of gastronomy and cultural studies was very important in shaping this book. The many conversations that I had with Diane and Priscilla over good food or coffee will become "food rituals" by the time this manuscript is published.

I am also very grateful to David Stark for introducing me to the fascinating "world" of innovation and its connection with organizing and organizations. Conversations at his Center for Organizational Innovation (COI) at Columbia University have played an important role in my research since its very early stages. Finally, the "creative chaos" that emerged from my interactions with Harrison White was highly influential in my work. I hope that this book can reflect, at least in part, the valuable advice that I obtained from each one of them and the privilege of having them as my mentors.

In developing this book, I was fortunate to work closely with Darío Rodríguez and Ramón Sangüesa. Ever since I was an undergraduate student, Darío has not only read everything that I have written (including quite unpolished versions of this book), he has also fostered my sociological imagination in ways that I would never have expected. I am very proud to say that he continues to be my dear friend and mentor to this day. Ramón joined me in many of the adventures involved in this research and was a constant source of positive energy behind my work. I am very thankful for the opportunities he has given me and for all the doors that he has helped me open.

This research was supported by a Fulbright grant and by a grant from the Technical University of Catalonia (#C08505) awarded by Telefónica Digital. I am deeply indebted to Pablo Rodríguez for his constant support and relevant comments at various stages of this investigation, and also to Oriol Lloret, María José Tomé, and Lars Stalling for their continuous encouragement and insightful suggestions. Telefónica Digital provided me with a stimulating space to write while I was in Barcelona and to present my ideas when they were still under development. I am extremely grateful for this.

In the final stages of my project, I had the opportunity to be part of the Mellon Fellowship at the Interdisciplinary Center of Innovative Theory and Empirics (INCITE), Columbia University. I also helped form and joined the Initiative for the Study and Practice of Organized Creativity and Culture (ISPOCC) at the Columbia Business School. The lively dialogues that I shared with these groups greatly inspired this book. In this respect, I am particularly thankful to William McAllister and Damon Phillips for their kind mentorship and constant support.

Friends and colleagues made this book a better one by providing substantive intellectual and practical support. Special thanks to Constanza Miranda for writing with me and for pushing me to search for the unknown; to Consuelo del Canto and Diana del Olmo for accompanying me at all stages; and to Rosemary McGunnigle-Gonzales for the countless phone conversations that we had about my work. Many thanks to Fabien Accominotti for sharing his great knowledge of the art worlds with me and for always being open to discuss new ideas, even if they were largely unrelated to his work. Thanks to Ifeoma Ajunwa, Juan and Jean Capello, Alfonso Cruz, Daniel Fridman, Carmen Gloria Larenas, Federico Leighton, Anna Mitschele, Kristin Murphy, Olivia Nicole, Trinidad Vidal, and Anna Zamora for their friendship and advice at various stages of this book. My foodie friends, Michael Nixon and Naja Stamer, read earlier drafts of the chapters and gave me comments when I much needed them. Thanks to Adriana Freitas for our long walks in Barcelona, and to Laia Sanchis for offering me a wonderful place to stay. The help of Katie Kashkett and Deanna Villanueva significantly improved this book by incorporating their editorial skills into this project, for which I am extremely grateful. Special thanks to Patricia Yagüe for making this a fun project by introducing her design skills into it, and for stimulating many creative sparks that are part of this book. Finally, my conversations with Dora Arenas during my coffee breaks provided much inspiration and joy to my otherwise lonely days of writing.

I am enormously grateful to Ferran Adrià and the elBulli team, and to each one of my respondents for being generous and curious enough to contribute to my research and, ultimately, to make it happen. My gratitude also goes to two anonymous reviewers at Columbia University Press for their insightful readings of an earlier manuscript and for their helpful and inspiring comments and criticisms.

Last but not least, I want to thank my family, and the love of my life, Jose. My dad, Eduardo Opazo, was the first to encourage me to contact elBulli, and he later read successive drafts that kept pushing me forward. My mother,

Maite Bretón, was always there for me to talk about my work, and in doing so, she brightened (and continues to brighten) each one of my days. My sisters Magdalena and Maite greatly contributed to this book by engaging in active discussions about my ideas while they were still being cooked. My husband, Jose, has been my companion in every step of this process and my greatest source of inspiration and love. *Jose, tú eres el motor de mis sueños.* I dedicate this book to him and to our daughter, Amanda, who recently arrived to transform our lives when we thought that things could not get any better.

Appetite
for Innovation

Introduction

T he backstage view of one of the world's most intriguing restaurants looked like perfectly organized chaos. In elBulli's kitchen, more than forty cooks coordinated in almost seamless ways to prepare a menu of thirty to forty courses that would be served that night, one of the last nights of the elBulli restaurant's existence. On one side of the large kitchen, two head chefs were working on something that looked like a big balloon covered by a thin, white membrane. And, on the other side, an apprentice made small spheres and later dropped them with a spoon in a yellowish liquid. At the kitchen's center was Ferran Adrià, elBulli's chef and co-owner. Rather than supervising the cooking process, however, Adrià was insistently making notes and diagrams in several documents that were spread out on the bar and on a wooden table next to the kitchen. Supposedly, this is also where Adrià sat at least twice a week to test the consistency of elBulli's menu. By the time of my visit, Adrià had already announced the unusual decision to close his successful restaurant to build a new research center for innovation under the name of "elBulli Foundation."

As I watched how this scene unfolded, I tried to make sense of what I was seeing. While a diner would probably have remarked on the meticulous preparation involved in each of elBulli's "magical recipes," from a sociological perspective, I was most intrigued by those seemingly insignificant yet systematic actions that make an organization's production of innovation possible.

I knew that in the last decades, elBulli and Adrià had not only created new food preparations, they had also become a key driving force behind the establishment of a new movement in the gastronomic field,[1] often interchangeably called molecular, techno-emotional, or experimental cuisine by the mass media. Years earlier, along with Chefs Heston Blumenthal from Fat Duck, Thomas Keller from French Laundry and Per Se, and Harold McGee, who has written seminal books on the topic of science and cooking, Adrià had published a statement in the newspaper, *The Guardian*, advancing the principles of a "new cookery." This approach, he announced, proposed culinary innovation in the form of new techniques, equipment, and new information in general, while building on the conventional knowledge of gastronomy.[2] By the time of my visit to the elBulli restaurant, Adrià and elBulli's presence was so significant in the gastronomic landscape that many chefs who were at the top of the culinary rankings had been trained in elBulli's kitchen.

Further, by then anyone familiar with the latest trends in fine dining would know that, from 1997 to 2011, the elBulli restaurant had received the coveted recognition of three Michelin stars; and it had been declared the Best Restaurant in the World for an unprecedented five times by *Restaurant Magazine*, another influential culinary ranking. It was also common knowledge that interested diners would wait for years to be able to eat at elBulli. Roughly two million people wrote an e-mail every November to ask for a reservation at the restaurant, but only 8,000 diners got to eat there every season.[3] The level of exclusivity at this restaurant seemed simply impossible in practice.

In some way, I had experienced this extreme exclusivity myself. In 2007, after six years of waiting, my parents received an e-mail offering them the opportunity to dine at this acclaimed restaurant. Months in advance, they had planned their vacation so as to drive from Madrid, where they lived at that time, all the way up to Cala Montjoi, the natural reserve in the province of Girona, Catalonia, where the elBulli restaurant is located. While in my home country, Chile, I remember receiving pictures of them sitting at one of the tables in the restaurant's terrace, just a few steps above the beach, ready to start their meals. Back then, the food being served looked indeed quite intriguing, at least to the eyes of an outsider. As my mother said when she described one of the dishes that she had that night: "It was like an edible gold brooch . . . but one that exploded in your mouth while you were eating it!" Despite the restaurant's beautiful location and how stimulating the food was purported to be, back then I could not stop wondering how it was possible for reservations at a restaurant to be in such high demand, or for that matter, why potential clients would wait for years to be chosen to dine there. What was it about this restaurant elBulli? What was its secret?

By the time of the restaurant's closure in 2011, it had also become unbelievably competitive for culinary professionals to work at elBulli as unpaid interns or apprentices. Every year 3,000 highly trained professionals from all over the world applied for a slot as a *stagiaire*, but only thirty or so were accepted. Part of the difficulty of getting a position at elBulli derived from the fact that the restaurant was open only six months a year, in order to dedicate the other six months to experimentation and creativity. Allegedly, this closing period enabled the restaurant to fully renovate its menu each year, presenting ever more exotic and ingenious creations to customers season after season. As a result, just as interested guests could not predict whether they would be chosen to dine at the elBulli restaurant, they were also not permitted to select what they wanted to eat once they had arrived there.

The mystical aura around elBulli was continuously reinforced by accounts of the restaurant's leader, Ferran Adrià. For over a decade, the mass media has portrayed him as a genius, a visionary, and a sorcerer of cuisine. And, beyond cuisine, Adrià has been frequently compared to icons of creativity such as Salvador Dalí and Pablo Picasso. With no English skills, Adrià has traveled all over the world giving talks about innovation and creativity; and without holding a college degree, he had stepped into the academic world as the keynote speaker of a course being taught at Harvard University called Science and Cooking. After the first iteration of the course in 2010, the number of students who wanted to enroll in the class was so great that a lottery had to be designed to determine who would get to participate. Thus, just as at the elBulli restaurant, students were not able to predict whether they would be chosen to be part of the class or whether they would have to try their luck during a subsequent year.

Months prior to my visit to elBulli in 2011, Adrià had announced the transformation of his mysterious restaurant into a think tank of creativity, which would reopen in 2015.[4] Yet, when reading about elBulli's reinvention from my office at Columbia University, I had realized that there was something puzzling about this new organization too. Despite my efforts, I hadn't been able to understand what the elBulli Foundation was going to be about—an interesting fact in itself. And when searching the Internet, I had come across the vast amount of historical records and detailed accounts of elBulli's creations, which, for the most part, were made available by the organization itself. In fact, I would later recognize these records when observing Adrià's preparation of one of his restaurant's final meals.

Curious about all this and with the intuition that there was much to be learned from the workings of elBulli from a sociological and organizational perspective, I prepared a two-page document describing my interest in conducting research at elBulli. I sent it that same week to the elBulli team. To my surprise, I seemed to be among the lucky ones, because a few days later I received a reply that said something like this: "Thanks so much for your e-mail on Ferran [Adrià's] behalf. We find your project interesting and we would like to know what we can do to help."

In my first encounters with Adrià and his team, I tried to explain to them my interest in studying elBulli as an organization whose experience could inform practices undertaken by other organizations concerned with the production of innovation. I would soon find out that the moment I had chosen to conduct my research was particularly fortuitous, given that my fieldwork was going to take place precisely when the organization was undergoing its most radical transformation and elBulli's members, especially Adrià, were themselves questioning and evaluating the structures that sustained the organization's operation.

Later, when I started collecting narratives from professionals in the gastronomic field both connected and unconnected to elBulli, I noticed that, like the mass media, many of them used expressions such as "genius," "visionary," or "God-like" to describe Adrià's qualities. Many of my interviewees, for instance, intimated that they believed Adrià "was able to see more than others can see" and attested to this by pointing out his "magical" or "extraordinary" capacities to create. As a sociologist, however, I was not interested in examining the psychological features of Adrià's personality, or in writing a biography that detailed his personal life (which is in fact already available for interested readers). Instead, my goal was to consider elBulli as a case that can expand our knowledge of how innovation can be enacted by an organization and, in so doing, provoke changes in the larger system of which it is part. Accordingly, Adrià's personal beliefs or motivations were interesting to me only as long as they unveiled aspects of the role played by a charismatic leader in sustaining innovation over time.

ElBulli was able to mobilize changes in the culinary field for over two decades, as we will see—changes that gradually percolated into other fields such as design, science, and technology. New culinary techniques and concepts developed by elBulli such as foams, frozen airs, spherifications, and deconstruction increasingly made their way into haute cuisine kitchens around the world. And, by the time the restaurant closed, elBulli had already entered people's homes by marketing "molecular gastronomy kits" that offered the opportunity to introduce elements of elBulli's cuisine into everyday meals. In addition to cooking techniques, organizational practices pioneered by elBulli had also spread into the high-end restaurant sector. Several recognized avant garde restaurants around the globe, for example, now have test kitchens or cuisine laboratories of their own, and also close for a definite period of time so as to fully dedicate their staff's energy to creativity.

How was it possible for a restaurant in the middle of nowhere to reach and have an impact upon the world that resided outside it? How did a self-taught cook with no English skills come to be recognized as an international icon of creativity and innovation? In some way, elBulli has managed to stay creative for several years and continued to captivate the public's attention during its periods of intermission. This book analyzes the process through which this occurred, not only by illuminating the underlying factors that explain Adrià's "visionary" capacities but also, and most importantly, by examining the processes and dynamics that enable an organization to produce systematic and radical innovation.

My investigation will make clear that while many good ideas may emerge from random creative sparks or from an individual's talent, the relentless production of innovation cannot be explained only by this. The research will show that innovation that is able to enact changes in a field is rather the result of concrete and collective practices that make it possible for new knowledge to be understood, recognized, and legitimized by the public. The experience of elBulli will illustrate that institutionalizing innovation involves the construction of an organizing structure that is able to win the support of a coherent group of people that helps to disseminate and maintain a new cause.

To understand the processes behind elBulli's production of innovation, I examined the organization's history and the different factors, both internal and external to the organization, that enabled it to become an avant garde restaurant, and that allowed Adrià to be recognized as a worldwide icon of innovation. Tracing the organization's past, as we shall see, was critical in understanding the organization's present, as it offered possibilities to identify the patterns that explain elBulli's growing trajectory. Moreover, instead of limiting my analysis to the internal workings of elBulli, I examined the organization's interaction with the wider context of its operation, what organizational scholars refer to as the "institutional environment." This involved including the views of people who had directly witnessed the inner workings of elBulli and, therefore, could provide me with insights regarding what was distinctive about the organization. It also required the inclusion of the perceptions of people who were not connected to elBulli and, hence, who could tell me about how the organization was able to reach and influence outsiders.

Given that the culinary field is multidisciplinary, I gathered narratives from a wide variety of participants in the contemporary gastronomic industry in two different yet interconnected sites: Spain and the United States, mainly Barcelona and New York, cities considered culinary hubs. My interviewees included current and former members of elBulli, elBulli purveyors and collaborators, and former elBulli apprentices, most of whom were chefs at renowned restaurants at the time of my interviews. I also collected narratives of elBulli's outsiders including gastronomic critics, chefs, faculty members of culinary institutes, and food scholars. During my fieldwork, furthermore,

I attended gastronomic conferences and events advertised as platforms organized for chefs and by chefs, and had exclusive access to the elBulli workshop and to original documentation while the new foundation was being constructed. For a detailed account of the data collected and the subjects who participated in the study, please refer to the Appendix.

In this book, readers will find that while words like "visionary" or "sorcerer" have been repeatedly used to describe the personality of elBulli's leader, the organization's methods for developing innovation are far from incidental. Rather, plenty of purposeful action is involved in making innovations effective within the organization and recognized by those outside it. As is the case with every organization, at elBulli, specific practices were mobilized on the ground in order to reach the world outside its boundaries and, thereby, to consolidate its reputation within its field.

Ultimately, this book represents a journey into a puzzling organizational model that pushes itself to its limits. Readers will notice that, unlike other organizations engaged in the development of innovation, elBulli is not concerned with the production of final products or services, but with encouraging permanent processes of discovery. For this reason, rather than reproducing successes, elBulli chooses to continue to innovate. To do this, the organization built a dynamic structure to sustain innovation over time. This study offers a close look into the vision of this innovative organization, and the social arrangements that were generated to make this vision effective in reality. It explains the internal and external practices that were at play in the workings of elBulli, and that eventually mobilized the entire reinvention of the organization itself.

My work expands on existing accounts written about elBulli and Adrià in a number of ways. First, it constitutes an extensive analysis that goes beyond the organization's limits (and of its leader's individual capacities) to understand its functioning. It also expands sociological studies of haute cuisine by providing a new window of observation into the development of innovation in the gastronomic field, from the late twentieth century to the beginning of the twenty-first century. This is important, given that the culinary landscape has undergone significant changes in the last few decades. Among these is a new role for chefs in society, a phenomenon usually called celebrity chefs—a category in which Adrià is considered an iconic figure. Moreover, nowadays recipes and culinary experiences at restaurants are widely circulated throughout the Web by food professionals, food bloggers, and food aficionados alike. Cuisine, thus, has become a topic prevalent in society, manifested in the growing number of TV shows related to food and the increasing number of books and magazines that focus on cooking from different perspectives. By providing an in-depth analysis of one iconic organization in the contemporary culinary landscape, this book offers a peek into the inner world of chefs, and thereby into some of the dynamics that encouraged the gastronomic revolution that has taken place over the last two decades.

Finally, this investigation proposes a new way to think about innovation that extends beyond the production of new ultimate products. Too often, innovation is examined by looking at an organization's final outcomes (such as patents) and by analyzing the conditions that lead to those outcomes. The major concern of this book, instead, is to show *how* innovation can be systematically mobilized in and by organizing systems. In doing so, it attempts to unveil the concrete practices that enable new ideas to have a sustained impact upon a wider population.

The structure that I chose to organize the book reflects the different processes involved in the enactment of radical innovation, from envisioning and implementing, to socializing and legitimating. Chapter 1 sets the groundwork for understanding the origins of elBulli's new ideas, and retraces the historical development of the organization prior to starting to propose new ways of doing things in cuisine. Chapter 2 examines the inner functioning of the organization by looking at how the vision of one individual was adopted by a group of creators who were all working toward a common goal. It also examines how teams, time, and space were managed at elBulli, and how the crafting of a "language," accompanied by systematic documentation, became a central mechanism for sustaining innovation within the organization.

Chapter 3 deals with the social dynamics that made it possible for elBulli's "new cuisine" to be understood and recognized by the gastronomic community. It describes the vehicles that were generated by the organization to stabilize a new basis of knowledge within its field. Chapter 4 examines the unintended consequences of the relentless production of innovation, its connection to the closure of the elBulli restaurant, and the need for the organization's reinvention.

Finally, Chapter 5 engages with the ongoing construction of elBulli's new organization, the elBulli Foundation. The transformation of the restaurant is used here as an opportunity to test and refine the practices found to explain the organization's innovative capacity—from making new recipes, to making new organizational structures to innovate, to making an entirely new organization. The chapter also offers readers the opportunity to explore the uncertainty surrounding elBulli's new project, and the limits of an organization's search for radical innovation and endless reinvention.

In analyzing the case of elBulli as one that can expand our understanding of how innovation works, this book addresses a number of themes that are central to sociology and to the study of organizations in general. On the one hand, it offers a close look into the phenomenon of charisma by examining the organized efforts made to sustain an organization and its leader's charismatic authority. On the other hand, from a methodological standpoint, my investigation can be used as a resource for the study of other extraordinary populations. Sociologists tend to be experts in studying the outcasts or the socially marginalized, but not to interview and study those who are recognized as extraordinary creative minds. Readers who have conducted fieldwork might anticipate that this is not at all an easy task. In my case, my bilingualism was an essential resource that helped me deal with this type of personality, which is often complex and unpredictable, and also to eliminate the mystery around Adrià and his team. On repeated occasions, I found myself speaking quickly and assertively, as I saw them do in their interactions, so as to get my ideas and questions across. Yet it was only when I started to act as a mirror for them (that is, to develop diagrams and maps similar to the ones they did to show how I saw their work) that they started to see me as a different kind of expert and, accordingly, to treat me as an equal and sometimes even as a confidant.

While my research is valuable in the ways indicated above, it also has a number of limitations that are important to outline. First, as a case study, it does not include any exhaustive cross-case comparisons, but only considers the experience of other organizations (such as restaurants) to unveil the specificity of the case under study. Nevertheless, there are numerous universes that, like elBulli, have been a central force in driving innovation within the gastronomic field and in other fields, examination of which would shed light on the findings obtained from this study. Second, given that my goal was to understand *how* elBulli's creations came to be recognized as innovations, the focus of my research is on success. I do hope, however, that my examination of the organization's growth shows that favorable outcomes are neither necessary nor impossible for an organization's development. Third, consistent with the ethnographic nature of my research, the analysis is restricted to the sites selected for the study and does not attempt to be representative of a general population. Thus, this book's objective is not to provide definite answers that can be invariably applied to diverse contexts, but simply to offer insights for future studies and applications of innovation.

One final aspect that shaped this book and that I find important to share is that, during the course of my research, I was in constant interaction with different types of audiences: from academics to business professionals to chefs. While having these different audiences introduced additional complexity to the project, it also provided diverse and insightful feedback that greatly influenced this work. The writing style that I use is a reflection of this process. In my work, I try to avoid jargon as much as possible so as to make my analysis accessible to a wider readership, including people who are familiar with elBulli's story and the maneuverings of the gastronomic field and those who are not, as well as people who are acquainted with sociological theories and empirical approximations and those who aren't. In keeping with this goal, I use copious quotations, pictures, and diagrams in the hope that they will better convey the richness of the world that I encountered while doing fieldwork. I also present a recipe of elBulli at the opening of each chapter. These recipes retrace the historical development of the organization, and illustrate central arguments made throughout the book. In the end, I hope my study will provide readers with an opportunity to enter the workings of a mysterious organization, and to realize that if one looks closely enough, things might not seem that mysterious after all.

0.1 and 0.2 (*top*) Ferran Adrià at his restaurant, and (*bottom*) elBulli's terrace during the restaurant's last week of operation; Cala Montjoi, Roses, Catalonia, Spain.

A Brief Note on the Meaning of Innovation

Innovation has become a fashionable term, widely used across disciplines and industries. Yet the widespread use of the term has rendered its meaning largely ambiguous. As a result, the term *innovation* is often used interchangeably with similar-sounding concepts such as change, entrepreneurship, or creativity. While there is a thin line that distinguishes all these terms, it is important to clarify it for the purposes of this investigation.[5]

Innovation is not equivalent to change; innovation corresponds to the *capacity to drive change.* Any living system, an individual or an organization, is in constant transformation and evolution. Living systems cannot avoid change. Innovation, however, does not refer to inevitable, innate change. It involves the *purposeful action* of mobilizing change. As such, it implies a decision-making process through which uncertainty is turned into risk, risk that comes with the responsibility of having decided.[6]

Like innovation, entrepreneurship is the capacity to drive the development of a given enterprise. Yet, while entrepreneurship is typically associated with business activities, the management of risk that characterizes innovation may or may not be oriented toward making a profit. In this sense, innovation represents a broader term that incorporates, but is not restricted to, entrepreneurship.

Finally, innovation is not equivalent to creativity. Creativity refers to the envisioning of original ideas, whereas innovation corresponds to the process through which new ideas are developed and implemented in practice.[7] This distinction is important as it implies that not every creative process will necessarily lead to an innovation. Innovations must have a social impact and be recognized by a community. Therefore, even if there might be plenty of creativity involved in the creation of, say, a new mobile device, a new delivery system, or a piece of art, these products and services are not innovations unless they have an effect upon a given audience.

The distinctions among these three terms are important for recognizing the case of elBulli as one that can expand our knowledge of how innovation works. The evolution of elBulli was marked by a series of turning points that led it to become a famous, avant garde restaurant. While some of the decisive moments in this organization's development were intentionally conceived of or enacted by the organization, others were mainly the result of external circumstances. However—and here comes the organization's agency in *enacting change*—these defining moments were actively mobilized or reinterpreted decisions that were made by elBulli, mainly by Adrià. Further, they were defined as decisions that coincided with or strengthened the organization's ultimate goals.

In relation to the notion of entrepreneurship, in which every restaurant is in essence a for-profit venture, activities associated with creativity at the elBulli restaurant, which Adrià and his team conceived of as the core activity of the organization, were gradually decoupled from business activities. Consequently, the functioning of the elBulli restaurant per se was not directly associated with turning a profit. In fact, in its initial stages, the restaurant was not making enough money to pay its staff and, after gaining external recognition, the restaurant by itself was losing half a million euros per year. Adrià considered profitability and creativity to be two distinct sides of the same body and used the metaphor of Robert Louis Stevenson's famous novel, *Dr. Jekyll and Mr. Hyde*, to explain the relationship between the two. Accordingly, during elBulli's evolution, mechanisms were actively developed to keep profitability and creativity separated while, at the same time, nurturing each other.[8]

Ultimately, Adrià and his team were not solely idea men, but innovators. As we shall see, the knowledge and practices that elBulli developed somehow managed to trickle down from the isolated mountains of Cala Montjoi to be used and expanded by professionals around the world.

Lobster Gazpacho, #45 1989

© Franscesc Guillamet Ferran

Serves 4 people

To prepare the boiled lobster:

2 750-g (1.5-lb) lobsters
Salt

To prepare the base of the gazpacho:

500 g (2 cups) of boiled lobster
    water (above elaboration)
1 young 65-g (2.5-oz) spring onion
4 cloves of garlic
1 70-g (2.5-oz) red pepper
1 small cucumber
25 g (5 tsp) of Jerez vinegar
26 g (1 oz) of toasted pine nuts

To prepare the lobster gazpacho:

Main gazpacho (above elaboration)
Basil oil (prior elaboration)
60 g (1 cup) of not-entirely-
    whipped cream

Final touches and presentation:

1. Put all the brunoised vegetables in a bowl with a pinch of salt and olive oil, enough to make the vegetables stick together.

2. Make a vegetable quenelle with two spoons, and place it in the center of a plate.

3. Around it put 5 slices of lobster and 1 pincer.

4. Then add 2 stuffed cherry tomatoes and 2 stuffed spring onions.

5. On top of the vegetable quenelle, put a pinch of chervil and 2 stems of chives.

6. Add 2 pieces of toast with basil oil and 8 cucumber sticks distributed in pairs.

7. Finish the dish with 5 slices of padron pepper.

8. Finally, put the gazpacho, very cold, in a jar or in a tureen to be served by the waiter.

(Abbreviated for purposes of illustration.)[1]

1

Context and Vision

One Day at the elBulli Restaurant

The first commandment in a kitchen is not disturbing the work . . . so if you want to see how we function, you need to become invisible.

— Ferran Adrià at elBulli restaurant, Spain

The trip to Cala Montjoi, the natural reserve where the elBulli restaurant is located, involves a seven-kilometer drive on a thin road up from a town called Roses in Girona, Costa Brava, Catalonia. The deep blue color of the sea can be seen at the end of every corner of the road, occasionally interrupted by Mediterranean-style houses. During the restaurant's busy season, Adrià lives in one of those houses, just in front of the elBulli restaurant. Back in the 1980s, when Adrià first joined the restaurant, going to elBulli was literally an adventure. As one of my interviewees recalled, "The road had no pavement; you literally had to break your car to be able to have a meal there." Once arrived at the bay of Cala Montjoi, it is possible to distinguish a sign with printed letters that say "elBulli." It is common for tourists around the area to stop by and take a picture next to the sign. A stone stairway separates the restaurant from the beach. When I arrived there I could see three of elBulli's apprentices, *stagiaires*, wearing their chefs' coats, staring at the gentle movement of the sea. They were not talking or interacting with each other in any way. Rather, it looked as if they were mentally preparing themselves for what was about to come. It was the end of July 2011. On short notice, Adrià had allowed me to come to the restaurant to observe the work performed during the restaurant's final season.

At the entrance, there was a figure of a bulldog in gray and yellow, representative of the restaurant's name, elBulli. David Lopez, a member of the staff in charge of IT tasks and who also performed front-of-the-house tasks, took me through the main corridor that leads to elBulli's dining area. The restaurant's innovative and cutting-edge image stood in stark contrast with its old-fashioned interior decorations: reddish cushions and curtains, chairs with floral tapestry, lights that simulated candles, and random pictures of different sizes in different frames. It seemed ironic that avant garde food was being served there. I caught a glimpse of Adrià walking from one side of the corridor to the other. He was wearing a white chef's coat, black pants, and Nike shoes, and he was agitatedly talking on his mobile phone.

As was customary with elBulli's guests, I was first taken to the kitchen. It was a large kitchen, 340 square meters in size, illuminated by natural light that filtered through a big glass wall. At the front, the kitchen had a big sculpture of a bull's head. I could count around forty cooks, only three of them women, working on different tasks. I was not introduced in any formal way. In fact, nobody seemed to notice my presence, even though I was insistently taking notes and photos of what they did. I immediately recognized Oriol Castro, one of elBulli's heads of cuisine and director of the creative department, an additional kitchen station that functioned all year in conjunction with the restaurant's productive tasks. Next to Castro was Mateu Casañas, head of the "sweet world" or pastry station, and Eduard Xatruch, another head of cuisine, responsible for shopping tasks and relationships with purveyors. They were all very serious, working on some preparation with one of the apprentices. Adrià came into the kitchen explaining how especially hectic this week was; journalists from all around the world wanted to come to the restaurant, Adrià asserted, and he already had several interviews scheduled for that same day.

At exactly 2:00 P.M. Castro said, "Good morning, everyone, could you pay attention, please?" The brigade of cuisine rapidly lined up along the walls of elBulli's kitchen, roughly resembling a military formation. In a matter of ten minutes, and at a very fast pace, Castro explained the main issues that needed to be addressed that day. He first pointed out what went wrong the day before: "It is important to be a 'person.' If someone asks you something, you need to respond. If you don't want to, then you should leave. It is as simple as that. First and foremost, we need to be teammates and 'persons' with each other." Then Castro proceeded to explain the menu that was going to be served that day, paying special attention to the incorporation of a new dish, which he described as the elBulli restaurant's final creation: Peach Melba, the last dish of elBulli. Castro indicated that the new dish was inspired by a recipe created by Auguste Escoffier, the father of modern French cuisine, given that the number of this dish, 1846, coincided with Escoffier's birth year. He also pointed out that the dish would incorporate an old culinary concept created by elBulli, deconstruction, and a new one that the team had been developing in the last years and which aimed to advance a new presentation of dishes in the form of "sequences." Castro carefully detailed each of the ingredients, preparations, and plating involved in the new dish, using terms like "lyophilized peach seeds," "frozen molds," and "bitter almond oil":

> We'll start to do the 'Peach Melba.' Begin by preparing the lyophilized peach seeds. There are two peach seeds: the mold of frozen cotton with toasted almond and amaretto and the one with peach liquor. You freeze it and remove it from its mold.... Leave it in the small wooden box with a hint of bitter almond oil....
>
> (Field notes, Oriol Castro, head chef of elBulli's kitchen and creative director)

Castro spoke so fast that I found it difficult to follow what he was saying. He then concluded the meeting by explaining how the Peach Melba was going to be incorporated into the menu:

Yesterday we served it to a few tables, today we'll serve it to fifteen tables and on Tuesday to another fifteen. On Friday and Saturday [the last days of the elBulli restaurant's life] it will be fully incorporated into the menu.

(Field notes, Oriol Castro, head chef of elBulli's kitchen and creative director)

In a matter of seconds, the line of cooks split apart and each one of them retreated to a specific position to start working. I stayed in the kitchen, observing how the mise en place for that night's meal was being set up. Adrià walked the kitchen, interjecting clear-cut orders to elBulli's heads of cuisine. Using a yellow pencil that he had tucked behind his right ear, Adrià quickly checked the different documents, including the menus that were going to be served that night, lists of ingredients and preparations, or the recipes of the staff's "family meal," usually served at 6:30 P.M., before the clients' arrival.

At 4:00 P.M. I went to the dining room where the wait staff would gather. There were fourteen young men and women who were waiters and sommeliers' assistants. Juli Soler, co-owner of elBulli, was there too, wearing sandals, shorts, and a black t-shirt. The head of the dining room, Luis Garcia, started the meeting by reminding his staff that the diners who were visiting that night had made reservations up to eight months in advance and, most likely, had planned their vacations around the opportunity to eat at elBulli. The staff needed to make their best effort to offer customers "the most memorable meals of their life," Garcia said. "We need to make them feel comfortable and natural. Make people slowly fall in love with us. All our effort must go in between lines." This remark, though it would go unnoticed by me at that point, would later emerge as the fundamental pattern that characterizes the elBulli organization's efforts to mobilize a "new cuisine." Garcia also reminded the staff that the director of the Royal Spanish Academy of Gastronomy was coming that day to give elBulli's members a special recognition, so they needed to adjust their schedules "to make everything work to perfection." During the meeting, members of the wait staff actively shared their opinions about the service provided the night before.

Castro, head of the kitchen staff, explained to the waiters (again in exactly ten minutes) the ingredients, preparations, and serving modality of the dishes that were being prepared and, specifically, of the new and last dish of the elBulli restaurant, the Peach Melba. "We served it to a few tables yesterday and the result was magic," he told the wait staff. Castro provided great detail about each of the items that comprised that night's menu, clearly distinguishing between creations that were extended versions of dishes served in prior years, transformations or combinations of previous dishes, or completely new dishes. Along with the description of each dish, Castro specified the year in which it had originally been created, the "flashbacks" that inspired them, the exact way in which each dish was meant to be eaten by the diner (e.g., in one or two bites), and how it should be served (e.g., in a spoon or some other kind of dinner service, finished at the table or in the kitchen).

When the meeting was about to end, Juli Soler pointed out, laughing, "Look who is here, the kid, the kid!" It was Albert Adrià, Ferran Adrià's brother, who had worked at elBulli since he was fifteen years old, after dropping out of high school, and had left in 2008. Now he was running restaurants in Barcelona, including Tickets and Bodega 1900, with his brother Ferran as his business partner. For many years, Albert had been a central driving force of elBulli's creativity, and he continued to be associated with everything that elBulli did. "I wanted to show my friends elBulli," Albert said in a very casual way. His brother came to greet him from the kitchen. He seemed very happy and surprised to see him.

In the kitchen everything was being set up for that night's dinner. Noise came exclusively from the movement of cooks, who diligently formed small groups, worked on some preparation, and then split apart to continue working on something else. They did this for hours, mimicking a well-oiled machine. Oftentimes, cooks used the word *quemo* (the Spanish word for burning) to notify others when they were holding something that required caution. As Lisa Abend described in her detailed account of the inner workings of elBulli's kitchen, this word was employed as an umbrella term to coordinate the highly international crowd that composed elBulli's brigade de cuisine.[2] During the rest of the afternoon I took notes and photographs of the work within the kitchen and talked informally with members of elBulli's team, trying to remain invisible, as Adrià had indicated to me when I first came in.

Before going to the elBulli restaurant, I had been told that I needed to leave after the mise en place had been set up, a rule that is maintained to ensure the privacy of the diners. Yet, when I was about to leave, Adrià reached out to me and said in an almost unintelligible way, "Hey, this is just a glimpse for you to get an idea of what we do! . . . Understanding elBulli is very complex . . . there are years of history . . . there is too much to explain."

1.1 and 1.2 (*top*) From left to right: three stagiaires outside elBulli restaurant before the start of a working day, and

(*bottom*) Ferran Adrià in the elBulli restaurant's kitchen reviewing the orders to be prepared that night, July 2011.

1.3 Meeting of the kitchen staff at elBulli restaurant, July 2011.

Pyramid of Creativity: Ferran Adrià's Vision of Innovation

A restaurant is a chef's skin.

—Personal interview, chef and owner of haute cuisine restaurant, United States

In the organizations literature, restaurants have been described as "individual-business models" typically built around a chef or restaurateur's goals and vision.[3] In this sense, considering Adrià's internal drive and beliefs is very important in understanding the workings of his organization. As elBulli's leader, Adrià's motivations are likely to reveal relevant aspects of how innovation was enacted by his organization over time and of the role that he played in shaping the organization's development. One haute cuisine chef in New York City supported this interpretation, saying that restaurants are the medium through which a chef expresses his creativity. A restaurant is a reflection of a chef in the same way as your skin is a reflection of who you are, he remarked. Trying to separate the two is impossible, as they are two sides of the same unity:

> ElBulli is who Adrià is. You wear your skin. Adrià wears his skin, which is elBulli, and I wear mine. This is something that is not selected. It is something that you grow into. It is something that you are, that lives with you, grows and evolves. As you get older, your skin changes, but it's always a reflection of who you are [as a creator].
>
> (Personal interview, chef and owner of haute cuisine restaurant, United States)

The binding connection between the role of chefs and restaurants has also been pointed out in academic studies of haute cuisine that consider the chef–restaurant dyad (as opposed to only one or the other) as a main unit of analysis in examining institutional change.[4] This chapter describes Adrià's vision of innovation and explores how this vision illuminates the central beliefs and motivations that were decisive in shaping the organization's development. As a sociologist, my intention is not to explore the psychological mechanisms that explain an individual's beliefs, but to understand the relationship of these beliefs with the social system to which they are associated.[5] In this case, it is the elBulli organization. A brief overview of the organization's historical trajectory will lay the groundwork for the subsequent examination of the concrete practices that enable the mobilization of radical innovation. This preliminary analysis will suggest that vital aspects of the production of innovation are left unexplained if we look only at an organization's new ultimate products or final invention stages. Instead, the development of radical innovation emerges as an unfolding *process* that is built through intertwined movements across different patterns of creation.

Over the years, Adrià's beliefs of innovation acted as a powerful force that mobilized and shaped the entire elBulli organization. Informed by more than thirty years in gastronomy, Adrià developed a metaphor to explain his vision of innovation, which he calls "the pyramid of creativity." This metaphor identifies four different modes of innovation—reproduction, evolution, combination, and conceptual creativity—each of which represents an increasing disposition to novelty.

(1) Reproduction. This is the least innovative mode of creativity, as it corresponds to the replication of an existing culinary creation. It is the culinary mode of novice cooks, who follow a recipe, deviating little. This method of creation is very similar to the act of copying, yet, given that circumstances change, the end result also tends to differ every time a recipe is executed. Adrià situates this mode of creation at the bottom of his creative pyramid due to the lower level of inventiveness and originality that it requires.

(2) Evolution defines minor changes introduced to existing products (e.g., recipes) that are conducive to a novel overall outcome. A good example of this in the culinary world is the incorporation of a new ingredient into a traditional elaboration. Adrià explains this by using the example of introducing tomato sauce into a traditional Italian dish of pasta, which gave rise to a completely new output, namely the recipe known as Spaghetti Pomodoro. In this case, the novelty of the outcome tends to be a by-product of the circumstances, such as creativity emerging from encounters between different culinary cultures.

(3) Higher on the scale of creativity, Adrià situates combination, which identifies the rearrangement of old and new elements (products, technologies, preparations, or styles) into new formats. Novel combinations in cuisine may emerge from the discovery of new cooking products (e.g., a new herb, seaweed, or powder), merged with the incorporation of new equipment into the kitchen (e.g., sous-vide water oven, a Pacojet machine to thicken liquids, or a food dehydrator), new sources of inspiration (e.g., nature, childhood memories, sense of humor) or even through exposure to entirely new genres of cooking (e.g., Asian cooking, Mediterranean cooking, or avant garde cooking). This notion coincides with traditional conceptualizations that define innovation as the combination of old and new ideas as well as the blending of knowledge across disparate domains, a conception originally derived from Schumpeter's 1934 account of innovation as the "carrying out of new recombinations." According to Schumpeter, recombinant innovations range from the creation of new goods to new methods of production, or even entirely new markets. Over the years, this recombinant conception of innova-

tion has been expanded in multiple directions and used to explain creative dynamics in a wide variety of contexts, ranging from the emergence of good ideas among business groups, to the invention of cellular phones, medical devices, and fashion jeans, to the production of Web designs by new media firms, to name just a few examples.[6]

(4) At the apex of his pyramid Adrià places conceptual creativity. He identifies this as the search for new words and sentences aimed at expanding the repertoire or language of a given community. For Adrià this mode of creativity in gastronomy primarily involves the active quest for new *concepts* and *techniques* with the capacity to expand and enrich a given culinary language. For instance, revolutionary cooking techniques incorporated in haute cuisine in recent years include rapid freezing through the use of liquid nitrogen and gelation via the use of alginates. Examples of cooking concepts are deconstruction (breaking apart traditional dishes), "vegetal cuisine" (situating vegetables as the main focus of a dish), and adaptation (positioning established culinary styles into new contexts).

The fact that Adrià places conceptual creativity at the apex of his pyramid says a lot about the actual development of his organization, elBulli. For Adrià, being innovative entails nothing less than producing the highest degree of novelty possible, and, in his view, this is achieved by the invention of new cooking concepts and techniques. Accordingly, elBulli's ultimate goal in creating, unlike many other restaurants, is not simply to develop something that brings pleasure to clients or to generate new flavor combinations.[7] For elBulli, providing a pleasurable experience (in the gustatory or aesthetic sense) is only one condition that the restaurant's culinary creations seek to fulfill. Rather, elBulli's ultimate goal in creating is to develop something that can produce breakthroughs of knowledge in the field—something that elBulli's members and other culinary professionals have never seen before and which, therefore, needs to be invented.

ElBulli's emphasis on the generation of new culinary concepts and techniques, as opposed to new dishes or recipes per se, responds precisely to the importance that Adrià assigns to mobilizing radical knowledge in his field.

Culinary techniques and concepts have a higher potential for the production of novelty in gastronomy, both from a quantitative standpoint (by offering the possibility to develop infinite numbers of new dishes or culinary creations) and from a qualitative standpoint (by proposing new ways of doing things both within the organization and in the culinary field at large). Based on his experience and intuition, Adrià has developed an example to explain the significance of creating new techniques and concepts in gastronomy through the popular Spanish preparation of the potato omelette:

> One day, someone had the idea of making an omelette [new technique]. It is likely that someone simply broke a couple of eggs in a frying pan and thought, 'What is this!?' . . . but later on, someone else had the idea of making a round omelette . . . then, to add tomato, onions, parsley, or whatever else was at hand. . . . The French omelette was invented! . . .
>
> With this [new technique] one can make thousands of different omelettes! But if it hadn't been for the first one, all the rest would not have been possible!
>
> (Public talk given by Ferran Adrià as part of the tour "Partners for Transformation" with Telefónica Company, November 2011, Argentina)

Another example commonly used by Adrià to explain the relevance of conceptual creativity is the creation of puff pastry, a relatively simple culinary technique that nonetheless makes it possible for the user to produce incredibly complex results. The technique of puff pastry creates a simultaneously soft and crispy texture that can be used in dishes both sweet and savory. It is possible that Adrià's focus on conceptual creativity might have derived from modern French chefs who regarded cooking essentially as a repertoire of culinary techniques and not of products.

From an analytical standpoint, Adrià's conceptualization unveils an important distinction in examining innovation. Unlike final products, the significance of culinary concepts and techniques relies on the fact that they are portable in essence, whereas dishes or recipes—especially highly idiosyncratic ones—might not be. Recipes are tied to the materiality of food and typically to the context of restaurants, whereas culinary concepts and techniques can be removed from their context of creation and applied to a wide variety of situations. As a result, the potential of concepts to trigger changes is greater because they can lead to developments that can be undertaken and reproduced by other actors in the system.

Let me explain this further by proposing an analogy within the music industry. Culinary techniques are to chefs what rules of harmony are to musicians.[8] Just as mastering the underlying harmonies of music enables musicians to create and reproduce songs, knowing a repertoire of culinary techniques makes it possible for chefs to generate endless numbers of food compositions. Note here the difference between the rules of harmony and the final tunes that may result from them. Sociological studies of jazz performance, for instance, have highlighted that it is this formulaic character of music that ultimately explains the ability of musicians to perform together proficiently, even if they have never played together in the past.[9] Knowing the rules that support the development of final compositions enables practitioners to effectively navigate their way through songs they might have not heard before and also to extend known songs in new directions. Something similar happens in dance. As expressed by the famous New York choreographer Twyla Thwarp, "the more technique you have, the more freedom you can have as a dancer and the better performer you can be."[10]

This distinction between final products and new concepts and techniques— what I call conceptual innovations—also applies to the development of innovation in fields like art or technology. Creating a new painting or sculpture is different from generating new conceptual developments that, in some cases, may give rise to entirely new artistic movements. Impressionists, for example, developed a number of new artistic concepts and techniques (such as the use of thick brushstrokes, tubes of paint, pre-prepared canvases, and observations made outdoors) that aim to depict modern life in more direct and powerful ways. This set of conceptual innovations, in turn, promoted a revision of old paradigms and a shift in artistic taste. Prior to the Impressionist movement, only mirror-like images of reality were counted as art, and any deviation from this was considered erratic or unskilled.[11] Similarly, the new rules behind Cubism enabled its creators, Pablo Picasso and Georges Braque, to develop multiple pieces of artwork of different kinds, and later evolved into an avant garde movement that was joined by other artists in the early twentieth century, and even extended to other fields such as literature, architecture, and music.

Another example can be found in the technology industry, specifically, in Apple Inc. and its charismatic cofounder, Steve Jobs. There is a difference between this company's production of new final products (or improved versions of those products), say Mac computers, iPhones, or iPads, and the generation of new technological concepts with the capacity to offer endless possibilities of creation within the company and for other companies in the technology industry. Examples of these new concepts might be the notion of a personalized computer or a smartphone that functions based on software applications and the use of a touch screen. The underlying conceptual and technological developments behind these inventions are what I call *conceptual innovations*. At Apple, the development of innovation is aimed at offering users a "new technological experience," not new technological devices per se—much in the same way the elBulli restaurant's goal was to offer customers a new culinary experience and not merely the opportunity to taste new dishes or representations of food.

Finally, within academia, scholars seeking to advance a line of knowledge in any given discipline might generate several or even hundreds of final products during their careers (e.g., academic papers or books as analogous to a restaurant's dishes or recipes). These ultimate products, in turn, may play an important role in building the academics' status and reputation within their fields. Yet it is possible that only a few of those final products (or perhaps none of them) advance a concept or method that the academic considers truly groundbreaking and, as such, able to serve as a platform for the generation of numerous final products (again, academic papers or books) developed either by him or by other members in his scholarly community. Conceptual innovations, therefore, are different from the outcomes that might result from them.

As in the fields of music, dance, art, technology, or academia, in cuisine, concepts and techniques can be easily detached from final food compositions and applied to a wide variety of contexts, irrespective of the chef's particular background and culinary preferences or the diners' local tastes. In this sense, techniques and concepts represent stronger cultural markers that can be borrowed from one culinary paradigm for another while still sustaining their independence from each other. This is what happened, for example, between the classical and nouvelle cuisine movement in the 1970s. While exploiting their foundation in classical techniques, nouvelle cuisine chefs like Paul Bocuse, Michel Guérard, Roger Vergé, Alain Chapel, and Pierre and Jean Troisgros advanced a new set of conceptual developments (such as greater simplicity in recipes, the use of fresh ingredients, and imagination) that distinguished their work from existing conventions. What is most interesting about elBulli in this respect is that, following Adrià's vision, the organization's main goal is to constantly rebuild and expand the existing repertoire of concepts and techniques that supports the craft of cooking.

To better understand elBulli's vision of innovation, however, it is important to understand the dynamics of the culinary field. Especially since the 1980s, haute cuisine's French identity has been challenged by its increasingly global scale. A number of culinary approaches have started to gain prominence in the culinary field, such as the slow food movement, the farm-to-table movement, and more recently, the Nordic cuisine movement, just to mention a few examples. The experimental or "molecular cuisine"[12] movement in which elBulli and Adrià are recognized as a key driving force is another culinary approach that achieved recognition at the turn of the twenty-first century. Like other movements in haute cuisine, however, the experimental approach encouraged by elBulli did not involve the total replacement of old paradigms. That is to say, the gastronomic field did not experience a totalistic shift toward elBulli's new culinary vision; nor did Adrià and his team detach themselves from classical or modern styles of French cookery such as those developed by Chef Antonin Carême and later by George Auguste Escoffier. Yet this does not mean that we should underestimate its importance. In the course of mobilizing a new cuisine, elBulli was able to establish a new basis of knowledge, mobilize supporters, and get that knowledge recognized within and beyond its field, all while being declared "the most influential restaurant in the world" by the time it closed in 2011.[13] It did so, I will argue, not only by recombining existing creations, but also, and most importantly, by mobilizing a new set of knowledge and epistemic practices that enacted changes in the paradigmatic ways of doing things in haute cuisine.

Conceptually, the approach proposed by elBulli differed from nouvelle cuisine chefs in its approximation of innovation. While nouvelle cuisine chefs used new technologies to do things better or faster, their approach to cooking remained bound to new representations of food. Following the principles that had guided the invention of Modern French cuisine since the nineteenth century, especially post-Carême, the work of nouvelle cuisine chefs continued to focus on pleasing customers through the presentation of enjoyable food. The work of elBulli and Adrià represented a paradigm shift in this respect insofar as it proposed a change in focus from new representations of food to the development of conceptual innovations. To put it simply, elBulli aimed to take creativity to an extreme by offering the interested public not merely new dishes, but new concepts with the potential to present opportunities to think differently about food, sometimes even at the expense of pleasure.

Moreover, unlike classical French conceptions in which discoveries are generated while creating a meal, at elBulli the act of discovery is a goal in itself. The meal is essentially defined by the creator and is ultimately aimed at opening the guests' palates and minds to novel possibilities. While the importance that elBulli assigns to process is also a feature of other culinary approaches, such as those that emphasize the authenticity of food, what is distinctive about elBulli is that its efforts deviate more and more from food to instead enter a conceptual realm. ElBulli's understanding of innovation, then, is not associated with extension or improvement, but with the notion of *invention*.[14] Accordingly, the organization's objective is not to relentlessly produce innovative products, nor to indefinitely rearrange combinations that have proven successful. Instead, elBulli's ultimate goal is to encourage *permanent processes of discovery* with the capacity to shift the rules that shape a field.

One could say, therefore, that a voracious appetite for radical innovation is the kernel of Adrià's vision, and, as we shall see, it is also the key characteristic that permeates every aspect of the elBulli organization. Whereas typically an entrepreneur would advance the development of a new enterprise by carefully examining potential competitors and associated risks and by gathering information on the existing expectations that the new product could fulfill, in directing elBulli, Adrià takes a quite different approach. ElBulli is managed by devoting the largest amount of energy and time to the advancement of conceptual developments that can introduce changes in the typical ways of doing things. Once having achieved this, elBulli's members then think about the ways in which the invention—a new concept or technique—can become accessible to and accepted by a relevant audience in the form of final outcomes, such as dishes or recipes. From elBulli's approach, then, the management of expectations operates in the reverse way: They come from the mind of the creator or group of creators and are subsequently transmitted to the public. Stemming from this way of reasoning, Adrià and his team strive to get to that instant in which they *know* that they have found something truly new. In this process, uncertainty is not a problem for the organization. On the contrary, members of elBulli are constantly looking for ways to encounter uncertainty, because their experience has shown them that this is where radical novelty comes from. Rather than being afraid of uncertainty, the elBulli team, and especially Adrià, are afraid of getting locked into reproducing modes of creativity—copying their own creations or others', or continuing to recombine existent creations—as this would mean that they have fallen into what Adrià considers inferior modes of creativity, such as that of novice cooks or recombinant cooks, a category with which elBulli does not want to identify.

In short, for Adrià and elBulli, creativity is not a matter of food, eating, or liking something; it is a matter of expanding the repertoire of words that compose the culinary language. To explain Adrià's desire for radical novelty, which later spread across his team, a member of elBulli mentioned something that occurred during the filming of the documentary *ElBulli: Cooking in Progress*, produced by a German film company and released in 2011. There is a very special moment in that movie, elBulli's member noted, a moment that only people who know Adrià well would be able to recognize. Adrià is used to being around cameras; he does not even notice them by now. Hence, during the entire process of filming the movie, he did not look at the cameras at any time—except for one moment. It is a moment in which Adrià is in the kitchen and Oriol Castro gives him something to try that he has been testing for the new menu. In that instant, only for a few seconds, Adrià looks straight at the camera because he has *seen* something and his excitement is such that he disregards everything else around him. Adrià cares only about that instant of the process in which he realizes that he has found something "[radically] new." Then, the elBulli member concluded, "over the years Adrià's zeal for getting to this moment has been distilled within a group, yet it is Ferran [Adrià] who has driven all of us toward this end. The demanding work required to get to this 'spark' or 'click,' is what he wants never to diminish at elBulli. He wants [this spark] to remain forever."

In this book, I identify two different types of innovation (final products and conceptual innovations) according to the degree to which they can enact changes within the larger system. By doing this, I do not mean to say that recombinant approaches to innovation are unimportant. In *The Structure of Scientific Revolutions*, Thomas S. Kuhn described how the progress of normal science is marked by the blending of old and new ideas that further articulate the paradigm itself.[15] Accordingly, as we will see, these processes appear to be at play at elBulli, and I repeatedly address them in my study. However, I am most interested in making sense of conceptual innovations, namely innovations that can lead to paradigm shifts or scientific revolutions. While these ultimately affect the production of final outcomes, I will suggest that they do not correspond to it. These are two different yet interrelated types of innovation. Final products such as songs, paintings, sculptures, or recipes may be *reproduced*, *extended*, or *refined* by other actors in the industry, but conceptual innovations are generative in nature and, thus, able to produce a *flux of new ideas* that can lead to the emergence of new paradigms.

Revolution or Evolution? elBulli Restaurant's Historical Development

The elBulli restaurant is widely known for its innovative approach to cooking. Especially from the early 1990s onward, first in Spain and later around the world, haute cuisine chefs and restaurants began to introduce elements of elBulli's distinctive culinary style into their own cuisine. In 2010, Adrià was declared Chef of the Decade by *Restaurant Magazine* and, especially during the last stages of the restaurant's life and even after it closed, elBulli's work started to attract prestigious universities and corporations and to be featured on the cover of well-known magazines from widely disparate fields, including the *New York Times Magazine, Le Monde, Time* magazine, the design magazine *Matador*, and the technology magazine *Wired UK*, to name a few. Although these exceptional characteristics of the elBulli restaurant have been consistently pointed out by the mass media, less attention has been paid to the historical trajectory of the organization and how it started to develop a new set of knowledge and practices that challenged standards of haute cuisine. In fact, elBulli's movement toward becoming an innovative restaurant was an unfolding and intertwined process that extended for decades. Examining the restaurant's development, therefore, can expand our knowledge about the dynamics that characterize an organization's movement from being a mainstream one to being an innovative one within a creative industry—in this case, the culinary industry.

If a restaurant mirrors a chef's inner motivations and beliefs, then Adrià's metaphor of a pyramid of creativity can tell us not only about his personal views of the originality imprinted in a given culinary creation; it can also illuminate the process through which his organization, elBulli, moved from being a mainstream restaurant to being an innovative one within its relevant institutional field, namely other restaurants within the fine dining segment. In effect, building on its leader's vision, it is possible to identify four turning points in the elBulli restaurant's trajectory, each of which follows the modes of creativity proposed in Adrià's pyramid: reproduction, evolution, combination, and conceptual creativity. Quite distinct to Adrià's conception, however, these creative modes appear to be interwoven in the organization's development as opposed to clear-cut steps leading inevitably toward increasing originality. Here I use Adrià's conceptualization as a theoretical tool to briefly retrace the organization's trajectory and to clarify the mixed dynamics that characterized elBulli's seemingly dramatic departure from conventional standards of cooking and, later on, its transition from a restaurant to a research center for innovation (readers already familiar with elBulli's historical trajectory may decide to skip this part and go directly to chapter 2).

As my rotated pyramid of creativity in figure 1.4 illustrates, elBulli's development over time traverses, in interacting ways, the different modes of creativity outlined by Adrià, ending with the organization's extreme focus

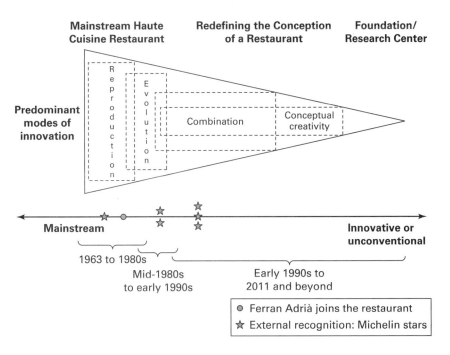

1.4 Rotating Ferran Adrià's "Pyramid of Creativity": elBulli's transition from mainstream to an innovative restaurant in the fine-dining industry.

on conceptual creativity in the present at the elBulli Foundation. The practices that explain the mobilization of elBulli's innovation both within the organization and in the organization's environment are analyzed thoroughly in the next chapters.

Reproduction: The beginnings of elBulli (from 1963 to mid-1980s)

Founded in 1963, elBulli evolved from a mini-golf course to a beach bar managed by a German couple and a few employees to an haute cuisine restaurant.[16] Like the majority of haute cuisine restaurants, elBulli started by following the norms of the dominant, or mainstream, culinary paradigm at that time, French nouvelle cuisine. During this period, the restaurant's creations consisted largely of reproductions of dishes developed by renowned French chefs who were part of this movement. The restaurant also followed the nouvelle cuisine principles by placing special emphasis on the use of fresh ingredients, simplicity in recipes, and presentation, among many others. In 1975, the elBulli restaurant's take on the nouvelle cuisine style of cooking led to the restaurant receiving its first Michelin star, a distinguished recognition in the high-end restaurant sector.

In 1983, Ferran Adrià, a native of Catalonia, joined the restaurant for a temporary internship during his military service. Unlike many haute cuisine chefs, Adrià had not had a mentor who taught him the basics of cuisine nor a family background connected to the restaurant world.[17] Instead, Adrià had started his professional career as a dishwasher in a French restaurant in Castelldefelds, a municipality close to the city of Barcelona. Through this connection, Adrià was encouraged by Miquel Moy, the first chef de cuisine for whom he ever worked, to study and memorize the traditional culinary creations of Spanish cuisine. His initial approximation to the craft of cooking was mainly intellectual rather than practical:

He [Moy] would make me study a book called 'El Práctico' and he would ask me for the dishes and the recipes every morning. After one year, I almost learned all those recipes by heart; from a theoretical stance, not from a practical stance. I had never cooked those recipes. This was very important for me, because classical cuisine was no longer new for me.[18]

Afterward, during his military service, Adrià had the opportunity to teach himself the classics of French cuisine. Being self-taught is different from having no formal training, Adrià emphasized when explaining his professional background.[19] When assigned to work in the army kitchens of an admiral, and after becoming head chef, Adrià had the opportunity to prepare a different meal every day and, in doing so, exhaustively studied and replicated classical French recipes. So, by the time Adrià joined the staff of the elBulli restaurant in the early 1980s, he was already familiar with the culinary paradigm that had for a long time governed haute cuisine—a body of knowledge that the elBulli team would exploit up until the last day of the restaurant's existence. During Adrià's first years at elBulli, and in collaboration with the restaurant's team, Adrià deepened his gastronomic knowledge in ways that followed prior culinary developments. Thus, at this stage the elBulli restaurant's primary mode of creation was based on reproduction. Things, however, soon started to change.

Evolution: "Creativity means not copying" (from mid-1980 to early 1990s)

A new phase in the elBulli restaurant's life began when Adrià became head of cuisine in 1984, which happened almost accidentally. As explained by one of my informants, after the former head of elBulli's kitchen suddenly decided to leave the restaurant, Juli Soler, manager of elBulli, asked Adrià if he was "enthusiastic enough and brave enough" to take the position. Adrià said yes. The first thing that Soler did was take him to France to experience firsthand the latest culinary creations developed by the gastronomic avant garde. During this trip to France, Adrià became familiar with the work of renowned vanguard chefs such as Pierre Gagnaire and Michel Bras. One gastronomic critic suggested that Adrià's experience in France was crucial for encouraging creativity at elBulli. It helped him to realize that there were "other worlds out there which could be introduced into elBulli's cuisine," he asserted.

In 1987 Adrià attended a talk given by Chef Jacques Maximin, who defined creativity in a way that Adrià would remember as especially significant in his career: "Creativity means not copying." With greater decision-making capacity at the restaurant due to his new position as head chef, and building on an in-depth knowledge of existing classic and modern culinary developments, Adrià guided the organization toward a new mode of creativity: the adaptation of established culinary approaches into new contexts. In this case, the context was the elBulli restaurant and its Mediterranean style of cooking. Unlike previous culinary approaches undertaken by the elBulli team, this approach challenged the conventions and principles encouraged by French cuisine. It did so mainly by introducing local ingredients and preparations that up to that point had not been incorporated into haute cuisine. An example of a dish from this period is one created at the elBulli restaurant in 1989 called Lobster Gazpacho (#45), the recipe presented at the opening of this chapter. This recipe included a classic ingredient used in haute cuisine (i.e., lobster) accompanied by a popular Spanish preparation, gazpacho, a tomato-based cold soup originally from the southern region of Andalucía. Interestingly, the modality chosen for serving the dish was an exact reflection of the underlying creative process that gave rise to it: When brought to the table the dish would appear to the eyes of the diner to be a conventional lobster salad. Waiters would then pour the gazpacho in the salad to finish the dish. Only then, knowledgeable diners, familiar with the standards of French haute cuisine, would be able to appreciate the innovation involved in the recipe produced at elBulli by the introduction of local ingredients and preparations. What about less knowledgeable diners? They would still be able to experience the greatness and magic of a dish cooked to perfection, Adrià would say.

In sum, during this period, the primary mode of creativity employed at elBulli resonates with the second phase in Adrià's scale of creativity—evolution—yet it strongly built on the mode of creativity that preceded it, reproduction. To be sure, the elBulli team took the most immediate environment as a source of inspiration (in this case, Mediterranean gastronomy) to bring new knowledge into their cooking, and then incorporated local culinary customs into the dominant culinary paradigm of French cuisine.

The dynamics of innovation revealed in this stage of elBulli's trajectory is aligned with those proposed by Burt in his study of innovation in business groups.[20] As the recipe Lobster Gazpacho illustrates, intersecting otherwise disconnected worlds can indeed lead to good ideas—in this case to good dishes—that extend the inventory of new final products produced by an organization. But this dynamic does not explain how a new set of ideas and epistemic practices are mobilized and get recognized in order to stimulate changes in the ways of doing things within a field.

A second star awarded to elBulli by the Michelin Guide in 1990 justified the creative reorientation undertaken by the restaurant. Also in 1990, Adrià's decision-making power at elBulli expanded further when, together with his partner Juli Soler, he became owner of the restaurant, elBulli S.L. A book entitled *The Taste of the Mediterranean* synthesized the organization's initial efforts to develop a distinctive style of cooking.[21] When I talked with Adrià about this stage of his organization more than two decades later, he said to me: "We could have kept doing the Mediterranean style forever. Even today there are chefs in Spain that still do that. But we didn't. I don't really know why." He paused for a few seconds and then stated firmly, "Well . . . we got bored. That's why."

ElBulli's attempts to continually rebuild the organization's creative repertoire, however, were not just due to boredom. As subsequent chapters will show, these attempts were primarily driven by the team's eagerness to generate conceptual innovations that could alter the norms that shape the gastronomic field and, equally important, by Adrià's concern with maintaining the restaurant's standing as a charismatic, avant garde restaurant.

Combination: Recombining existing and newly developed creations (late 1990s to 2011)

The elBulli team's search for a unique style of cooking intensified during the following years.[22] Mainly from the late 1990s onward, elBulli developed a number of concepts and techniques that enabled the team to start combining the organization's own repertoire of knowledge with existing ideas in novel ways. As we will see in detail in the following chapters, examples of new culinary techniques implemented at elBulli during this period are foams, airs, and spherifications (small caviar-like spheres of liquids); and examples of new concepts are deconstruction and minimalism, or the incorporation of "snacks," or "avant desserts," as a new item on the menu of a fine-dining meal. Another innovation pioneered by elBulli at this stage was the removal of the traditional à la carte menu, first instituted by Escoffier in 1899, and its replacement with a tasting menu, which radically altered the fine dining experience: At elBulli, now only the chef would decide what customers would eat. While there were other haute cuisine restaurants that had tasting menus, completely eliminating the à la carte menu was a change mobilized by elBulli, especially among Michelin-starred restaurants. One former member of elBulli recalled how this change occurred in practice. It was a complex process that involved years of negotiations, until Adrià came to a final decision:

> I remember that when the menu was definitively eliminated in 2002 we had to write a letter to the Michelin [guide] explaining why we were going to do that. Indeed, because one of the rules of the Michelin guide was that there should be a menu from which the customer could choose his meal. And at elBulli, suddenly, customers were not allowed to choose anymore. . . . We had to maintain the menu for three years, because the Michelin [guide] could not decide whether this was a positive thing or a negative thing. . . . But the moment came when Ferran [Adrià] said: 'we are going to take the menu out because when a client asks for the menu it breaks the rhythm of the

kitchen and this is not our way of cooking. This is not what we want to show our clients!'

(Personal interview, chef and former member of elBulli)

As a result, the fine dining meal offered by elBulli began to depart from the conventions encouraged by classical culinary approaches and also the Mediterranean haute cuisine style that the organization itself had developed. Gradually, changes enacted by elBulli started to trigger changes beyond the restaurant and to motivate other actors and institutions in the gastronomic field such as chefs, culinary critics, and ranking systems to rethink their notions of what a meal is and what a restaurant is. In this stage, the organization's primary mode of creativity shifted from being mainly adaptations of prior culinary developments to being *combinations* of old and new developments, yet again, while still maintaining a strong basis in the knowledge that the organization had previously acquired. One chef from New York City summarized the shifts enacted by elBulli in standard conceptions of a fine dining meal as follows:

> Twenty years ago, anything larger than [a] six- or seven-course meal would be quite a foreign idea, whereas now that is not so foreign [an] idea doing twenty, thirty, plus courses. [ElBulli also influenced in] scaling things down; now you can serve one bite and call it a course. Delivery systems; not everything needs to be eaten with a fork and knife, not everything needs to be served on a plate. Sometimes a course can be a liquid, something you drink. Sometimes something that you normally drink can be a salad!
>
> (Personal interview, pastry chef of haute cuisine restaurant, United States)

By stretching the boundaries of fine dining, the elBulli restaurant worked to redefine the rules of the game that, up until then, had dominated haute cuisine.

In one century from Escoffier to Robuchon, the measure of a chef was to make one thing, one style, perfect. And everyone made the same style in all the best restaurants in the world. . . . Okay, that is one century to make the same food.

Now, you have ten years, right? And everything changes. Because now, there is something called 'new technique,' not 'existing' technique. So whatever you call it, it just changed the whole thing. It changed the entire game.

(Personal interview, apprentice at elBulli, chef and owner
of haute cuisine restaurant)

Arguably in recognition of its culinary innovations, the elBulli restaurant received a coveted third Michelin star in 1997 and was declared the Best Restaurant in the World by *Restaurant Magazine* for an unprecedented five times between 2002 and 2009. Broadly, these awards represent the social recognition obtained by the restaurant in the gastronomic field. While these dynamics reveal a pattern of creation that is no longer limited to the development of new final products, it still represents recombinant innovation in a normal science framework. As we shall see, the strategy of recombining old and new developments to innovate will persist all through the organization's development. However, the last years of the elBulli restaurant's life were marked by a growing emphasis on generating *inventions* that could lead to a paradigm shift in cuisine.

Conceptual creativity: A new culinary language (mid-1990s to 2011 and beyond)

Already in 1994, elBulli's team had made the exploration of new culinary techniques and concepts a primary concern of the organization. Adrià and his team emphasized a conceptual approach to cooking by searching for new words that could expand the language of cuisine. Several transformations enacted within the organization during this period support this claim: the consolidation of a system of documentation as a basis for innovating, the incorporation of a development station as an additional yet leading kitchen station within the restaurant, and the creation of a research and development laboratory working alongside the restaurant during the off-season. Importantly, at the time of their implementation, these organizational arrangements were at odds with the conventions of the high-end restaurant industry. In general, these changes incorporated into the functioning of elBulli demonstrate the organization's incremental movement toward Adrià's utmost mode of creativity—conceptual creativity—driven by the systematic study of gastronomy. Like the other modes of creativity, however, this mode actively built on and exploited the foundations of knowledge that had previously supported the organization's development.

The most obvious manifestation of this conceptual reorientation is elBulli's transformation in 2011 from a restaurant into a think tank called the elBulli Foundation. Whereas one might think that the main goal of a restaurant is to provide a pleasurable dining experience to customers, the elBulli Foundation's main goal is to become "a place of reflection through cooking." As stressed by Adrià:

> In high-end cuisine, the big difference that elBulli has made is that before people cooked for others to like what you do; we [instead] cook to create. [We cook] for you to have an experience, regardless of whether you would like it or not. It is an experience; the incorporation of provocation, of sense of humor, all these in the meal, is something that is not normal in cuisine. . . . We have transformed elBulli in a place of reflection through cooking.
>
> (Personal interview, Ferran Adrià, chef and owner of elBulli)

In sum, when we apply Adrià's vision of innovation to examine the historical trajectory of elBulli we find that, quite distinct from what Adrià's pyramid would predict, elBulli's development was not the result of the replacement of one pattern of creation by another. Rather, elBulli's evolution was defined by a continuous rearrangement of different orders developed both by the organization and by other actors in the industry. The organization then encouraged its own development by actively building on and challenging the existing knowledge and practices of its field. Therefore, like all organizations, elBulli's attempts to innovate cannot be understood in abstraction from its concrete framework of operation, as they represent alterations of that framework.[23] As Harrison White reminded us of in his book *Identity and Control*, identities (in this case organizations) are built from both structure and fresh action.[24] Getting action in an orderly world does not involve a clearly differentiated movement from one domain to another, but the *fluid crosscutting across preexisting orders*. ElBulli's purposeful actions involved in generating and stabilizing a new basis of knowledge are the major themes of this book.

Existing Knowledge as a Starting Point

There is one additional aspect that is important to highlight in order to fully understand the historical trajectory of the elBulli restaurant. The process of developing innovation in haute cuisine appears to be strongly attached to the foundations of knowledge that support the gastronomic field. As claimed by a Michelin-starred chef in Spain, "if one wants to do something new, one needs to know what has been done and have an understanding of the basics and what is classic. Otherwise you cannot do avant garde cuisine." Another chef confirmed this by saying that being able to bring about culinary magic is by no means a simple task: "You need to know the basic knowledge; otherwise it's just tricks."

In the world of cuisine, there are skills and knowledge that chefs need to acquire for the development of what they call a well-informed "gastronomic criterion," which serves as a basis from which to innovate. They do so by mastering classic and modern culinary techniques, preparations, and styles from which they can build their creativity. Having this solid basis of knowledge is seen by culinary professionals as crucial to the development and appreciation of innovative culinary creations.

As stated earlier, in the case of elBulli, members of the organization had already mastered the standard knowledge of gastronomy before they started to challenge the conventions of their field. The elBulli members' in-depth knowledge of classic and modern culinary approaches is manifested in the several culinary prizes and awards that were given to the restaurant during its initial stages. In this regard, Adrià remembered how in his initial search for originality he had to force himself to put away all the books and notes that, up until then, guided his creative endeavors, as only by doing this would he be able to develop a unique culinary approach. "There is never a rupture when innovating. It is always an evolution, even if it is a revolutionary evolution," Adrià said to me in one of our personal conversations.

The elBulli team's departure from preexisting knowledge and conventions as a basis for moving beyond those conventions was seen by my interviewees, connected and unconnected to elBulli, as a key aspect of the organization's capacity to mobilize changes within its field:

> You need to be a great chef to make these new ingredients properly shine. You need to understand how to draw flavors and bring flavors onto the pedestal that you want to. And then, have fun with these newer ingredients in our pantry where we can now probably manipulate into textures and shapes that we weren't able to do before. . . . They [elBulli's team] were in the right situation.
>
> (Personal interview, pastry chef of haute cuisine restaurant, United States)

> Ferran [Adrià] is a master of the classics foremost, and then he sat down in the creative role. He knows how to use salt first before anything else and that is what a lot of people forget these days. It is the importance of knowing the classics and the basics.
>
> (Personal interview, chef and owner of haute cuisine restaurant, United States)

The above quotations reveal the paradoxical nature of innovation: Innovation is ultimately a matter of professional consensus. It is defined precisely by what it seeks to deviate from and, as such, it exists only when a legitimate group of experts recognizes its value and contribution.[25] My conversations with other professionals in the gastronomic industry confirmed that this dynamic also applies to the development of other crafts such as music or painting.

> Great practitioners throughout history—and it doesn't matter what discipline— are grounded in the classic traditions in history of whatever it is: In music you tend to learn the classical approaches to things when you are learning how to play an instrument. . . . Or painting: Picasso was an expert at pencil

and paper drawing and realistic renderings of objects before he could really delve into cubism. And I think that same is true now.

During the nouvelle cuisine movement, it became clear who were the chefs grounded in classic fundamentals and who weren't, and the same is true with modernist cuisine or avant garde cooking, whatever you want to call what Ferran [Adrià] has been a driver of. There are practitioners out there who are doing all these kinds of neat stuff, and it is not good, because they don't have that basis of understanding, they don't have that depth of knowledge that allows Ferran [Adrià] to be great.

(Personal interview, faculty member of a culinary institute, United States)

More often than not, therefore, breakthroughs emerge out of knowing and exploiting the boundaries of knowledge within a given field. This is especially true if the aim is not only to generate new products but to advance new avenues of knowledge, what elBulli was aiming to achieve. The evidence presented thus far suggests that innovation may be better understood by looking at an organization's adaptive *process* rather than an organization's final outputs or invention stages. When examined in retrospect, overlapping changes may come into view as part of the natural evolution of an organization. However, evidence from elBulli's development depicts innovation as a chain of transformations that are built into both the internal structure of an organization and its network of relationships with external actors and institutions. An organization's transformation occurs as syncopated changes that are intertwined in time and social space, between order and disorder.[26]

ElBulli is what it is because of its stages, because of the vast cultural heritage that it carries. It is an evolutionary process. . . . [ElBulli's] dishes are [just] expressions of a series of innovations that, little by little, provided the foundations for a gastronomic revolution.

(Personal interview, faculty member of culinary school, Spain)

Innovation is not the result of sudden transformations, but of adaptive and purposeful change.[27] It involves the continuous rearrangement of how different orders are intertwined rather than the substitution of one order by another.[28] Generally, when we look at an organization's trajectory, it is possible to identify a series of turning points that allowed the organization to become innovative within its field. This is the case with elBulli and the case of many organizations in other creative industries. As we will see, the organizing model of elBulli suggests that innovation is not inherently chaotic or disruptive. It is, rather, an unfolding process that gradually crystallizes over time. Organizations that we call innovative, misfits, or mavericks at one and the same time swim in the mainstream and against it.

Veal Marrow
with Caviar, #186
1992

Serves 4 people

To prepare the veal marrow:

    4 veal bone marrows (1,000 g
    [2.25 lb] each)

To prepare the cauliflower purée:

    150 g (5.5 oz) of cauliflower
    50 g (¼ cup) of light liquid cream
      (35% fat)
    30 g (1 oz) of butter

Other:

    100 g (3.5 oz) of caviar
    Osietra salt
    Wheat flour

Final touches and presentation:

1. Flour the bone marrows lightly
   and slow cook them in a pan, like
   cooking a duck foie gras escalope.

2. Place the cooked bone marrow on
   a rounded plate.

3. Concurrently, prepare a quenelle
   of hot cauliflower purée.

4. Finish the dish with 25 g (0.9 oz)
   of Osietra caviar over the veal bone
   marrow.

(Abbreviated for purposes of illustration.)[1]

2

From Chaos to Order

elBulli's System of Continuous Innovation

A Creative Attitude

In public talks, Adrià has repeatedly pointed out that people tend to overestimate creativity. "Creativity is an attitude," he claims. "It is simply a mixture of curiosity and the commitment of trying every day to find out something that one did not know before." Accordingly, hard work, commitment, and a relentless quest for improvement are conceived as key elements of elBulli's operation. However, although Adrià's creative attitude has certainly been fundamental in the daily functioning of his organization, elBulli's story is not so simple. Behind individual attitudes, there were collective practices implemented throughout the organization over time. These practices are critical in explaining the organization's effectiveness in mobilizing innovation, both internally and externally. This chapter explores the inner workings of elBulli and the internal procedures designed to produce systematic and radical innovation.

By the time of its closure in 2011, Adrià and his team had managed to develop a total of 1,846 recipes by systematically incorporating new products, technologies, modes of serving food, and, most importantly for the elBulli team, including completely new concepts and techniques into their cooking. Nonetheless, what is most significant about elBulli from an organizational standpoint is not what they actually did—that is, the concrete culinary creations that resulted from their work—but *how they did it*. Behind the talent, gastronomic knowledge, and creative attitude that supported the daily work of elBulli, there was a specific *way of doing things*, a set of *know-hows* or epistemic practices that enabled the team to systematically envision, recognize, and implement new ideas. These know-hows were comprised of a set of shared beliefs, logics, methodologies, and codes that fostered the production of innovation inside the organization in ever-increasing ways. In fact, according to my informants, both connected and unconnected to elBulli, the organization's way of doing things was a critical aspect—if not the most important one—that filtered into other kitchens around the world and, in so doing, contributed to overturning central dogmas of haute cuisine.

Like opening a clock to see how all of its pieces are put together to make it function, this chapter looks at the ongoing construction of an organizational system designed to produce relentless and radical innovation. It reveals key practices that made it possible to coordinate belief and action within the organization toward the pursuit of a common vision. Understanding the different ingredients that compose the elBulli organization can inform the practices of other organizational forms engaged in the development of creativity and innovation, both in the gastronomic field and in other fields.

Organizing for Change

The practices that support elBulli's inner workings, which will be examined in this chapter, illuminate an important dilemma faced by organizations in the twenty-first century: the difficulty of not focusing on old certainties or needs but, instead, investing in searching for new opportunities. James G. March used the terms "exploitation" and "exploration" to refer to this quandary. While exploitation is associated with the refinement, selection, and execution of existing alternatives, exploration corresponds to processes of search, risk-taking, and experimentation with possibilities that are new to the organization.[2] Applied to my proposed distinction, processes of *exploration* are associated with an organization's efforts to produce conceptual innovations that can later be *exploited* for the development of new final outcomes.

In the business literature, this quandary also resonates with the so-called "innovator's dilemma," which has been said to be key in determining an organization's ability to develop and endure.[3] By studying firms in the industries of steel, department stores, and disk drives, Christensen found that many well-managed firms advance their own failure as a result of paying too much attention to improving product performance in the short term rather than developing new technologies that could offer novel opportunities for them in the future. The innovator's dilemma, then, is very much associated with the efforts of organizations to sustain an appropriate balance between exploiting and exploring knowledge or, as I propose, between developing final outcomes and conceptual innovations.[4]

Currently, organizations that are concerned with the development of innovation tend to invest large amounts of resources and capabilities (e.g., infrastructure, human resources, financial resources, etc.) in support of the discovery of new products or services that could enhance their competitive advantage and increase their differentiation from other organizations within their field. Once an achievement has been made, organizations are likely to engage in demanding cycles of production, distribution, and improvement of the new product or service, so that after a period of evaluation and testing, the organization can decide whether or not to reproduce, redefine, and redistribute the product (in a similar or in a different form). If successful, organizations may continue doing this for decades, slightly adjusting their results according to the demands and expectations of its public and their relative position in the market. Some organizations may be involved in many of these cycles of production at once. Yet, even if the complexity of these dynamics is higher, the underlying organizational vision with regard to innovation remains focused on the reproduction or refinement of ultimate outcomes, rather than on exploring new possibilities of discovery.

With the advance of globalization and the rise of an increasingly interconnected society, changes enacted at all levels—individuals, groups, organizations, or larger collectivities—occur with a greater velocity than ever before. Furthermore, these changes have consequences that are increasingly difficult to predict. In this context, proposing a new way of doing things within any given domain (either by extending an existing idea or practice, transforming it, or proposing a radical change) has an exponentially higher potential to generate permutations at a systemic level, within the same domain or across domains. This fact has important repercussions for contemporary organizations as it suggests that an organization's ability to develop and implement new knowledge and practices is central for its endurance. Failure to recognize and act upon rapidly changing conditions can not only lead an organization to lose profits or market shares, but can also lead to the sudden realization that the rules that had once governed the game have changed. Now more than ever, mobilizing change—in the form of both normal and revolutionary innovation—is not only beneficial to organizations, but even a requirement for their survival.

Faced with this dilemma, contemporary organizations need to develop a dynamic structure that enables them to engage in the constant generation and reassessment of their internal practices, down to their core areas of expertise. How can an organization organize for change? What kinds of organizational models allow for the continuous development of innovation at these different levels, namely final products and conceptual innovations, exploitation, and exploration?

As mentioned earlier, unlike organizational models focused on reproduction or scalability, elBulli's main goal is to generate breakthroughs that can alter the rules of the game that shape the field. To accomplish this goal, elBulli struggles to preserve an *ever-changing structure*, and it does so by incorporating procedures that enable it to sustain both the exploitation of existing knowledge and the exploration of new alternatives. The former is encouraged by a set of highly defined processes through which knowledge is methodically integrated, recorded, and analyzed by the organization's members—a process that resembles the laboratory practices used in the development of scientific achievements, as described by science and technology scholars such as Fleck and Latour.[5] The organization's efforts to explore new possibilities, on the other hand, are defined by elBulli's attempts to continuously rebuild its repertoire of knowledge through generating new scenarios to create and figuring out "in progress" alternatives that could better accomplish the organization's vision—and, thus, that should be pursued—and leaving the rest latent for future exploration. As we shall see, this explains why there appear to be no failures in the elBulli organizing model, but only learning. Although unique, the case of elBulli is highly informative with regard to how innovation is mobilized within contemporary organizations and to how they struggle to integrate both exploitation and exploration into their functioning so as to ensure their survival and, thereby, to mobilize changes within their fields.

To examine the internal practices behind elBulli, however, we must start by analyzing the belief system that supported the organization's operation and which extended beyond the beliefs of its individual leader, Adrià. *Belief systems* are defined as a set of related ideas that are learned and shared by a group and which have some permanence. As a social phenomenon, belief systems have a supra-individual nature that operates independently from a group of followers, yet they rely on the commitment and validation of those followers for their existence.[6] However good or inventive elBulli's ideas might have been, the organization needed to breed an acceptance within a group for its innovative efforts to work in practice. In the following I describe the set of shared beliefs that supported elBulli's functioning, and then examine the organization's attempts to encourage commitment and validation among its members.

Culture or Cult? From Individual Beliefs to Shared Beliefs

Some people have said that we are a cult . . . there might be some truth to that.

—Field notes, member of elBulli

The sociologist Robert K. Merton used the notion of the self-fulfilling prophecy to explain a puzzling social phenomenon: In the real world, people's beliefs in positive or negative visions of the future can eventually become fulfilled by their actual behavior.[7] This happens all the time in our daily lives: Thinking that we might fail a test is likely to influence the actual results that we obtain, and believing that we can achieve great things can ultimately lead us to make those things happen. The notion of the self-fulfilling prophecy has a lot to say about the dynamics that support the development of innovation, especially when talking about radical innovation.

Imagine a creative individual, in any field, who tries to persuade others to believe in an idea that he considers unique and remarkable, yet who at the same time acknowledges that the idea might be too difficult to accomplish or even be unfeasible in practice. Given that the individual's purpose is in itself extraordinary, the most probable reaction that the individual might obtain from his audience is skepticism or, in the best-case scenario, indifference. Talent and knowledge aside, an innovator's capacity relies first on the individual creator's belief and confidence in his own capacity to develop extraordinary things.[8] This was true of Adrià. From his first years at the elBulli restaurant, Adrià had the strong conviction that the invention of a "new culinary language" was possible, a language that was different from all those that had existed so far and that he knew by heart. One former colleague of Adrià's at this stage, who owns a three–Michelin starred restaurant declared among the world's best, explained the puzzling way in which Adrià's initial prediction seemed to have made itself come true:

> At a time when everyone was convinced that nouvelle cuisine was the big revolution and that, from then on, everything has been said already, he [Adrià] said: 'No, no, no, no! There is more, there is another language.' This is something that he saw, and when he saw it, all of us thought that he was a bit crazy.
>
> But ultimately he [Adrià] has created it. He has created it because he envisioned it. He had it so clear in his mind, that at the end it has occurred.
>
> (Personal interview, chef and owner of haute cuisine restaurant, Spain)

My ethnographic accounts reveal that Adrià's strong belief in himself as a creator—a belief that, as we will see, he maintains to this day—was a necessary precondition for his predictions to come true. As a matter of fact, a leader's devotion to an internal calling is required to instigate revolutionary movements in any context.[9] In the case of elBulli, along with Adrià's vision-ary capacities and perseverance, his ego appears to be another decisive factor in his ability to take on huge projects and push them until they are realized in practice. As one interviewee pointed out, "His strong belief in himself has allowed him to be what he is. In order to be a surgeon you need to believe in yourself, you need to believe that you will be able to cut someone through and then sew him back up. Similarly, with huge projects, you need to believe that *you* can do it. Adrià truly believes that *he* can create enormously, that he can take on projects on a global scale." For these kinds of projects to be effec-tive, this interviewee concluded, "we need people with ego." However, for Adrià, assuming the responsibility of making such a complex vision a reality was not possible without sacrifice. On several occasions he has intimated that when the time came for him and his wife to decide whether or not they would have children, they realized that it was either the project of elBulli or having a family. "We decided not to have kids," Adrià once said to me. "ElBulli is my kid."

An individual creator's conviction of his extraordinary capacities, none-theless, is not a sufficient explanation for the spread or perpetuation of his beliefs. There is yet another aspect of driving radical innovation that needs to be accounted for: making *others* believe in those capacities too, that is, building a community of followers around the creator that can support and help him to make his claims come true. As stated by Max Weber, the author-ity of a charismatic leader—in this case, of Adrià as a creator—relies on his or her ability to obtain social recognition.[10] To sustain his status, Weber explained, the leader must continuously show proof of his extraordinary qualities; that is, he must demonstrate again and again that he is worthy of his followers' devotion. If he is not able to convince others, the individual creator runs the risk of losing credibility and, as suggested by the informant quoted above, being labeled as crazy.

An innovator's ability to surround himself with supporters and to incorpo-rate them into his cause is especially important in the context of haute cui-sine, given that the work performed within restaurants is essentially performed in groups. Both *inventiveness* and *reproduction* are necessarily intermingled in the workings of haute cuisine restaurants. While an executive chef might be able to develop three or four original techniques or dishes, he is not able to systematically reproduce them for his clientele. Thus, chefs need to find ways to transmit their convictions to their teams so those team members can help them to transform their ideas into reproducible products that can be systematically served to customers. As an avant garde chef, unconnected to elBulli, indicated, "You need a team to reproduce your vision, and that is very hard to accomplish. Because you are not only transmitting measures, you are conveying a philosophy, affection, and passion." As in any high-end restaurant, therefore, elBulli required the work of a team for its leader's beliefs to reach its primary audience, diners. "Someone might be very exceptional," one member of elBulli emphasized, "but in cuisine, if you want to do something big, it is very difficult for one person alone to do it."

At elBulli, through the years, Adrià built a close-knit community of ten to fifteen talented people who not only believed in his cause, but also devoted most of their lives to trying to see it realized. All the closest members of Adrià's team had worked with him for longer than a decade and had received most of their training, if not all, with him at elBulli. "We've been raised by Adrià," one of elBulli's heads of cuisine said to me when I asked him about his professional background. "Everything we know about how to run a restaurant comes from our experience here. I am elBulli, elBulli is me," another chef remarked. The intense rhythm of work during the restaurant's season not only regulated the elBulli members' workday, which is usually long in any high-end restaurant (from twelve to fourteen hours a day), but also dictated the amount of time they got to spend with their families. This was especially true for those members whose families did not live near Cala Montjoi, the remote natural reserve where the restaurant is located. These members explained how the intense work during the restaurant's season made it very difficult for them to spend time with their wives and, for others, to participate in the first years of their children's lives. In fact, two of elBulli's head chefs usually spent the week at the restaurant and only visited their families on the weekends. For a period of six months, these chefs' personal and social lives revolved only around elBulli's kitchen; they lived like monks in a secluded monastery:

> Those six months were like being in confinement, especially for me and the other head chef, since we slept above the kitchen. That is, we finished the work at the restaurant and then we went up a staircase and there was our room. Then we woke up, walked down the stairs and went to the kitchen. This demanded huge concentration! During the next six months you could go to the doctor, to your nephew's baptism . . . that small range of freedom was not permitted [during the restaurant's season], in fact, we didn't even dare to ask.
>
> (Personal interview, former member of elBulli)

Several characteristics of a "total institution"[11] can be identified at elBulli. As described by Goffman, total institutions often include a small number of fixed members and incorporate elements of both formal organizations and domestic communities. These institutions' totalizing character derives from the fact that they separate their members from the outside world by establishing a set of formal and informal rules that guide the individuals' daily activities. Monasteries, religious cults, work camps, and military groups are examples of these types of institutions. Very much like what happens at these organizations, almost all aspects of elBulli's members' lives were controlled during the restaurant's season and subordinated to the organization's goals.

However, despite the personal sacrifices that many of elBulli's members had to make, they all expressed a profound pride in being able to work at elBulli and a great belief in the figure of Adrià as the organization's leader. For them, elBulli was not merely a place to work; they saw it as their home, as a project of their own. After all, they consistently stated, they had spent more time with Adrià than with their wives and kids. It comes as no surprise, then, that workers of elBulli often used the word "family" to refer to the organization's permanent core.[12]

But what sustained the commitment of elBulli's team members? Their commitment to Adrià specifically was largely grounded in the team's belief in his extraordinary talent, knowledge, and profound awareness of everything that happened inside elBulli. When describing Adrià's abilities, for instance, members of elBulli insistently emphasized his exceptional gastronomic criterion: "He can smell things, he has that vision, the best gastronomic criterion that I have ever seen in my life." And also pointed out Adrià's visionary capacities: "He can see things that others cannot see." In this respect, while they all recognized Adrià's exceptional ability to learn from others and to modify his actions accordingly, they also acknowledged that "he is almost never wrong."

Adrià's detailed knowledge of what happened outside elBulli is another key aspect that sustained his authority inside it. During the restaurant's off-season, Adrià constantly traveled to all sorts of countries, which gave him the opportunity to visit other restaurants, attend conferences, meet influential people, and give talks around the world. Given the secluded lifestyle of the majority of his team members, Adrià's deep awareness of the outside world led them to describe him as their Google or, as someone else noted, as "the eye that sees all." This sense of admiration and loyalty toward Adrià was confirmed by outsiders who worked as interns during one of the restaurant's seasons and witnessed the dynamics that took place inside the restaurant: "[In cuisine] you need to make others follow you to be the best . . . and they [elBulli's members] are beyond loyal to Ferran. They would die for him! [I guess] because he is Ferran, I don't know why!" one perplexed former apprentice claimed. In sum, members of elBulli saw Adrià as an institutional leader, that is, as the unique possessor of a systemic perspective and, thus, able to make decisions regarding the pressures that might be affecting the organization and the actions that could be undertaken to ensure its survival.[13]

Members of elBulli offered many other reasons to explain why they stayed at elBulli instead of, for instance, trying to gain experience working in other restaurants or learning about other culinary approaches. On a personal level, they stated that elBulli provided opportunities that were unthinkable at other high-end restaurants. At elBulli they were trained by "the hand of the best" and were able to continue developing the kind of cooking that they loved and with which they felt most comfortable. Further, while it was true that during the restaurant's season the daily work did not leave much time for them to do other things, the six-month period in which the restaurant was closed, as I will explain later, provided a window of opportunity for its members to travel and explore other culinary cultures and restaurants and to devote large amounts of energy to investigation and research. Thus, especially during the elBulli restaurant's final stages, the organization offered its members plenty of opportunities to further their training and to learn from different people and cultures in a way that would have been impossible at other restaurants. "ElBulli is not a normal restaurant, not at the level of the [culinary] offer nor at the level of the work that we do," one of the head chefs said. He also stressed that elBulli provided them with the opportunity to see the world—a world that, as we now know, was shaped by the organization's own vision and beliefs. "As a chef, one would not normally know the world, [one would not] meet interesting people. . . . You would not have time to create. We feel privileged to be next to Ferran," a head chef of elBulli remarked.

The popularity achieved by the organization over time reinforced the commitment of its members. Year after year, with the growth of the restaurant and its increasing recognition, Adrià demonstrated to his team that all the sacrifices they had endured had been worthwhile. In explaining how he stayed at elBulli for longer than a decade, one member emphasized how his commitment had been systematically strengthened by being assigned new responsibilities and projects to undertake:

I remember that on my first day [of work] I wanted to leave. I was young; it was my first serious job. But every so often I was given more responsibility, more projects appeared. You could do things [at elBulli] that at other restaurants you couldn't. And every time something new came up, I said to myself, 'when I finish this I'll go,' but before I finished something, another exciting thing was starting, which made me want to stay. It kept me motivated. So I stayed and stayed.

(Personal interview, member of elBulli)

The outside recognition obtained and the organization's growth represented proof that reinforced elBulli's members' commitment and validated Adrià's status as the institutional leader of the organization. Yet, regardless of how significant all these personal motives were for elBulli's members, there was a more profound purpose that pushed them all to stay next to Adrià: At elBulli, they believed that they were contributing to a larger cause or, to put it in their terms, to a "global cause." They all had the conviction that elBulli was a central agent in the gastronomic avant garde and that, in the end, their efforts in expanding the boundaries of knowledge in their field would have repercussions that would live beyond them. They stayed because their work at elBulli would also stay, even after their deaths.

> Here we are, sacrificing our lives for a project. Because we believe in it, we believe that we belong to it and we are super convinced.
>
> Some of us are leaving our families, our kids.... This is not something that we do for money or because we feel like it; we do it because we coldly believe that it is something that is growing, and we can see [that growth] every year... it is not about prestige. We are doing something that has a meaning, a base, a philosophy. It is something solid, with strong supports; it is like a building, a building that will keep standing.
>
> (Personal interview, member of elBulli)

Members of elBulli's core team, therefore, were not simply hired workers with specialized training, but members who dedicated their working days to the organization. Parallel dynamics have been found in the political field, for instance in Philip Selznick's classical study *The Organizational Weapon*.[14] In examining the workings of the Bolshevik party, Selznick highlighted that cadres (the party's permanent core) were "dedicated men" who had a personal commitment to the organization up to the point of assuming significant risks and sacrifices. He stated that the maintenance of the cadres' commitment was a primary objective of the party given that their emotional involvement constituted "the indispensable vanguard of the revolution." Personal commitment enabled the organization to turn the workers association into

an instrument, a "weapon" that could be deployed for the continuous con-
quest of power. Like elBulli's core team, therefore, communist cadres not
only agreed with the organization's program, but also accepted its discipline
and actively worked toward the achievement of the organization's vision.

In conclusion, the belief system that supported elBulli's operation suggests that the organization's development did not represent a linear progres-
sion toward a specific end. Rather, innovation emerged at the organization as
a vision and as a way of being—a *project* that fulfilled itself over time. In this
case, an individual's appetite to drive change later extended to a community
of believers who worked to see their leader's vision realized. The level of
agreement around the organization's vision, however, should not be overesti-
mated. As we will see, not all of elBulli's members fully understood the significance of this vision, but the majority believed in it, since their sense of belonging to the organization depended on their compliance with it. It was
through a set of concrete practices and dispositions that the elBulli team
found ways to transform an initial vision that had formed in the mind of one
individual into something that, quite opportunely, looked very much like
what Adrià had predicted in the first place.

The Methodology Behind the Vision

The elBulli team's pursuit of a common vision was a matter not only of pure
determination or conviction, but also of methodology. One can have a strong
vision of the future yet leave its accomplishment to the mysterious workings
of faith or destiny. But this is not what happened at elBulli. Although the
fame and success achieved by the organization and its leader were not in
themselves premeditated, a particular infrastructure to mobilize innovation
became established at the organization so as to advance a new basis of
knowledge and practice in its field.

Members and collaborators of elBulli consistently highlighted a key characteristic of elBulli's creative process, one that differentiates the workings of
the organization from other organizations in the gastronomic field. Following

Adrià's lead, at elBulli, as much emphasis was put on searching for novelty as on finding ways to better organize and control the work. A member of the organization referred to this, saying, "If there is one thing that Adrià enjoys as much as cooking it is to rationalize, optimize, and plan . . . to generate protocols of how to do things." This characteristic led those outside the organization, connected and unconnected to it, to depict Adrià as being different from "regular chefs." Whereas chefs usually operate based on feelings, soul, and instinct, one chef remarked, in managing elBulli Adrià instead "attempts to leave little to chance; he works more like a scientist." Accordingly, after Adrià joined elBulli and especially after he became co-owner of the restaurant in 1990, a number of different methodologies and logics were implemented, aimed at coordinating belief and action inside the organization. Through a series of formal interventions, both deliberate and ad hoc, an *organizing structure* for the development of innovation was established at elBulli, a structure that made it possible to systematically convert "creative chaos" into effective innovation. The importance that Adrià assigns to the organizing system behind his restaurant is such that, in retrospect, he has claimed that elBulli could not have succeeded without it. In his words, "it is impossible to be creative without good organization."[15]

At the Beginning There Was Mainly Chaos

From the early 1980s when Adrià joined the elBulli restaurant until its closure in 2011, elBulli's team evolved from being a group of seven to ten friends who worked in fairly chaotic and intuitive ways to a "disciplined army of food professionals"[16] that worked in largely predictable ways, as noted by Anthony Bourdain, the chef and television personality, after his visit to the elBulli restaurant a few years prior to its closure. By then, elBulli was composed of over fifty cooks and twenty kitchen staff members, as well as administrative staff and professionals from other creative fields, all of whom worked with the precision of a "Swiss clock," as one of my interviewees observed. These structural qualities that characterize the workings of el-

Bulli did not emerge all of a sudden. Rather, they became consolidated over the course of the years and as a result of several interventions mobilized in and by the organization.

When Adrià first became head of elBulli's kitchen he was only twenty-three years old. As mentioned previously, this position had been unexpectedly assigned to him after elBulli's former head chef had resigned. "Now, I realize that this was a huge stroke of luck! It is very strange for someone to become head chef so early in his career," Adrià would say to me decades later. During that time too, and mainly due to economic reasons, the elBulli restaurant began to close during the winter period. The underlying motives for this were simple: The municipality of Roses, where the restaurant is located, is mainly a tourist region and nobody was coming to the restaurant during the winter. So during these months, there were many days they would make zero in profits. "These were hard times," Adrià and members of his team recalled.

As a young head chef, Adrià formed his brigade by inviting colleagues whom he knew well and with whom he shared common characteristics: They were all about the same age, originally from Catalonia, and had a common passion for cooking and haute cuisine. Many chefs who participated in elBulli's brigade at that time are now famous chefs who work or own restaurants ranked among the best in the world, like the chef I cited earlier in this chapter. The common background among the members of Adrià's original team was very important in their creative ventures, as those connections turned the team members' attention toward a common source for inspiration: their most familiar context, Mediterranean cuisine. Together, these chefs would explore the confines of fine dining by introducing their local culinary customs, which would later become known as elBulli's Mediterranean style of cooking. One renowned chef who participated in Adrià's brigade at this stage remembers this as one of the most exciting moments of his career. "It was an environment filled with passion and talented people. . . . You could sense that something big was going to emerge out of there." Yet he also acknowledged that if Adrià had not positioned himself as the "sergeant of the army," the whole enterprise would have been futile. Adrià was the one ensuring that all the talent did not go to waste, the chef claimed, by constantly trying to find ways to channel it into a concrete direction, even if neither of them, including Adrià, knew what direction that was. Controlling the group was not an easy task, the chef stressed. Back then they were all in their twenties and, although they all worked hard during the day, they also wanted to go partying every night. "All of us," he remarked, laughing, insinuating Adrià's involvement too.

> We all went partying every night. . . . So it was very hard to wake up in the morning. If no one had taken on the role of the sergeant of the army, it would not have worked. He [Adrià] was always alert, making sure that nothing we were constructing would fall apart, even without knowing, at that point, what it was that we were building. . . . But there was the inquiry, the search for something new.
>
> (Personal interview, chef and owner of haute cuisine restaurant, Spain)

Over the following years, the elBulli team's initial chaotic search for a new culinary language was mobilized in increasingly structured ways.

Time and Space to Create

To cope with the economic difficulties that the restaurant was facing, in 1995, Adrià and his business partner, Juli Soler, decided to launch side business projects that could financially support the restaurant. One longtime member of elBulli recalled, "He [Adrià] had it very clear from the beginning. To do research one needs money. He [Adrià] said: 'we are not going to become known because, suddenly, we are doing things differently. We need to find ways to potentiate this capacity that we have in different directions.'" As a result of this, the development of business activities would become the organization's main source of revenue and continue to expand until the restaurant's closure in 2011.

Starting in 1995 as well, another significant change was mobilized inside the organization: the six-month break for the off-season began to be used as an opportunity to experiment with new food preparations in a separate location from the restaurant: first the Talaia Mar restaurant (1995–1997) and later the Aquarium (from 1998 until 2000), both located in Barcelona. Looking back at the organization's trajectory, Adrià identified this as the most important intervention that was ever made to potentiate creativity at elBulli. Yet it is worth noting that, although this change involved the purposeful action of the organization's members, it was initially motivated by external constraints that the restaurant was facing.

Back then, the practice of separating creative tasks from productive tasks had been widely recognized as beneficial for organizations concerned with the development of innovation. Already in the 1980s, major modern corporations such as IBM or 3M, to name just two examples, had established a division between the operating organization and the innovating organization (often called R&D departments), each functioning according to specific tasks, processes, structures, and reward systems.[17] Yet at the time elBulli introduced this separation into its functioning this was not a common practice among high-end restaurants, despite the potentially significant benefits that it might bring within the field of gastronomy. Serving customers every day (and in most haute cuisine restaurants, twice a day) involves highly demanding chores that leave little or no time to devote to creativity. In fact, the majority of the chefs that I interviewed recognized that they had very little time to think or evaluate new ideas during their daily work. So at elBulli, having designated time and space dedicated exclusively to R&D tasks soon proved to be key in advancing the now shared belief that the invention of a new basis of knowledge in the form of a new culinary language was possible.

Adrià's brother, Albert, who directed the research team during the off-season, stated that working in a new setting, away from the restaurant, radically altered the way in which they approached creativity at elBulli. Similar to the way a child becomes an adult, Albert explained, "Our games became directed searches, missions." Thus, at the new location, the organization's initial abstract vision started to be broken down into concrete missions that were carefully compiled into lists that were handed over to the team to accomplish. While some of the tasks listed corresponded to well-defined ideas, such as the discovery of warm ice cream or warm jellies, others were merely hints of ideas for further exploration, such as "work on gellifications" or "go to eat at X and Y places." Working in a new space, members of elBulli noted, expanded the team's opportunities to question and reexamine aspects of the craft of cooking that were largely taken for granted in the context of a restaurant, such as the rigid organization of teams, the focus on immediate and tangible results, and the unavoidable aversion to risk and failure that the management of the restaurant required. Importantly too, the new location provided them with the necessary equipment to test and evaluate new ideas in increasingly methodical ways:

> We reflected upon every single aspect of cuisine . . . such as why is there a savory section [in the kitchen] that is separate from a sweet section? Can't it be all the way around? What happens if we change it? Well, perhaps we cannot change completely. . . . And what about the spices? Why do I put vanilla only on desserts? Can't I use it for savory dishes too? And what about ice creams? Could they be savory? If they're made out of fruit, technically they can also be made of vegetables. . . . There was continuous reflection, in which everything was questioned and everything was tested.
>
> (Personal interview, member of elBulli)

In *Innovation: The Missing Dimension*, Lester and Piore pointed out that unlike the broadly used analytical perspective on innovation—characterized by the search for solutions through exchanges of precise information—an interpretive perspective seeks to find *new* problems and opportunities by means of open-ended and fluid conversations. The account presented above suggests that an interpretive perspective predominated in the work performed at elBulli's new location. Whereas at the restaurant, roles, tasks, and goals were highly defined, the new space offered the possibility for new procedures, team structures, and schedules to emerge.

During the off-season, while in Barcelona, Albert and two other members of elBulli's team would buy high-quality ingredients in the city's main food market, Boqueria, and go to the new location to test their ideas through continuous processes of trial and error. To support their work, they developed lists of the ingredients and preparations that they had tried, while specifying the results obtained in each of the experimentations. Also, following Adrià's indications, they synthesized the experimentations performed by recording them into what they called "files of creativity," later organizing them into folders, complete with pictures that illustrated the whole process. To better manage the work at the new location, calendars were developed that carefully dissected the otherwise highly flexible time off from the restaurant into specific tasks that could encourage their investigations. The new schedule included the search for new products or research trips to other restaurants and cities as an integral part of the work, tasks that the restaurant's daily exigencies left little or no time to accomplish. As Albert Adrià recalled:

> We were just three people and one computer, because my brother [Ferran] was afraid that we would turn into bookworms and forget about cooking. So we had to synthesize everything very quickly, first on paper, and then visualize it and put it into the only folder that we had. . . . My brother has always been a maniac of documentation, of archiving. . . .
>
> (Personal interview, Albert Adrià)

As in the elBulli restaurant, the learning processes at the new location were based on learning by doing. The same sense of immediacy that characterized the work in the kitchen was imprinted onto the creative processes performed at the new space, yet it was brought to an abstract level. Members of Adrià's team described these processes in the following way: Every day, hundreds of ideas were tried out one after the other, just as if they were preparing dishes that needed to be instantly served to customers. Creative processes were never stopped while in progress. Rather, theorization always occurred after the fact. When something was not working, one member recalled, Adrià would tell them to set it aside and start working on something else: "Leave it for now! Don't get stuck! Save it and keep moving." The act of instantly recording what they did made it possible to detach themselves from those processes that were not working, yet keep them available for future explorations.

During a working day, at intervals the team would gather to quickly summarize the results obtained and identify which ideas might be further explored and which ones might not by developing lists, diagrams, charts, and timelines to visualize the information, a practice they maintain to this day, as we will see in chapter 5.

In summary, establishing a separation from the routines and logics of the restaurant provided the elBulli team with greater flexibility to explore new alternatives, both in cuisine and in the organization of creativity in cuisine. What's more, similar to what Bruno Latour described in his examination of Louis Pasteur's laboratory,[18] elBulli's new location was gradually equipped with technologies that fostered the search for novelty and which provided means to confirm the validity of the results obtained, at least within the controlled conditions of elBulli's test kitchen.

After a few years of working in this way, members of elBulli started to see the first traces of what they saw as a truly original approach to cooking. The emergence of this new approach became apparent by the discovery of new culinary concepts and techniques that the organization's members realized could be used for the creation of endless new final outcomes (dishes or recipes) that would embody elBulli's unique cuisine. Some of the culinary techniques that were developed during these years included warm jellies, foams, and savory crocants; new culinary concepts included deconstruction, minimalism, and pluralism, which will be described later. What is most important to notice here is that for elBulli members these new culinary creations were not conceived as mere accidents or good ideas that could be exploited to develop new products and later move on to something else. Rather, they saw these creations as the first syllables of a unique vocabulary; what they had long been searching for. Their capacity to see beyond mere culinary products did not happen out of thin air. It was rather the result of principles, procedures, and a set of codes that were mobilized within the organization and which directed the team's attention toward a broader goal.

Creative Principles

According to Albert Adrià, the key to elBulli's effectiveness during this period was the "velocity" that characterized the team's creative processes. In his words, "We reached conclusions because we were moving at a high velocity, very high, we were super effective [in creating] through constant communication, dialogue, and doing." Indeed, Albert's use of the word velocity resonates with an important characteristic of the internal organization of elBulli's creative team: In creating, the organization's members were not merely moving fast—they were moving in a common direction. Let me briefly explain what I mean by this. Whereas the term speed defines how fast something is moving, velocity refers to moving toward something. Thus, while the former might allow an individual or a group to cover long distances, it would not necessarily lead it to advance toward the fulfillment of a shared goal. This is an important distinction to make because, while elBulli's system of working indeed encouraged its members to not stand still, it also provided them with a value framework, what they called "creative principles" or a "philosophy," that aligned the team's actions and beliefs in the pursuit of a collective goal.

On his free days, Adrià examined the results obtained from the experimentations to try to identify patterns between the findings and the most fruitful directions that could be pursued. An important part of this analysis was to extract creative principles that could orient the team's work toward the achievement of a common vision. Some of the creative principles defined during this period at elBulli were: understanding the "essence of ingredients" (as opposed to being influenced by personal preferences or by the ingredient's price in the market), exploiting the boundaries between the sweet and savory worlds in cuisine, and considering the five human senses—smell, touch, hearing, vision, and taste—as equally valid points of departure in the development of new culinary creations. In 1997, an additional "sixth sense" was added to elBulli's list of creative principles, which defined the incorporation of emotions such as irony, humor, or provocation as a constitutive part of the fine-dining experience. Unlike the five physical senses, elBulli's sixth sense called on diners to reflect on the message hidden in the restaurant's creations. On a daily basis, these principles provided a set of tight rules that oriented the creative processes, making it possible for the team's members to distinguish which of their actions fit with the organization's mission and which did not, and decide accordingly.

Along the lines of elBulli's attempt to innovate according to specific principles, studies conducted in the computer industry have found that the organizing models of agile organizations emphasize both structure and anarchy as part of their functioning. Organizations do this by implementing a small set of fixed rules that define a framework of operation, while maintaining a flexible structure out of which creative responses can emerge. With too little structure, the organizations' attempts to integrate and exploit existing knowledge would be unproductive; and too much structure within organizations may hinder the organizations' ability to generate new knowledge and search for novel opportunities.[19] A small set of rules, then, provide the organizational system with the rigidity necessary for members to make sense of change and to recognize new possibilities.

At elBulli, the establishment of creative principles had important consequences in the workings of the organization. The originality achieved in the team's culinary creations during the mid-1990s and on still awed its leader, Adrià: "This was the moment in which we set the basis, the philosophical pillars of what elBulli would be in the future. From here onward we decided that we were going to do avant garde cuisine and every change that we have made ever since has followed this direction." Considering the results obtained from their work, it was also decided that they would accomplish this by following a specific path: the creation of new techniques and concepts that would serve as building blocks for the development of a new language—as we already know, a mode of creativity that Adrià places at the top of his creative pyramid. From Adrià and his team's perspective, the high level of inventiveness that this quest required could support the invention of a groundbreaking language, different from any other culinary language that had ever existed before. Besides a creative attitude and commitment, a new set of principles and procedures for organizing the work was gradually set in place in order to bring this vision closer to completion.

A New Way of Organizing

Although the months working at a separate location proved to be very productive for the development of creativity, the elBulli team soon realized that the findings obtained were not easily transportable to the restaurant and, hence, that new procedures needed to be established in order to enhance the synergy between the work developed during the restaurant's on and off periods. In 1994, a first step was taken by incorporating an additional station at the elBulli restaurant's kitchen, which would function in parallel with the other stations that normally divide the work within kitchens. This new station was called the development station, and a newly specialized creative team was established to run this station. Furthermore, it was determined that the creative team would consist of the same members who had participated in the experimentations during the off-season, and that they would be in charge of translating the findings obtained into edible dishes or recipes that could be served to clients at the restaurant.

The importance of having a separate space and time to create at elBulli was such that Adrià later decided to officially establish a laboratory of cuisine. In 2000, he bought an apartment located in the center of Barcelona, right across from the Boqueria food market where they went to buy products to experiment with, and baptized it with the name "elBulli workshop." From that year onward, this workshop operated as a test kitchen and became the center of operations of elBulli's creative team during the restaurant's off-season.

Since the early 2000s, therefore, two distinct yet interconnected branches of the organization—the restaurant and the R&D workshop—would nurture each other for the development of the type of innovation that elBulli was ultimately aiming to achieve, namely conceptual innovation. Similar to what had happened in the previous years, the structural separation of time and space between the two locations made it possible to assign different goals, teams, and schedules to each side of the organization. The internal functioning of these two locations and their feedback mechanisms in producing innovation can be summarized as follows:

(1) elBulli workshop: From October to March, elBulli's creative team gathered at the off-site location, which they called *el taller*, to conduct research and development tasks aimed at fulfilling the organization's primary goal: the creation of new culinary techniques and concepts. The results and findings obtained from these months of experimentation were carefully recorded in files, folders, and visual representations that served as the basis for the generation of new final products (i.e., dishes or recipes) later at the restaurant.

(2) elBulli restaurant: From April through August, the information and knowledge generated at the elBulli workshop gradually filtered into the restaurant through the work conducted at the development station and was converted into edible and reproducible dishes that could be served to diners. Waiters in the restaurant recorded the diners' feedback in order to improve the dishes currently being served (i.e., mainly feedback on dishes that were left mostly uneaten).[20] While at the beginning of each season the dishes on the elBulli restaurant's menu were the same as in the previous season, they began to gradually change with the introduction of good ideas developed during the off-season and their implementation into new dishes. By July, all the dishes on elBulli's menu were completely new. Then, once the restaurant's season was over, the information generated at the restaurant was transferred back to the elBulli workshop and used by the creative team as a basis for the investigations that they would conduct over the following six months.

ElBulli's organizing model, therefore, consisted of processes that combined both rigidity and fluidity in the system by systematically generating new scenarios to create, each operating according to specific goals, logics, and routines. While the restaurant focused on the execution of precise tasks and creativity in the form of new final outcomes, work at the elBulli workshop fostered the search for new alternatives in the form of conceptual innovations.

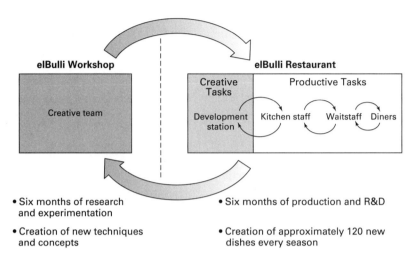

elBulli Workshop

Creative team

elBulli Restaurant

Creative Tasks

Development station

Productive Tasks

Kitchen staff   Waitstaff   Diners

- Six months of research and experimentation

- Creation of new techniques and concepts

- Six months of production and R&D

- Creation of approximately 120 new dishes every season

2.1 Cycle of innovation production at elBulli (restaurant and workshop).

Hence, the interrelation between these two branches encouraged the organization's advancement of knowledge by making different types of innovation possible (see figure 2.1). In this respect, the workings of elBulli resonate with the notion of "ambidextrous organizations," which describes organizations that reconcile exploitation with exploratory activities by establishing architecturally distinct units that are at once tightly coupled internally, yet loosely coupled with each other. Like elBulli, exploiting and exploring units have different cultures, team configurations, and incentives. While the former emphasizes team efficiency and control in the short run, the latter fosters experimentation and opportunity creation in the long run.[21]

As one would anticipate, elBulli's organizing system required strong financial foundations to maintain itself. Since the late 1980s, an important source of revenue had come from side business activities developed during the restaurant's off-season, as mentioned previously. In 1995, however, a separate branch of the organization was officially instituted for the development of business projects, first called "elBulli catering" (1995) and later "elBulli Carmen" (2001), once again run by a separate team supervised by Adrià.

Mostly under the brand Ferran Adrià, as opposed to elBulli, this branch of the organization would initiate consulting projects and collaborations with a wide array of companies during the organization's trajectory, including Chocovic (chocolates and other derivatives from cacao), Hacienda Benazuza and NH Hotels (hotel management and catering), Oils Borges (oils and vinaigrettes), Caprabo (supermarket), Lays (potato chips), and Estrella Damm (beer), among many others, some of which resulted in substantial failures. The underlying logic for using the name Ferran Adrià instead of elBulli for most of the business is associated with Adrià's dilemma of creativity versus profitability, which, as I noted, he considered analogous to the strange case of Dr. Jekyll and Mr. Hyde: While elBulli's brand was meant to be associated with high quality, the avant garde, and exclusivity, the name Ferran Adrià could be employed for commercial purposes such as the development of popular and mass-produced culinary products with only small touches of originality. One member of elBulli explained this principle of separation in the following way: "If you want the public image of elBulli to sustain itself, you need to keep it virgin. We want elBulli to be linked with high-end cuisine. So you cannot poison it! Regardless of how good the [commercial] potato chips we made might be, we cannot use the brand of elBulli, because it is not haute cuisine."

Prior to continuing to examine how the elBulli team came to accomplish their vision, that is, to establish a new language and basis of knowledge in cuisine, let me briefly stop here to describe the social organization at the elBulli restaurant and at the elBulli workshop. This analysis will provide details that are important to consider in understanding how innovation was manufactured within the organization and also, as we will see in chapter 5, in understanding the continuity and separation of elBulli's new research center of creativity, the elBulli Foundation, from its preexisting organizational form.

Two Organizing Logics: elBulli Restaurant and elBulli Workshop

Two different modes of organizing coexisted at elBulli. At the restaurant, the work was aimed at producing new final outputs (dishes or recipes) through the systematic *exploitation* of knowledge. The operation of this branch of the organization was characterized by a strict standardization of time and motion in the workers' activities, an emphasis on discipline and control, and a top-down administration that mimicked the hierarchy of military institutions. In this sense, the elBulli restaurant resonated with the bureaucratic forms of organizations described in the investigations of Taylor, Weber, and Fayol in the beginning of the twentieth century, which presented rationality and efficiency as axiomatic criteria.[22] On the other side, the work at the elBulli workshop was oriented toward the search for new paths of discovery through procedures aimed at encouraging the collective *exploration* of uncertainty. It was the coupling of these different pieces of elBulli's system that sustained the dynamism of the organization as a whole.

At the elBulli restaurant, the staff was organized in a very hierarchical way. Adrià was at the top of the hierarchy, supervising the preparation and plating of every dish that was served to customers and selecting the new culinary creations to be incorporated into the menu. Next to him was Juli Soler, his business partner, with his brother Albert as head of the development station. After Albert left elBulli in 2008 for reasons that will be later explained, Oriol Castro, one of the head chefs at the restaurant, succeeded him as creative director. On several occasions, Adrià told the press that he and Soler were like a married couple in their management of elBulli. Their distinct roles complemented each other in the restaurant's daily work. Members of elBulli indicated that while Adrià injected tension into the team, Soler tried to lighten the mood and keep things from getting too serious. During the service, Adrià was backstage, making sure that everything was being executed to perfection. Soler, in contrast, was in the front, keeping track of all the information about the people who were visiting each day (e.g., food allergies, beverage preferences) and greeting them as soon as they stepped into the restaurant. Soler constantly used humor to generate a warm environment, which contrasted sharply with Adrià's serious personality. For instance, members of the wait staff recalled a typical phrase used by Soler while he was guiding elBulli's guests to their tables, knowing that they had probably traveled long distances to arrive to the restaurant's isolated location: "I hope you didn't come here to eat! Because if eating is what you want, there are plenty of other places where you could go!"

The differences in roles between the Adrià brothers also played an important function in the daily work at elBulli. Ferran's methodical approach was complemented by Albert's romantic and artistic approach to cuisine, elBulli's insiders explained. Within the organization, Albert was recognized as having an extremely sensitive mental palate, that is, a remarkable capacity to remember the taste of the most delicate flavors without needing to physically try something. This capacity made Albert a key facilitator of the creative processes that happened inside of the organization. By the time Oriol Castro replaced Albert as director of the creative team to become the right hand of Ferran Adrià, Oriol had developed the same palate as Adrià. As one informant noted, "they can look at each other when trying something and figure out what they are thinking without even talking."

Further down in the chain of command was a permanent team of ten to fifteen staff members who occupied management positions in the different sections of the elBulli restaurant, specifically the kitchen, service, and administration. With the passing of time, and due to the restaurant's increasing recognition, the staff expanded to include a growing number of unpaid interns or apprentices, commonly called *stagiaires* in the high-end restaurant sector. These apprentices were usually highly skilled professionals who traveled from far away to dedicate their time to working with and learning from Adrià and his team. As a rotating group, each season the apprentices represented the highest proportion of the workforce necessary for implementing elBulli's culinary creations in exact ways, as opposed to executive creative tasks—a role that often generated frustration and resentment among many of them. These internal tensions that were part of the workings of elBulli's kitchen had been well documented in Abend's 2011 book, *The Sorcerer's Apprentices*, which narrates the journey of elBulli's interns through one of the restaurant's final seasons. During my fieldwork, I noticed that Adrià was well aware of the frustrations experienced by elBulli's apprentices. In a personal conversation, he went so far as to say that the apprentices were "not a real part of elBulli's team," adding that "saying the opposite would be a lie." However, while elBulli's apprentices were primarily additional hands in implementing the daily service, they supplied additional gains that were critical in sustaining the organization's recognition and status within its field, as we will see in chapter 3. Because of their different backgrounds, moreover, the apprentices provided fluidity to elBulli's working system by introducing new information that allowed the organization to continue running smoothly. As a member of elBulli pointed out, every season the apprentices "injected new blood" into their work by infusing the permanent team with new energies and skills from which they could all benefit.

One apprentice who spent seven months at elBulli described how Adrià asked newcomers for new ideas at the beginning of the season. According to his account, Adrià offered a complete collection of elBulli books in exchange for a new technique. My informant decided to show a technique that he had learned working in a famous restaurant in the United States made with liquid nitrogen, which, he concluded, led him to win the contest set up by Adrià. During that season, elBulli's team used this technique to develop a dish that they informally refer to as "dinosaur eggs."

> He [Adrià] said at the beginning of the year: 'Whoever has the best idea will get a set of books.' . . . So I showed him this technique, they do it at [name of a famous U.S. restaurant]. . . . It is a good technique. You take the siphon and do truffle mousse. You roll the ball with liquid nitrogen and get a kind of balloon. . . . I showed him that technique, and he gave me all the [elBulli's] books.
>
> (Personal interview, apprentice of elBulli, sous-chef at an haute cuisine restaurant, United States)

At the elBulli workshop, the organization of teams followed a quite different logic from that established at the restaurant, one that resonates more with what sociologists have denominated "heterarchy." David Stark pointed out that heterarchical forms of organization are characterized by higher openness, reflective cognition, and management of uncertainty through the use of multiple evaluative principles.[23] In his ethnographic work, Stark showed that this kind of organization can be found in widely disparate settings, ranging from a manufacturing factory in the 1980s in Hungary, to new media firms in the era of the Internet boom, to financial companies and modern arbitrage. The innovative capacity of these organizations, Stark stated, relies on their ability to keep diverse logics at play, which enables coordination toward a general objective. Similar to the work performed by the elBulli team at the workshop, Stark showed that manufacturers, media professionals, and traders did not know what they were looking for until they found it, but they did share a set of principles that oriented their search for the unknown and which supported the development of complex and heterogeneous collaborations within organizations.

At the elBulli workshop, given that no customers needed to be served every day, time could be used for different purposes, which created opportunities to establish connections with individuals and institutions outside the organization, such as culinary schools, food companies, and also with professionals from other creative fields. The practice of taking time off from the restaurant once a year and of using this time to initiate new relationships and to visit new scenarios was described by members of elBulli as an "oxygenation" process, which introduced "fresh air" to elBulli's operation.

Interestingly, in a way similar to how members of elBulli joined the organization and stayed for decades as new projects arose, professionals from different disciplines who began working with Adrià and his team on specific projects also continue to collaborate with the organization to this day. An enterprise that bolstered elBulli's creativity in several directions was one established with Luki Huber, a Swiss industrial designer based in Barcelona. As Albert recalled, none of the members of elBulli had any experience working with a designer. "[Huber] was just a young guy on a skateboard who said that he had made cans for cockle and candle spaghettis. . . . We thought he was nuts and asked him for his phone number." After a call from his brother, they were working with Huber on the design of new kitchen utensils and equipment that could further develop elBulli's cuisine. As it was common within elBulli, they started by sharing with Huber a particular line of inquiry: They needed to find a surface on which elBulli's cold preparations, served during the hottest months of the year, could be nicely presented while maintaining their temperature and state. After doing some research and based on his background in design, Huber proposed that they use slate due to its capacity to maintain extreme temperatures and started working on ways in which this material could be incorporated into elBulli's service, in particular, into the restaurant's marble plates. Soon after starting to work with the elBulli team, Huber realized that the work of designers and chefs had many things in common: They were both ultimately oriented toward the creation of a concrete object and aimed to be accepted by an end user. Yet the velocity with which the elBulli team tried out new ideas caught Huber's attention:

> When I got there [the elBulli workshop] I immediately noticed that I was encountering a well-oiled machine. They worked in a very systematic way and I had to adapt. . . . Later I realized that the reason they went so fast was because in the restaurant they had to work in a very disciplined manner . . . and they applied this same way of working to creativity.
>
> (Personal interview, Luki Huber, industrial designer, collaborator with elBulli)

An interaction that began as a one-time experiment, Huber remarked, gave rise to a "ping pong match" that has lasted more than a decade. New questions systematically emerged out of the interdisciplinary interactions about new ways of serving and manipulating food. Examples of this are, for instance, the invention of an artifact created to cut elBulli's technique of warm jelly in the form of spaghetti, which made it reproducible and appealing to diners; or the creation of a siphon with a special adapter that allowed for the instant transformation of warm gelatin into the form of one long spaghetto. A dish called 2 m Spaghetto Parmesan, consisting of a six-foot-long gelatin spaghetti, was created using this artifact designed by Huber in collaboration with elBulli.

As mentioned earlier, at the workshop the creative team also planned research trips to food companies, restaurants, or other countries to foster their creativity. I will briefly revisit one of these trips to illustrate how this occurred in practice. One of the most famous culinary techniques developed by elBulli, "spherification," was discovered during a visit to a candy factory in 2003. As the story goes, the Adrià brothers had been in the factory for a few hours and when they were about to leave, Albert saw a big bowl filled with water that contained small spheres of something that he could not recognize. Without thinking much of it, Albert took one of the spheres and squeezed it. To his surprise, the sphere exploded! "What is this?" Albert asked one of the employees of the factory, while looking straight at his brother. The Adrià brothers would learn that the spheres were the result of a gellification process produced by submerging a liquid mixed with sodium alginate in a calcium bath. Although the process sounds difficult when it is described, it produces the most spectacular results by instantly generating a thin membrane around the liquid that makes it look like a small, caviar-like sphere without actually becoming solid in the interior. As soon as they came out of the factory, Albert attempted the process and . . . it worked! What is important to notice here is that in essence the technique of spherification already existed, but it was the elBulli organization's philosophy that directed Albert's attention toward recognizing its value as a technique that could be applied within cuisine and incorporated into elBulli's new language.

Yet, as so often happens during the creative process, once this was discovered, a new challenge emerged: The elBulli team needed to cope with the constraints imposed by their primary context of operation, the restaurant. That is to say, they needed to find a way to use this new technique to serve customers by making it reproducible in exactly the same way. The interdisciplinary collaborations cultivated at the elBulli workshop were very important in this respect. On this occasion, the elBulli team turned to the collaboration with Huber for new answers. Together they worked on the design of an artifact that could simultaneously create multiple spheres of the same proportion. The object that Huber designed consisted of many syringes positioned at the same height placed on top of a calcium bath. When dishes were ready to be served, members of the kitchen staff could fill the syringes with the same amount of a given liquid and, after submerging it in the bath, they would have many identical spheres ready to be plated. The first dish that was ever made at elBulli using this technique was called Spherical Caviar of Melon (2003). It contained multiple caviar-like spheres made out of pure melon juice served inside a can of caviar that said "Imitation elBulli" on the outside, also manufactured by Huber. Moreover, the dish epitomized one of elBulli's creative principles by evoking the sixth sense of humor and irony in customers, who after trying the orange-colored spheres would unexpectedly realize that it was not real caviar but fake caviar.

These external ties with professionals from other disciplines and institutions multiplied and diversified in the years to come.[24] To name one final example, in 2003, the elBulli team turned to the scientist Pere Castells to better understand the chemical properties of spherification, which opened new possibilities to incorporate this technique into the restaurant's dishes. These collaborations later extended to universities, institutes, and research

2.2 and 2.3 From left to right: (i) adapter for spaghetti of warm gelatin design by Huber, and (ii) dish 2 m Spaguetto of Parmesan (#920, 2003). *Source*: Courtesy of Luki Huber, http://www.lukihuber.com. Photograph copyright: Franscesc Guillamet Ferran.

2.4 and 2.5 From left to right: (i) caviar machine designed by Huber, and (ii) Spherical Caviar of Melon (#873, 2003). *Sources*: Courtesy of Luki Huber, http://www.lukihuber .com. Photograph copyright: Franscesc Guillamet Ferran.

centers, first in gastronomy and later in other fields. The productive friction that emerged from these interactions led Adrià to include them as part of the normal functioning of his organization. According to Hagel and Brown, productive friction emerges by bringing together people with different skills and perspectives.[25] The friction that results from their interactions brings benefits to the organization by prompting new answers to unanticipated problems. At elBulli, members of this interdisciplinary group received the name of "agitators," due to their capacity to bring creative chaos into the experiments performed at the organization and to generate new paths that helped them move forward. Equally important, these interactions offered the creative team a direct window into the outside world, enabling them to scan their environment for new information and to assess the originality contained in their own creations, a very important function if one considers the enclosed and restricted conditions that characterized the work during the restaurant's season.

In sum, at the elBulli restaurant, internal processes were structured to generate optimal results in the production of a perfect service. The focus of the work was the generation of new products (e.g., dishes or recipes) that could be diligently reproduced by the staff members, irrespective of their personal background or training, thus mimicking the inputs-outputs relationship that describes the workings of a machine. The internal management of the elBulli workshop, on the other hand, was oriented toward the collective exploration of new conceptual and technical developments that could generate returns for the organization in the long term. Importantly, the transfer of information between these two branches of the organization was guaranteed through the maintenance of the same group of people on both ends. Although this description might lead one to think of the elBulli restaurant and the elBulli workshop as two sides of a continuum between hierarchal and heterarchical forms of organizing, it is important to note that unlike heterarchies, in which no central authority can be identified, at elBulli, both branches of the organization had one leader orchestrating all the work: Ferran Adrià.

In examining *The Success of Open Source*, Steven Weber pointed out an important disadvantage of centralized organizations in mobilizing innovation, specifically with regard to keeping an appropriate balance between exploitation and exploration.[26] Unlike organizations in which decision making is highly centralized, the open software industry operates based on a disaggregated community. Each participant in the community ("developers") can autonomously decide how to invest his time and energy, given that they all have access to the same source code. While some may decide to focus on exploitation—say, improving the existing technology by debugging activities—others may decide to focus on exploring new design architectures that can produce substantial changes in the technology. According to Weber, the disaggregated character of this community makes it possible to preserve a balance between exploration and exploitation by increasing the chances that on average the returns obtained will be positive for the organization. The case of the open source software industry stands in stark contrast with organizations like elBulli in which decision making is concentrated within a group or even within one person. While the latter kind of administration might facilitate the implementation of formal interventions within an organization, as we shall see, it also increases the probability of encountering problems in dealing with the trade-off between exploiting and exploring knowledge. This is because the survival and development of the organization is exclusively dependent upon the decisions made by people in higher ranks, which might lead to favorable outcomes but can also lead the system to its demise.

The establishment of a specialized team, schedule, and space, and of external collaborations, played a significant role in facilitating new ideas in the elBulli organization, both at the restaurant and at the workshop. Yet, as

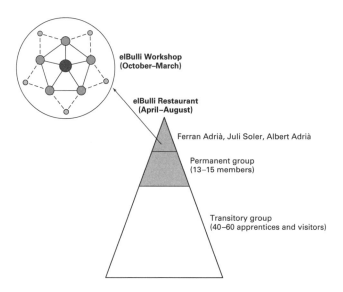

2.6 elBulli's team configuration (restaurant and workshop).

Internal organization of the elBulli restaurant and the elBulli workshop, from 2000 until 2011. The pyramid illustrates the organizational form that predominated at the elBulli restaurant, the branch largely responsible for productive tasks. The highly interconnected network represents the organization of teams at the elBulli workshop, mainly horizontal and multidisciplinary in character, and largely responsible for the organization's creative tasks (nodes in dark gray represent elBulli's creative team and nodes in light gray represent collaborations with professionals and institutions from diverse fields). One central authority, Ferran Adrià, can be identified on both sides of the organization.

2.7 and **2.8** On the top, elBulli's brigade de cuisine preparing one of the last meals of the elBulli restaurant in July 2011. In the center of this picture are two of elBulli's head chefs, Oriol Castro and Eduard Xatruch, and in the back, several of elBulli's apprentices. The picture on the bottom depicts a few members of elBulli's creative team working at the elBulli workshop, specifically, the chefs, Oriol Castro and Ferran Adrià, and the scientist, Pere Castells, in January 2013.

I mentioned prior to this intermission, elBulli's ultimate vision was not to generate isolated creative sparks, but to generate and institutionalize a new basis of knowledge, a new language in cuisine. In trying to achieve this, the elBulli team came to the realization that, irrespective of how imaginative their achievements were, if they were not organized into a coherent whole they would not be understood by others, not even by themselves. So in an effort to look for ways to effectively manage the work inside elBulli, a classification system to make sense of the information generated was developed, one that could be collectively recognized and expanded upon by the group and, perhaps, even by those outside the group.

Do Not Lose Track of Your Creations!

After 1987, when Adrià heard Chef Jacques Maximin's phrase "creativity means not copying," the elBulli team had taken a step back from the existing culinary approaches to try and develop their own language in cuisine. In order to not copy others, they needed to find a unique voice, one that could be recognized as distinct by themselves and by others. One way members of elBulli found to push themselves into thinking outside the box was by looking at possible combinations between pairs of ingredients that had never been put together before, an exercise that they would later conceptualize as "impossible combinations." To do this involved looking for gaps in knowledge instead of staying locked into existing ideas.

The creation of an iconic dish in 1992 called Veal Marrow with Caviar (#186), presented at the beginning of this chapter, exemplifies this stage of elBulli's search for novelty. As one of my interviewees recalled, Adrià was in the kitchen, desperately trying to envision a novel flavor combination. The most straightforward way he found to do this was by looking at the ingredients that he already had. First, he saw caviar, a highly valued ingredient in gastronomy; then he saw veal marrow, a soft and fatty product that is rarely seen in haute cuisine. What would happen if one put these two together?

"Bone marrow and caviar, it is so strange!" Adrià thought. While the combination of these two products was itself unique, members of elBulli knew that it also represented an existing culinary concept, typical in Catalonia, their common region of origin—namely the fusion of products from the sea and the mountains. The underlying idea for the new dish was then set: Based on a known culinary concept, the elBulli team would develop an innovative flavor profile through the mixture of two elements that, to the team's prior knowledge, had never been put together before. By doing this, they were indeed going to be able to fill in a blank in haute cuisine!

Though this might have first been experienced as a *eureka* moment, Adrià and his team soon realized that this type of creativity could only go so far before encountering serious limitations. The collision of heterogeneous bits of knowledge might indeed lead them to good ideas, but not to the generation of new conceptual and technical developments that could serve as the basis for a new genre in cuisine. The recipe Veal Marrow with Caviar represents precisely this turning point in elBulli's trajectory: from a chaotic and recombinant creativity to a strategic and conceptual creativity encouraged by an organized search for a new basis of knowledge and epistemic practices in cuisine.

Put simply, creativity expressed in a recombinant way might indeed have directed the elBulli team to fresh gastronomic results, yet not to develop a new gastronomic language that could be understood and spoken by others. Without the support of a coherent framework—an underlying "grammar"—any attempt to develop a new foundation of knowledge would be doomed to fail. Let's revisit a known example in the world of literature to see how this can be so:

'And only one for birthday presents, you know. There's glory for you!', [said Humpty Dumpty].

'I don't know what you mean by "glory",' Alice said.

Humpty Dumpty smiled contemptuously. 'Of course you don't—till I tell you. I meant "there's a nice knock-down argument for you!"'

'But "glory" doesn't mean "a nice knock-down argument",' Alice objected.

'When I use a word,' Humpty Dumpty said, in rather a scornful tone, *'it means just what I choose it to mean—*neither more nor less.'

'The question is,' said Alice, *'whether you can make words mean so many different things.'*

'The question is,' said Humpty Dumpty, 'which is to be master'—that's all.[27]

Despite Humpty Dumpty's claims of authority, it is a well-known fact that language is necessarily a social phenomenon,[28] which implies that new words have meaning only when they are shared and understood by a given community.[29] Accordingly, a person who only makes up new words, yet is not able to communicate, is likely to be considered absurd or crazy—not an innovator able to develop new ideas and to effectively turn them into accepted inventions. This highlights the importance of channeling innovations, especially radical innovations, in interpretive ways so that they can be understood and recognized by others. Adrià in particular might have known this from reading and reproducing the work of Carême and Escoffier, two of the most influential minds in modern cuisine and whose culinary inventions Adrià knew by heart. In the early 1800s, Carême generated an exhaustive system to codify his cuisine, which, by the turn of the century, had been modernized by Escoffier and had not only become widely used across the gastronomic community, but had also been decisive in reformulating the rules that governed haute cuisine.[30]

The crafting of a new culinary language at elBulli was mobilized by specific practices and methods, despite the fact that to the eyes of the organization's members these changes appeared to have happened in a natural way. In 1999, when elBulli's recently established creative team was working in a location separate from the elBulli restaurant, the business branch of the organization, elBulli catering, launched a consultancy project with a hotel chain in Seville, Spain, called Hacienda Benazuza. This project was aimed at "expanding the culinary magic of elBulli to 24 hours a day,"[31] for which the elBulli team embarked on the task of designing a new signature menu. Given that the elBulli restaurant's customers only got to try dishes made exclusively for one season, the project with Hacienda Benazuza could offer an opportunity for guests to gain familiarity with elBulli's cuisine of previous years. Consequently, the new customized menu would include a selection of the elBulli restaurant's historical dishes, that is, a compilation of elBulli's "greatest hits."[32] In order to create this customized menu, Adrià decided to mobilize his team toward gathering as much information as they could about every dish that had been made at the organization since he had joined the restaurant in 1983. Yet, as usually happened with elBulli, actions that at first seemed to be oriented toward achieving a definite goal evolved into larger projects that had multiple ramifications. In this case, a mission that began as the elaboration of one menu eventually became a massive venture that required not only the participation of elBulli's current members, but also that of its former members, some of whom had left the restaurant decades before.

Soon after the elBulli team had started to collect information about older dishes, Adrià realized that the effort that this task required could contribute to a larger purpose: Possessing detailed information about all of elBulli's past creations could become a rich basis of knowledge for their present and future creative endeavors. Intuitively, he realized that these efforts could serve to develop an organizational memory that could be distributed among the team. A chef who participated in elBulli's brigade de cuisine back in the early 1990s mentioned that the majority of the participants in the project did not really understand why they suddenly needed to pay so much attention to archiving instead of to cooking. "We are cooks after all, we are not used to being around books and papers," he said. The restaurant had just started to close during lunchtime and they all thought that this would allow them to have more spare time during the day, he noted. Yet only a few months later, Adrià had them begin to use all that extra time to study and to organize elBulli's archives, including old menus, files, and folders. In collecting this information, they also turned to the creative minds that had been behind elBulli's good ideas decades before and who no longer worked at the restaurant, namely the former head chefs and sous-chefs of elBulli's brigade:

He [Adrià] came to work every morning very early at elBulli and he was sitting there, at his table, working, full of papers, organizing. . . . The final result, at that moment, I could not see it clearly. I only started to understand more when I began to see Christian Lutaud, Jean-Louis Neichel, Xavi Sagristà, all the former head chefs and sous-chefs of elBulli, suddenly begin to appear out of nowhere! . . .

[Then I started to see it] It was all about remembering and refreshing those lost memories and anecdotes . . . about looking at the past, going back to the roots, the origins and remembering, cataloguing all that had been forgotten.

(Personal interview, former member of elBulli)

Following in Carême's and Escoffier's footsteps, Adrià asked the team members to catalogue every recipe developed at elBulli according to the ingredients and preparations that composed it and its date of elaboration. "Describe each recipe as if you were explaining it to a fool!" Adrià said, emphasizing detail in documentation. "Anyone must be able to understand it." By "anyone" he meant not only members of elBulli or professional cooks, but also regular people, basically anybody who might want to get acquainted with elBulli's novel approach to cooking.

The task of compiling and organizing all this information was massive, and the elBulli team soon realized that they were going to need time to accomplish it. So for the first time since Adrià's arrival at elBulli, they decided to take a sabbatical for one year to improve and expand the organization's work. Throughout 2002, no new culinary creations were going to be produced at elBulli. As a result of this intervention, the following year, the restaurant's menu would not include any new dishes. Over the course of 2002, instead, elBulli's members would be fully dedicated to gathering and synthesizing the organization's prior knowledge. Members of elBulli referred to this period as "the year of the retrospective." Here it is possible to see a conscious effort undertaken by the organization to explore new alternatives instead of continuing to extend existing knowledge.

Little was left to chance in conducting this massive task since a clear strategy was defined to approach it: While the records generated were ultimately going to be organized in chronological order, the process of synthesizing the information was not. Like piecing together a puzzle, the members of elBulli would start by collecting and examining the information that was most fresh in their minds (that is, the culinary creations developed during the prior year) and compiling it into a manuscript. This first manuscript, Adrià dictated, would serve as a model for organizing the information obtained during earlier years, reaching as far back as 1983, the year in which Adrià joined the elBulli restaurant. There was only one more challenge that needed to be overcome in order to lead this task to fruition: to define a suitable codifying system that could be used to organize elBulli's prior knowledge into a coherent whole. Whereas Carême's and Escoffier's culinary creations had been structured based on existing cooking categories, such as cooking bases, soups, entrées, and desserts, elBulli's gastronomic corpus needed to be organized according to a new framework, one capable of conveying the unique properties of the new cuisine that elBulli aimed to advance.

The majority of the chefs I interviewed claimed that they saved the information about previous creations "in their minds" or in notebooks and computers, and voluntarily shared this information with their teams when necessary. This informal way of cataloguing an organization's knowledge has also been found to be present in the field of design. In an ethnographic study of the design consulting firm IDEO, Andrew Hargadon and Robert Sutton found that information about previous projects was mainly stored in the designers' minds, personal written records, and on the final products that they generated.[33] This enables each designer to act as a "technology broker" within the organization by using their unique background in developing new recombinations of existing ideas. These methods for acquiring, saving, and retrieving an organization's knowledge, however, continue to be bound to the minds of its individual members. The processes that I found operating within the elBulli organization had a different character: They were based on a formal catalog that was distributed across the organization. Also, in line with elBulli's goals, this catalog did not focus on final products but on the underlying materials that led to those products. A major implication of this documenting system is that it generated a collective memory that was ready to be used and exploited by the organization's members in their search for new problems and solutions.

Crafting a Language Platform for Innovation

Developing a new language platform to describe elBulli's culinary approach did not happen by chance. It required a taxonomic effort that was quite different from the practical activity of cooking that members of elBulli's brigade or any such brigade are used to performing. It involved several intellectual exercises of mapping, in the simplest way possible, the elements that could represent elBulli's new cuisine. To do so, Adrià and a few members of elBulli gathered at the organization's headquarters, the restaurant in Cala Montjoi, with the objective of brainstorming a way in which their work could be integrated into a coherent structure. One of the participants in these meetings recalled this as one of the most exciting moments in the history of the organization. Using a paperboard and a pencil, as he usually does, Adrià sketched different elements that could be used to describe elBulli's work. Every time a set of elements was selected, the group tested its validity by evaluating whether or not it could also be used to describe the work of other chefs or even the work of professionals from other fields such as art, literature, music, fashion, or design. They aimed for elBulli's framework to be applicable to the analysis of any creative work, culinary or otherwise. From time to time Adrià's brother, Albert, would enter the room and give the team his opinion on the combination of elements that had been chosen. While on some occasions Albert would point out aspects of elBulli's cuisine that were missing from the diagram outlined, in other cases the elements chosen appeared to be inappropriate to the description of the work of other crafts. So, just as if they were creating a new recipe, the process of crafting a codification system to account for elBulli's work involved multiple processes of trial and error until a satisfactory solution was reached.

> It was one of the most important moments [of elBulli], because we were trying to find a map that could work: 'of course, this one works!' [we would say]. But then Albert [Adrià] would come from outside, with a fresh perspective, and say, 'We cannot analyze our cuisine if we are missing this'... and then we would need to start from scratch again. It was like a ping pong match, but a very exciting one.... We would be there, from 10 A.M. until 2 in the morning, trying out [maps] with Ferran. The day we found it I was exhausted, but also thought, 'How happy I am!'
>
> (Field notes, member of elBulli)

It took the meeting's participants a long time to realize that, whatever framework they settled on, it was going to be better suited for crafts that are essentially practical or, more precisely, in which the ultimate creation is material in nature, such as cooking, fashion, or design. Literature, for instance, can be seen as the opposite example given that the craft of writing is intellectual in essence and has words both as the main medium and the end of expression.[34]

After multiple iterations, the team members who participated in this process decided upon a set of four elements that described elBulli's work. Each element, they stated, represented a distinct family of words and was built on an underlying organization and philosophy that provided the building blocks for making it work:

(1) Products: refers to the ingredients used in a culinary preparation. Examples of products are types of fruit, vegetables, dairy, sweets, grains, fats, and oils.

(2) Preparations: corresponds to concepts and techniques used to create new culinary creations. Whereas concepts refer to theoretical constructs or ideas, techniques refer to a physical phenomenon produced by a new way of manipulating food. According to elBulli, for instance, deconstruction is a

concept as it represents the idea of breaking apart the different components of a traditional dish in order to make it unrecognizable from a visual standpoint. From a gustatory standpoint, however, the taste of the dish will mirror that of the traditional recipe, allowing it to be recognized by the diner. An example of a technique, on the other hand, is foams, as they are the result of a new cooking procedure, in this case, using a siphon to produce a light and soft texture in an instantaneous manner.

(3)   Technologies: corresponds to the kitchen equipment used to manipulate and utensils used to serve food.

(4)   Styles and characteristics: represent different culinary approaches and overall features of elBulli's cuisine. Examples of culinary styles developed at elBulli are the Mediterranean style mentioned earlier, developed early in the history of the organization, and which consists of the incorporation of traditional Mediterranean products and preparations into haute cuisine; or Natura, which is defined by creations that attempt to resemble sceneries of the natural world. In 2008, Albert Adrià wrote a book titled *Natura* that synthesizes this culinary style.[35]

According to elBulli's team, different combinations of these elements led to the production of new dishes and recipes, the restaurant's ultimate creations.[36] Also, as has been stressed, the team regarded the development of new preparations—that is, new concepts and techniques—as the main characteristic of elBulli's cuisine due to their capacity to generate truly unique designs.

The dish Spherical Caviar of Melon described earlier can be used as an example to explain how this framework was believed to work in describing elBulli's cuisine: The central *product* used in this dish is cantaloupe melon, a very common ingredient in Spanish cooking, and it is prepared by using a new culinary *technique* developed at elBulli: spherification. Both the *equipment* and *utensils* used for this dish were created at elBulli as well, as we know, in collaboration with the industrial designer Huber. These included an artifact designed to produce several caviar-like spheres simultaneously and a can of caviar with the label "Imitation elBulli" on it, which was specially manufactured for that dish. Finally, the dish's *style* and *characteristics* corresponded to elBulli's technical-conceptual approach to cooking, given that the underlying idea of the dish is based on one of elBulli's techniques (i.e., spherification). Another characteristic of the dish that elBulli considered part of its signature style was the explicit attempt to evoke diners' sense of humor and irony through a unique and amusing presentation.

In the same way as this framework could be used to map out elBulli's work, it could also be used to describe other crafts. A member of elBulli explained this to me by using the example of fashion: If I am a dressmaker, he said, first I would have to organize myself to create; I would need a team, a schedule, a workshop. I would also need a philosophy, to have an idea of what I want to do and how it would materialize into my final creations. The main products that I would work with are, for instance, fabrics, buttons, etc. The equipment and utensils that I would use are scissors, sewing machines, pins, thimbles. My styles and characteristics could be the use of rare fabrics, exotic color combinations, or the design of casual or vintage clothing. With all that, the member of elBulli concluded, I could create final products that are my own. In the case of a fashion stylist, these could be unique suits, dresses, or whatever else he wants to create.

Classifications are segmentations of the world.[37] They involve determined actions of sorting things out in ways that are meaningful to a given community, and, thereby, they change that community. In examining different classification systems—ranging from classifications of diseases to race to mortality—Geoffrey Bowker and Susan Star proposed that these systems should have the following characteristics: They should be based on unique classificatory principles, contain categories that are mutually exclusive, and aim to be complete. Similarly, as we can see, elBulli's attempt to build a system for codifying its cuisine was restricted neither to the organization nor to the world of cuisine. As in Bowker and Star's account, elBulli's classifications aimed to represent and encompass a world that was much broader than the organization's actual work, and aspired to influence a community that extended far beyond the organization, as we will see in the next chapter.

After settling on a set of elements, a discussion emerged among elBulli's members to decide the name that the new classificatory system should

Organization and Philosophy

Products

Preparations
(concepts and techniques)

Technologies
(equipment and utensils)

Styles and characteristics

New Final Products: Dishes and Recipes

2.9 elBulli's evolutionary map.

Sources: Author's own elaboration based on *A day at elBulli*: 515. Photographs courtesy of elBulli and Rosemary McGunnigle-Gonzales. Photograph copyright: Franscesc Guillamet Ferran.

receive. Two main possibilities were proposed: calling it either a "creativity map" or an "evolutionary map." They decided on the latter, as it would emphasize the unfolding and transformative character that was integral to the advancement of knowledge at elBulli, or at any other organization for that matter.

Once a framework was defined, old and new creations developed at the organization began to be classified according to the four families of words that compose elBulli's evolutionary map. One ex-member of elBulli explained how this process confirmed his belief in Adrià's extraordinary capacities. He drew on the biblical story of Genesis to support his claim by depicting Adrià as the God who, after having created the world, made Adam assign names to his creations:

Ferran was the pioneer of this kind of cooking, of this thinking process, so he had to be the one who named things. . . .

He is the God who, after having created the earth, named the tree 'tree,' the fish 'fish.' I believe that he is the creator, so it is normal that he had given names to things.

(Personal interview, former member of elBulli)

These internal practices of elBulli unveil an important aspect of mobilizing revolutionary innovation. Unlike incremental innovations or recombinations, which are bound to an existing background of knowledge, radical innovations require additional effort to be understood by others, even within the context of one organization. Their recognition, therefore, requires the invention of new words that can convey the new meanings generated and which can serve as "gears" or "transcribers" between actors and actions.[38] These dynamics also apply to the fields of music and art. Scholars have indicated that mobilizing radical innovations in music not only requires that practitioners engage in differentiation strategies from existing musical developments, but also that they entail a linguistic aspect encouraged by the creation of new concepts and styles that enable the establishment of a new paradigm.[39] Studies in the field of art have also pointed out that revolutionary innovations entail deliberate changes in the conventional language, which can then modify the character of the art works produced.[40] Mobilizing radical innovation, therefore, requires both the production of new content *and* new interpretative schemes that can orient the actors' perceptions toward the legitimizing of new facts. Thus by crafting a new language platform, elBulli moved beyond the mere production of new content to encourage new epistemic practices that proposed new ways of knowing cuisine.

Over time, Adrià and his team expanded elBulli's vocabulary by continuously incorporating new "words" into it, that is to say, new products, preparations, technologies, and styles. They did so mainly by extending and refining existing knowledge in haute cuisine (e.g., by incorporating popular ingredients or technologies into their work, such as a candy-floss machine to create a new dish, "cotton-paper"). Second, and most importantly for elBulli, they did this by introducing new concepts and techniques that could provoke changes in ways of thinking about food and cooking in general. In doing so, as we know, members of elBulli did not simply seek to generate new products or recombinations of products, but to expand the existing gastronomic vocabulary. This kind of effort resonates with Henderson and Clark's definition of "radical innovation" as being different from "incremental," "modular," and "architectural" innovation (the first, aimed at refining an existing design; the second, at introducing changes in the design's components; the third, in the relationship between its components).[41] Whereas these types of innovation follow a normal science framework, radical innovation involves the introduction of both a new set of concepts and new arrangements that lead to a new dominant design. The elBulli organization aimed to routinely engage with this latter type of innovation.

Establishing a "map" or classificatory scheme to organize elBulli's creations had significant repercussions in the achievement of the organization's goals. First, elBulli's evolutionary map provided the organization's members with a shared basis of understanding that allowed them to make sense of their world. This was especially important at elBulli, given that the world they aimed to create was different from what already existed. Having to invent new words to explain their creations thus reinforced the elBulli members' collective belief that what they were doing was truly original and unique. As related by one of elBulli's head chefs, "Realizing that there are no words to describe what you are doing, is the most obvious way of knowing that what you are doing is in fact new." Another ex-member of elBulli stressed this, saying:

> It is not merely that new concepts, techniques, and technologies were created. What is important is that a *new language* was created, because as with anything in life, if it doesn't have a name, it does not exist as such!
>
> (Personal interview, former member of elBulli, italics mine)

Second, gaining the skill of communicating via a codified vocabulary made it possible to connect the individuals' actions and beliefs with the organization's ultimate vision. In so doing, it provided a medium for the organization's members to navigate the new world that they were creating and to consolidate a community that had a shared foundation of knowledge and basis of cognition.[42] Having a "conceptual map" to orient their actions also allowed the organization's members to move their tangible creations to an abstract level from which multiple kinds of permutations could emerge. The map, then, represented a new medium to make innovation generative inside the organization.

In my conversations with elBulli's members, for instance, they explained how, after defining elBulli's evolutionary map, their experimentation processes were increasingly interrupted by conversations about whether a new discovery made was indeed a new concept or a new technique or, perhaps, neither. This change in behavior is significant, as it reveals that elBulli's codification was not a static system used to record what had been created at the organization and then stored in some hidden archive. Nor was it a conventional manual, a recipe book that simply listed the organization's end products. It was, rather, an operative system that was actively used by the organization's members to search for and implement new ideas. In this sense, elBulli's language functioned as a rigid yet flexible structure that directed the members' attention toward recognizing and generating opportunities for discovery. In the mid-twentieth century, organizational scholars called these structures "classification schemes";[43] later, when analyzing the workings of organizations at the turn of the twenty-first century, they called such structures "social technologies of search."[44] Interestingly, at elBulli the notions of classification and search do not appear to be opposites; instead, the organization's internal language constituted a *classificatory system* that guided and encouraged *search* within the organization.

Here it is worthwhile to mention an experiment presented in the influential book *Organizations* by James March and Herbert Simon, due to its potential to illuminate the significance of developing a *language* with definite categories and shared meanings within a social group.[45] The experiment was called "noisy marbles" and consisted of the following: Participants in the experiment were given a handful of marbles and were asked to determine the colors of each of them. While control groups were given marbles with unambiguous colors (e.g., blue, black, red, or yellow), experimental groups were given marbles that did not match conventional color designations in any way. Comparing the performance of the groups, the resulting evidence showed an interesting pattern: The performance of experimental groups was consistently hampered due to the lack of a formal vocabulary to describe the marbles. Most importantly, the data also showed that these groups' performance became equivalent to the control groups *only when* participants were able to create a *shared vocabulary*, that is, to generate categories that were accepted by all members of the group—quite similar to the taxonomic effort performed by elBulli's team in their attempts to innovate in cuisine.

Prior studies in the gastronomic field have revealed the lack of a technical vocabulary operating in the work within restaurants. In his seminal ethnography of professional kitchens, Gary A. Fine found that cooks mainly coordinated their daily work through a practical and improvised language, which he called a "sociolect."[46] However, the language that I found orchestrating elBulli's creative endeavors very much resembled the vocabulary found within the groups with higher performance rates in the noisy marbles experiment mentioned above. Rather than operating based on an improvised vocabulary, the elBulli creative team worked on the basis of a "strategic vocabulary,"[47] which allowed the organization's members to coordinate their actions toward the fulfillment of a common goal. Interestingly, I could not find evidence of the existence of such a collective accomplishment in my interviews with other culinary professionals, at least not in the form of a definite vocabulary like the one formally defined and deployed by elBulli's team. Besides allowing the organization's members to coordinate their present actions, the organizational practices outlined also allowed elBulli's members to evaluate their past and, in so doing, to create their future.

Auditing Creativity

Taste is subjective, so I had to generate a circle of objectivity to evaluate my creations.

—Public talk given by Ferran Adrià as part of the tour "Partners for Transformation" with Telefónica Company, June 2012, Chile

In the process of gathering information on elBulli's past culinary creations, Adrià and his team found something far more interesting than just the documentation of the data: Tracing elBulli's prior achievements made it possible to discover the underlying patterns that had led to discoveries and accomplishments and, thereby, to identify the unique features that characterized elBulli's cuisine. Since Adrià had heard the phrase "creativity means not copying," his biggest concern had been to create a distinctive culinary language. Therefore, examining the connections and disconnections among all of elBulli's creations offered the organization a perfect opportunity to examine how and to what extent its work had in fact deviated from the work of other professionals within the field and, hopefully, opened avenues that could help the elBulli team expand the gastronomic vocabulary at large.

In 2002, during elBulli's year of the retrospective, Adrià and his team embarked on the task of analyzing all the information gathered by using elBulli's evolutionary map as a common lens. They did so by carefully looking at finished dishes and detecting the components that made it a distinctive creation of elBulli, that is to say, an "elBullistic" creation. While some dishes might have involved a new product, concept, technique, or style developed at the organization, others included a combination of older ones. In fact, members of elBulli mentioned that the most interesting creations they invented lie precisely at the crossroads of the organization's vocabulary. If something elBullistic was identified in the dish under study, then it was incorporated into the organization's records along with an identification number that counted elBulli's own creations. If the opposite happened, that is, if the dish was deemed essentially a replication of someone else's work or if the personalized touch incorporated into the dish was not determined to be a significant contribution, then the dish was not included in the organization's records. Of particular importance here was the classification of those creations that incorporated a conceptual development into elBulli's creative inventory, which indicated the ways in which a new technique or concept had been implemented and the paths of discovery that it had opened.

A member of elBulli who participated in this process showed me a picture of one of elBulli's dishes in order to demonstrate how they interpreted and assessed their culinary work. The picture portrayed a dish that, at first glance, looked like a cocktail or a dessert (though I would later learn that it was a tapa, served at the beginning of elBulli's meal). The official name of the dish was written at the bottom: "Savory tomato water ice with fresh oregano and almond milk pudding" followed by the number "159."

> Look, this is a frappé of tomato, the first dish of our frozen-savory cuisine. From here onward, if we found that another savory frappé was done a year later, but if instead of tomato we did it with asparagus, then it wouldn't go into the analysis. But if rather than doing a frappé we said, 'Let's try to make it a sorbet,' and we realized that this had not been done before, then I would put it into the analysis of the next year.
>
> (Field notes, member of elBulli)

He continued to show me descriptions and pictures of dishes included in elBulli's records to further illustrate his point: "This was the first time in which a dish was served in a spoon," he pointed out while looking at another dish or, "This was the first time that we used this technique in a savory dish." Whereas the main innovation incorporated into the first dish, he stated, was the use of new cutlery and the incorporation of a new concept ("minimalism," used at elBulli to describe courses that can be eaten in one bite yet which are able to convey high levels of culinary magic), the main innovation in the second dish had been the introduction of the technique of caramelization into a savory elaboration (an example of what they call "symbiosis be-

2.10 Dish "Savory tomato water ice with fresh oregano and almond milk pudding," followed by the number, #159, 1992. *Source*: Courtesy of elBulli. Photograph copyright: Franscesc Guillamet Ferran.

tween the sweet and savory world"). In short, two main factors were used by elBulli's members in evaluating their creations: First, the extent to which *external references* were being used for the generation of novelty and, second, the extent to which *internal references* were being used to further expand that novelty. Adhering to these criteria, the elBulli team analyzed and classified each of the organization's creations starting from the year 1983 onward. As a consequence of their strict (and self-imposed) system of evaluation, the date of elaboration of the first dish ever created at elBulli was declared to be 1987, that is, four years after Adrià had joined the restaurant. This is because, based on the evidence analyzed, all dishes created before then had not been "truly elBulli's," but merely imitations or reproductions of existing culinary developments, especially of French cuisine. In sum, the elBulli team's efforts to systematize and analyze the organization's information offered a definite background against which new ideas could be collectively recognized and assessed by the organization's members, a process that Adrià calls "auditing creativity" and which, to this day, constitutes the basis of their creative endeavors.

The system of evaluation defined by elBulli represents the organization's attempts to actively build its identity as an avant garde restaurant and to maintain a strategic position within its institutional field. Organizations are "meaning systems" and, as such, they need to find ways to interpret their work and to determine their environment. To do this, organizations develop structures of shared meaning that are critical in supporting their functioning and endurance. These are not necessarily highly calculated structures but, as at elBulli, they are purposefully implemented by organizations to orient and shape the work performed by them.[48]

Over the course of 2002, using the same shared criteria of evaluation, the elBulli team examined not only finished dishes, but also procedures and practices that had led to new ideas. After realizing that the analysis of elBulli's creations made it possible to identify where and when creative sparks had occurred throughout the organization's history, Adrià and his team decided to codify and examine those as well. The results of this investigation were long lists of different creative methods that have inspired good ideas at elBulli (listed in table 2.1); records of the exact dates of trips to restaurants, food companies, or cities around the world in which discoveries had been made, along with exact descriptions of how they impacted work at the organization; and finally, a yearly report of unfinished ideas, namely potentially good ideas that had not made it all the way to the restaurant's menu. El-Bulli's team named these lists of unfinished ideas "what could have been but was not," emphasizing their latent creative value.

The unusual combination of a visionary mind and a disciplined way of working that is present in Adrià and his team has precedents in other iconic Catalonian innovators such as Ramon Llul, Pablo Picasso, and Salvador Dalí. In the thirteenth century, Llul developed a complex system of classification aimed at reducing all knowledge to specific principles, including knowledge from philosophy, theology, and natural sciences. Llul called his system "The Art," and proposed it as an all-encompassing rational tool to support the Catholic faith in missionary work. Picasso too, especially after his strong partnership with Braque when developing Cubism, kept meticulous journals of his work to monitor his creative process. Suitably, to this day Picasso is known for his detailed sketches and rigorous studies in the preparation of final art pieces. Finally, despite his eccentric and volatile personality, Dalí also devoted great efforts to develop a method that could grasp the irrational and unconscious images that characterized his work. He called it "paranoiac-critical method" and used it to methodically incorporate unconventional perceptions into art pieces.

TABLE 2.1 elBulli's creative methods

Inspiration (1987): Envisioning new ideas based explicitly on external references in gastronomy but also in art, design, the natural world, etc. (dishes of elBulli that use this methodology include, for instance, some that build on the work of Antoni Gaudi, the famous Catalonian architect who designed iconic buildings in the city of Barcelona).

Changes in the structure of the menu (1987): Transformations in the fine dining meal accomplished by eliminating traditional items on the menu (e.g., cheese trolley and dessert trolley), by introducing new items (e.g., snacks, tapas, avant desserts, morphings, and follies), or by blurring the boundaries between savory courses and sweet courses on a menu.

Local tradition as a style (1988): Turning to local products, cooking techniques, elaborations, and other characteristics to create (examples of this are the incorporation of cooking traditions from Catalonia, the use of the concept of tapas, and the inclusion of Mediterranean products and sauces, as well as sea and mountain dishes into haute cuisine).

Adaptation (1988): Creation of new versions of classic or traditional recipes served in a personalized way (i.e., according to elBulli's culinary philosophy).

Association (1989): Developing new ideas by selecting potentially fruitful combinations of products, cooking techniques, families of products, etc., through the use of predefined lists and records as well as the "mental palate" and "gastronomic criterion."

(continued)

Changes in the structure of dishes (1990): Altering the relationship between the elements that compose a dish (e.g., the main component, sides, or sauces) to propose a new disposition of the dish.

Symbiosis between sweet and savory worlds (1992): Incorporating ingredients, concepts, and techniques of one world into the other world to generate novel results.

New ways of serving food (1992): Creation of new molds, cutlery, or utensils for serving food or new ways of plating dishes (e.g., dishes finished by the waiter or the diner).

Technical-conceptual search (1994): Search for new concepts and techniques that give rise to novel results in different lines of development.

Creating with the senses (1994): Use of one of the five senses—vision, smell, touch, hearing, and taste—to create a new elaboration. Changes in the reference point may produce new shapes and proportions, new plating dispositions, new ways of "reading" a dish, or new product smells, textures, temperatures, and sequences.

Influences from other cuisines (1994): Incorporating culinary traditions from other geographic locations into elBulli's cuisine (for instance, trips to Mexico, Italy, Japan, China, and Thailand were particularly influential in elBulli's cuisine).

Deconstruction (1995): Disaggregating each of the elements of a known dish and changing its visual appearance by manipulating its texture and temperature, yet maintaining the essential taste of the original dish. In addition to the deconstruction of known dishes (e.g., potato omelet), known elaborations (e.g., mayonnaise) and products (e.g., asparagus) can also be deconstructed.

Commercial preparations and products in haute cuisine (1996): Incorporation of commercial products and preparations not common in haute cuisine.

The sixth sense (1996): Incorporation of new emotions and judgment criteria into a fine dining meal such as irony, transgression, provocation, childhood memories, surprise, games, decontextualization, culture, deceit, harmony, gastronomic memory.

Pluralism (1996): Creation of a new culinary elaboration based on one family of products.

Minimalism (1996): Obtaining the maximum "magic" with minimal elements, either in one bite, in one dish, or by using only one product or one family of products.

Reconstruction (2001): Reconstruct the core idea of a known dish by reassembling its components into a new version. Similar to the method of deconstruction, preparations and products can also be reconstructed.

Synergies: Use of different methods in combination to generate new dishes and styles or characteristics. In elBulli's cuisine this method was used especially during the last decade of the elBulli restaurant's existence.

Note: This table is organized according to the date on which the creative methods were first used or created, largely identified in retrospect by elBulli's team. ElBulli's creative methods can be applied in different levels to encourage the generation of new ideas: from the creation of ultimate culinary products (e.g., dishes or recipes), to components of dishes (e.g., ingredients, preparations, styles), sequences of dishes (menu), or to overall fine dining meal (e.g., service, presentation, etc). Although these methods originally referred to the world of cuisine, they could also be used to foster creative processes in other fields.

Source: Created by the author based on elBulli's catalogue, 1983–2002. Juli Soler, Albert Adrià, and Ferran Adrià, elBulli 1983–1993 (Barcelona: elBullibooks, 2004); Richard Hamilton and Vicente Todoli, Food for Thought, Thought for Food (New York: Actar, 2009).

At elBulli, the exhaustive analysis and recordkeeping resulted in definite documents that the members called "general catalogues," a collection of five volumes that analyzed all the organization's creations. The catalogues present pictures and descriptions of the dishes created each year, followed by lists of new products, preparations, technologies, and styles, also generated on a yearly basis. They also include descriptions of the organization's creative principles, methods, sources of inspiration, and ideas "that could have been but were not" . . . at least during the year under examination.

While elBulli's systematizing effort allowed the team to better coordinate their actions, it affected their actions as well. ElBulli's catalogues made vast amounts of information accessible and distributable among the organization's members. Suddenly, all of elBulli's work (including dishes, flavor combinations, methods, sources of inspiration, and potentially good ideas) were no longer the property of one visionary mind but were instead a distributed source of knowledge that could be collectively deployed in creative processes. In this sense, the recollection and analysis conducted contributed to the generation of a shared "mental palate" among elBulli's creative team that facilitated the experimentations performed within the organization. This explains why, during the final years of the elBulli restaurant's life, it was normal to hear a head chef say to the kitchen staff or the wait staff, "The new dish number A is an extension or a combination of the dish B and C, originally created in year D," or "This new technique X, developed in year Y, will be included in the new dish Z." In fact, I heard elBulli's head chef and creative director, Oriol Castro, say the latter at a meeting during one of the last days of the restaurant's existence, as referenced in chapter 1.

ElBulli's classifications, therefore, acted as representational devices that enabled the organization to interpret and evaluate its functioning according to the organization's goals. A similar practice can be found in other kinds of organization, such as in Edwin Hutchins's analysis of the inner workings of a cockpit system.[49] This study showed that coordination and "distributed cognition" were achieved within the organization through the use of "representational devices" that made it possible to remember tasks that were vital to the organization (e.g., remembering its speed via a speed card booklet or airspeed indicator). According to Hutchins, these devices ensured the system's effective operation by offering a medium for the crew members to collectively assess information and to modify their actions accordingly. In a similar way, the classifications generated at elBulli rendered the organization's information analyzable by the team toward the achievement of a shared goal.

After 2002, the organization of information into catalogues became a normal part of elBulli's functioning. Every year, during the restaurant's off-season, members of elBulli would gather to analyze the information generated during the previous year and synthesize it into catalogues. These catalogues, in turn, became an additional and more definite layer of the already existing recordkeeping system that supported the investigations of elBulli's creative team, composed first of the "files of creativity" (which constituted a short-term memory for the organization), followed by "folders of creativity" (a medium-term memory), and finally, the yearly catalogues, which represented a more permanent source of elBulli's recollections. Together these three types of records functioned as backup devices that fostered the development of new ideas in continuous ways. For instance, every year, the lists of ideas that-could-have-been-but-were-not were the first resource that members of elBulli drew upon for their experimentations at the workshop. As explained by a member of elBulli's creative team, once at the workshop, they did not start creating from scratch: "We first tried to go back to those [already explored yet unfinished] ideas, looking at their essence, trying to renew them, to recycle them, once and again." A similar process was undertaken by members who coordinated elBulli's side business projects, which used these developed and underdeveloped ideas originally generated for the restaurant, and explored their latent value in collaborations with external companies.

If one tries to be creative for one day or a few weeks, one can rely only on intuition or spontaneity. But if one's aim is to be continuously creative, and in a radical way, as elBulli's members attempted to be, one must also rely on established practices and methodologies that can help you to obtain that goal. In this sense, the compilation of elBulli's creative methods was another fund of knowledge that enhanced the creative processes within the organization. According to elBulli's members, from 2002 on, these methods were used often as intuition for the development of new ideas. The diagram in figure 2.11 illustrates the steps that constituted elBulli's creative processes during the last decade of the organization's life, as depicted by its members. It shows how elBulli's lists of creative methods, recordkeeping practices, and the analyses of the organization's achievements were systematically deployed for the development and implementation of new ideas. Overall, these practices developed at elBulli not only provided stability and dynamism to the system by pushing its members to continuously retrieve, evaluate, and reconsider old certainties, but also to systematically search for new gaps of knowledge that could offer new possibilities to create.

The data that I collected suggests that at the time elBulli was methodically documenting and analyzing all its work, this was not a frequent practice

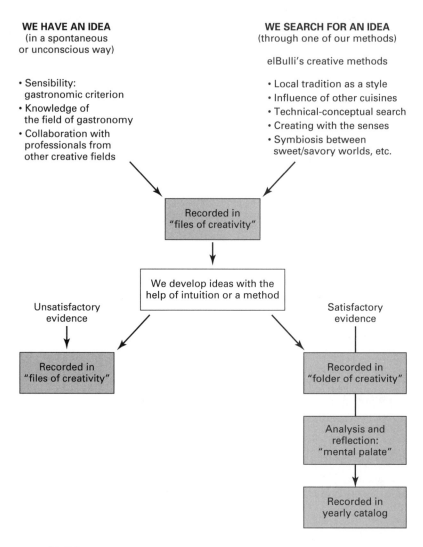

WE HAVE AN IDEA
(in a spontaneous
or unconscious way)

WE SEARCH FOR AN IDEA
(through one of our methods)

elBulli's creative methods

• Sensibility:
  gastronomic criterion
• Knowledge of
  the field of gastronomy
• Collaboration with
  professionals from
  other creative fields

• Local tradition as a style
• Influence of other cuisines
• Technical-conceptual search
• Creating with the senses
• Symbiosis between
  sweet/savory worlds, etc.

Recorded in
"files of creativity"

We develop ideas with the
help of intuition or a method

Unsatisfactory
evidence

Satisfactory
evidence

Recorded in
"files of creativity"

Recorded in
"folder of creativity"

Analysis and
reflection:
"mental palate"

Recorded in
yearly catalog

2.11 elBulli's creative process.

All instances of systematization in elBulli's creative process are included in gray boxes.
Source: Personal summary of a diagram seen at the elBulli workshop on July 2012.

among professional restaurants. As one chef told me, typically good chefs keep a notebook in the pocket of their chef's coat and take notes of what works during their daily work. But most of their culinary secrets are kept between the lines and left inaccessible to those who do not participate in the cooking processes. Other chefs mentioned that while they constantly wrote ideas on a board that they kept within the kitchen, they also asserted that the next day "someone would come and erase them." Alternatively, some of the chefs that I interviewed did publish cookbooks every now and then, especially those whose work had already been recognized by influential gastronomic institutions. Yet they also acknowledged that they did not analyze the information in exhaustive and systematic ways in order to find patterns in the data, as we know elBulli did. In this context, the long lists of recipes, flavor combinations, preparations, creative methods, and finished and unfinished ideas that were integral to elBulli's creative processes were something that caught the attention of other culinary professionals who encountered the organization's working system.

One purveyor who worked with Adrià and his team from the early 2000s pointed out that he noticed strong differences between how elBulli and his other clients approached creativity. Different from other haute cuisine chefs at that time, he observed, elBulli's team had seemingly defined its own rules of the game to develop a new cuisine:

> They would have these big whiteboards, and starting from these boards they would have these big white poster papers to write down all different techniques, all different preparations, all different ingredients, all different whatever. And then they would start doing crisscross. Almost to a point that it was like *a game*. It looked like backgammon or chess....
>
> (Personal interview, purveyor for elBulli)

Quite different from elBulli's initial chaotic and intuitive attempts to generate novelty by bringing together disparate materials, the experimentation processes performed at the workshop appeared to the eyes of this purveyor as defined by clear and shared procedures that determined novel points of departure to create:

> That's why they were able to break the barrier, because they weren't doing the traditional 'OK, take it in the kitchen and try it.' No, no! they were doing it almost like in a mathematical way . . . they were doing these crisscrosses of combinations which on paper you can see are possible, but if you were in the kitchen and have the ingredients in front of you and the pans in front of you, you would never have thought of it, never. . . .
>
> So that was the big, big difference: He [Adrià] made it almost scientific, *it wasn't creative and spontaneous necessarily. It became creative, and in the end it is creative, but it was a scientific way of being creative and not a random way.* . . . Otherwise, he would never have come up with a lot of these things.
>
> (Personal interview, purveyor for elBulli, italics mine)

Furthermore, one of elBulli's apprentices pointed out that the aspect of elBulli's system that had caught his attention the most was the documentation and classification schemes used within the organization. Soon after arriving at elBulli, he claimed, he could recognize the power that these practices had in defining the organization's future, even while its invention was in progress:

> Most restaurants when they feel that it's time to write a cookbook, they would need to go back, almost do research about dishes that they did and why they got there. Whereas like elBulli would be doing this while it was happening! It is so rare. It's almost impossible, it's like almost knowing that you're going to be great, you know?
>
> (Personal interview, apprentice of elBulli)

It has been mentioned that elBulli's classifications and documentations served as a common repository of knowledge that oriented and encouraged the experimentation processes inside the organization. Also, and perhaps more importantly, the conclusions obtained from the analyses of the recollection of elBulli's products, preparations, technologies, styles, creative methods, or

combinations of any of the former, were increasingly used at the organization as a toolkit for the construction of new "facts." The more equipped
elBulli's own repertoire and test kitchen became, the more the team could
build on the organization's own knowledge, rather than on external references, to generate and validate new ideas. In doing so, they consolidated
what Adrià calls elBulli's "creative patrimony" or "own tradition." At a public event in New York City, Adrià explained the underlying logic of elBulli's
attempts by saying, "We create words, with those words we create sentences
and with those sentences we create paragraphs . . . the more words we have,
the more unique our language will be."[50]

The results obtained through these practices indeed increased the organization's capacity to create new and exotic dishes. If we trace the genealogy of
elBulli's dishes, it is possible to notice an increasing symbiosis between
elBulli's own patrimony of knowledge with the creation of ever more unique

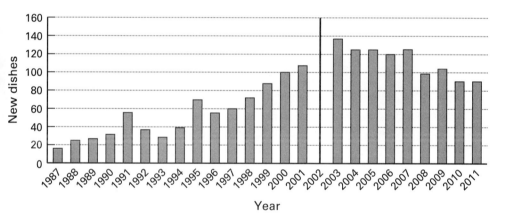

2.12 elBulli's new dishes (1987–2011).

Number of new dishes created at elBulli from 1987 to 2011 (from dish #1 to #1,846),
according to the organization's records. ElBulli's "year of the retrospective," 2002, is marked
with a black line. (During the years 2010 and 2011 the restaurant's seasons happened one
after the other with a total number of 180 new dishes developed. For the purposes of this
annual analysis, I divided this amount into two to make it correspond with each year.).
Source: elBulli's records.

and elBullistic recipes. However, as will become clearer in subsequent chapters, while this innovative capacity to relentlessly create recipes (or final products) became a trademark of elBulli and was considered noteworthy by other professionals in the gastronomic field, it was not what the organization ultimately aimed to accomplish. As can be seen from figure 2.12, Adrià and his team completely renovated the menu once a year, developing a total of 1,846 dishes in the restaurant's trajectory. The number of new dishes generated by elBulli expanded consistently from 2003 on, the year after the retrospective, by creating over 120 new dishes on average every season.

In sum, over the years Adrià and his team developed an infrastructure that coordinated action and belief inside the organization and that was characterized by a particular vision, set of codes, and methodologies. As in the invention of a game, elBulli's system proposed methods that distributed the roles that each participant would play, specified how time and space would be used, and indicated how knowledge would be acquired, stored, and deployed toward the achievement of the organization's final goals. What is most interesting is that elBulli developed a common language that was understood and spoken by the organization's members and that was used to collectively interpret, evaluate, and expand the work that was performed inside the organization. Alongside shared classifications, a system for documenting and analyzing the work was also instituted at elBulli, which rendered the knowledge generated available to all its members, irrespective of their background or the specific moment at which they had joined the organization. The result of this was a disciplined yet dynamic structure that fostered the production of innovation in various ways. The linguistic foundation that coordinated the work inside elBulli was a key element that provided dynamism to the system. As Weick mentions with respect to the dynamics of jazz improvisation, the acquisition of a common language supports the emergence of order and control, while at the same time it encourages fresh action and autonomy.[51]

To conclude, let me return to a question posed at the beginning of this chapter: How can an organization organize for change? What are the kinds of organizational models that facilitate the continuous enactment of radical innovation?

So far, my analysis has shown that elBulli achieved this by defining radical innovation as the core of the organization's functioning, then attaching symbolic meaning to the organization's creations, and finally by setting up shared systems of classification and search for the organization's members to detect when their creations were contributing to the fulfillment of the organization's ultimate vision and to what extent. The next chapters will reveal that once these internal practices became recursive, they made it possible for the organization to reproduce itself based on its own creations (both incremental and revolutionary) and change the organization's structures accordingly, to the point of reinventing the organization itself!

Taking all the evidence into account might lead one to conclude that establishing a self-referential structure and language of creation can enhance an organization's ability to bring about novel ideas. However, although this might work in practice, it can also be highly risky. Again, if one speaks a language that nobody else understands, one's ideas are likely to be indecipherable and meaningless to others and, therefore, likely to remain hidden. But, as we know, this is not what happened to elBulli's work. This is because in addition to generating an internal structure to innovate, the organization developed ways to get its ideas recognized and validated by external parties. ElBulli's members paid as much attention to making their new ideas accessible as to the originality with which they imprinted them. As a result of these external practices, the development of a distinctive cuisine was accompanied by an emergent community that also craved elBulli's culinary creations. The next chapter examines how the organization reached the world that resided beyond the remote natural reserve of Cala Montjoi to percolate into other kitchens around the globe.

Smoke Foam, #400
1997

Serves 10 people

© *Franscesc Guillamet Ferran*

To prepare the smoke water:

500 g (2 cups) of water
2,000 g (4.5 lb) of green firewood
500 g (17.5 oz) of green leaves

To prepare the smoke foam:

500 g (2 cups) of smoked water
   (cooking method above)
2 sheets of gelatin, approximately
   2 g (0.07 oz) each (previously
   hydrated in cold water)
1 ISI siphon of ½ liter (1 pt)
1 shot of N_2O

To prepare the croutons:

1 piece of sliced bread
   (100 g [3.5 oz])

Final touches and presentation:

1. Fill a shot glass with smoke foam.

2. Place two cubes of bread on top of
   the foam.

3. Season it with virgin olive oil.

(Abbreviated for purposes of illustration.)[1]

Diffusion and Institutionalization of Innovation

elBulli's Universe

When the elBulli restaurant closed on July 30, 2011, several of its apprentices traveled all the way to Cala Montjoi to help Adrià and his team prepare the restaurant's last meal. Adrià remembered this as the happiest day of his life. "We had never celebrated a party at elBulli. And I didn't think we should change. But I realized that I was wrong. It was unfair to the team."[2] So he decided to throw an unforgettable party on the last day of his restaurant's final season. The event consisted of a meal that retraced the historical trajectory of the restaurant by presenting its most emblematic dishes. According to the head chef, Oriol Castro, it included those dishes "which had an impact because of the [incorporation of a new] technique or concept."[3] Fifty diners, consisting of friends and relatives of the elBulli's "family," were invited to enjoy the forty-nine-course meal prepared especially for the occasion. The day of the elBulli restaurant's closing, magazines and newspapers worldwide carried pictures of Adrià wearing a white chef coat and a blue apron, with his arms up in excitement. Standing behind him were the members of elBulli's team and elBulli's former apprentices, who were now regarded as celebrity chefs—Joan Roca from El Celler de Can Roca, René Redzepi from Noma, Grant Achatz from Alinea, Massimo Bottura from Osteria Francescana, and Jose Andres from Think Food Group, among others. By then, elBulli had been acclaimed "the most influential restaurant in the world"[4] and, days after the event, the mass media used expressions like elBulli's "last supper" or "elBulli rises to the heavens"[5] to report on the event, suggesting that Adrià and his team had left the restaurant when they were at their best.

As this brief description of elBulli's "last supper" indicates, by the time the restaurant shut its doors, the elBulli team was far from being a group of

3.1 and 3.2 Gastroeconomy (www.gastroeconomy.com)/Marta Fernández Guadaño.

lonely creators, working in the isolated mountains of Cala Montjoi. On the contrary, through the years the organization's knowledge and practices had managed to spread far beyond the restaurant's immediate environment and were taken up and expanded upon by chefs around the world. Indeed, as this manuscript goes to print, no fewer than seven of the ten best restaurants according to the San Pellegrino list extensively incorporate into their cooking culinary techniques or concepts pioneered by elBulli. And, as we shall see, not only had elBulli's culinary creations found their way into other kitchens, but the key beliefs and methodologies that guided work inside elBulli had been adopted as well.

In sum, by 2011 elBulli had become a key driving force in the gastronomic avant garde, stimulating changes in previous conceptions of a meal, the internal management of high-end restaurants, and the relationships among chefs or between chefs and society. Beyond gastronomy, Adrià had become a public figure: *Time* magazine had nominated him among "the 100 most influential people in the world," he had been appointed "Ambassador of the Spanish brand" and had become the first haute cuisine chef to be invited to the Documenta 12 art exhibition of Kassel, and to receive the Lucky Strike award for designers, to name just a few of his honors. Furthermore, without holding any college degree, Adrià had been awarded degrees *honoris causa* in widely disparate fields, including chemistry, humanities, and food technology. In addition, since 2010 he had been the designated keynote speaker of a yearly course taught at Harvard University called Science and Cooking.

To explain the impact that elBulli had on its wider institutional environment, one haute cuisine chef, who was not connected to elBulli, associated it with the Big Bang theory, positioning Adrià and the restaurant as the catalyst in the emergence of a "new universe:"

For me, Ferran Adrià or elBulli is like a Big Bang, like an explosion that happened at a given moment in the gastronomic universe . . . the epicenter, the genesis of all this is elBulli and Ferran Adrià. Ferran Adrià in all his extensions, I mean, his team and him as the leader of this movement.

... If I were trying to explain to a kid what elBulli is, I would explain it like this. He [the kid] would not need to have an understanding of gastronomy to appreciate that suddenly an explosion happened and from that explosion many different rocks and planets began to form to create a whole new system.

(Personal interview, head chef of haute cuisine restaurant, Spain)

Although the above conception of the emergence and impact of elBulli as a Big Bang event is appealing, it does not correspond with reality. The Big Bang theory, as explained by the renowned physicist Stephen Hawking, describes the expansion of the universe that might have emerged spontaneously, prior to which events cannot be defined or observed.[6] Yet, as Fleck pointed out in relation to scientific discoveries, new facts do not emerge all of a sudden.[7] Just as there is not one sea toward which all rivers flow, Fleck claimed, there is no intrinsic logic that leads to discoveries becoming scientific facts. Thus, even if in hindsight scientific anomalies or innovations might appear to be logical or objective solutions, they are the results of concrete and systematic efforts that make it possible for new ideas to be recognized by a given "thought collective," that is, a group of people who share a common base of knowledge and who can therefore assess the value of ideas and help expand upon them. Similarly, at elBulli, new ideas and practices were carefully crafted by the organization against a background of accepted knowledge, and they were mobilized by a thought collective which allowed them to *become* successful.

In the field of art, Becker pointed out that the success of new creations does not depend on their intrinsic aesthetic value, but on their ability to *ideologically* and *organizationally* rebuild the existing network of collaborations or to create new ones.[8] In particular, revolutionary innovations need to be processed, and this requires building a new "art world" around them that enables them to achieve some permanence. Cubism, for instance, could not have emerged without offering possibilities for other artists to recognize unfamiliar languages and to learn about the new vision, techniques, and activities that were being proposed by the movement.

Hirsch too highlighted that new ideas in the industries of book publishing, recordings, and motion pictures need to be discovered, endorsed, and carried to the public by organizations in order to meet an intended audience.[9] In the publishing industry, editors must meet regularly with writers to find ideas for new books, and popular music artists must achieve coverage on the radio in order to generate a consumer demand. The emergence of swing as a new musical style, for instance, followed this trajectory: It occurred only after swing tunes had been played on the radio stations, when the term *swing* had already been established among young jazz aficionados, and when iconic swing figures, such as Benny Goodman and Glenn Miller, had coordinated tours across the United States or developed glossaries on how swing music should be played.[10] Altogether these examples show that if new creations are not processed favorably by the system of collaboration of which they are a part, they are doomed to fall into oblivion, regardless of how original or inventive they are.

One counterexample to this seems to be the work of Don Van Vliet, alias Captain Beefheart, whose experimental approach to rock music in the 1960s, while highly creative, remains followed mostly by a specialized group of aficionados. Unlike his acclaimed high school friend, Frank Zappa, Van Vliet did not like to play in public and only performed a few concerts when his Magic Band was at the peak of its fame. Moreover, experts have observed that Van Vliet's compositions seemed to lack musical forms that could be detached from his individual talent and thus easily reproduced by other practitioners.[11] This might explain why obituaries after his death characterized Van Vliet as a "musical maverick," whose original musical compositions remain largely part of a "cult obsession."[12]

At elBulli, in contrast, alongside the internal "circle of objectivity" that the organization constructed to guide, evaluate, and validate the team's creative endeavors, an added external circle of objectivity was also carefully built by the organization, which allowed outsiders to understand and recognize the value of the organization's work. In what follows, I propose a framework of three dimensions to analyze how elBulli mobilized new ideas and practices in order to reach an intended audience. This framework consists of, first, a conceptual dimension, that is, the development of a new concept of fine dining. Second, there is a spatial dimension, corresponding to the vehicles developed to make the organization's knowledge and practices accessible to others. And third, there is a social dimension, engaging the social dynamics that fostered the creation of a new art world around elBulli's work and encouraged the recognition of the organization's claims.

The value of this analytical framework relies on the fact that it proposes embeddedness and institution building as a constitutive part of innovation, and especially of radical innovation. In other words, it emphasizes that one cannot talk about *inventions*—that is, innovations that are able to percolate within a field—without taking into account the socializing and institutionalizing practices that enable them to have an impact on and be undertaken by a given audience. People or organizations might come up with new and good ideas all the time, but it is *how* those ideas are mobilized on the ground that ultimately determines their social appreciation and influence.

When I asked my informants, connected or unconnected to elBulli, about the factors that might explain elBulli's impact on the gastronomic field, different elements were mentioned: (1) the distinctive character of elBulli's culinary creations; (2) the restaurant's exotic location; (3) the exclusive system of reservations; (4) the various awards given to the restaurant by prestigious institutions inside and outside of the culinary field; and (5) the continuous and penetrating exposure of the elBulli restaurant and, most notably, of Adrià to the mass media and the press. In table 3.1 I present a selection of quotations from my in-depth interviews that illustrate the significance of each factor. Details on the subjects interviewed and the internal variability of the data collected can be found in the Appendix.

Although all these factors are indeed critical in explaining elBulli's influence and fame, by themselves they do not tell us about the *how*, that is to say, the processes whereby elBulli's new ideas and practices came to be understood and recognized by the gastronomic and other fields. On the one hand, the distinctiveness of the restaurant's cuisine and its geographic location were the main preconditions that encouraged the interest in elBulli in the first

TABLE 3.1 Factors mentioned by interviewees to explain the influence and impact of the elBulli restaurant in the gastronomic field

Factors	Examples of Quotations
Distinctiveness of culinary creations	• "It has to do with Ferran's search for offering something new and not replicating what others were already doing. Not having fear of failure or fear of doing something different. This fearlessness, coupled with the quest to do things well and strive for perfection, allowed elBulli to attain the status it has today." (Personal interview, apprentice at elBulli) • "I think Ferran was legitimately doing new, cutting-edge, and innovative things. And that captured the imagination both for us and, most importantly, of colleagues throughout the world." (Faculty member of a culinary institute, United States)
Location	• "The location was very unique. I mean, two hours away from Barcelona in a very small village on the sea in Costa Brava and the Cala Montjoi; such a beautiful place in the mountains that was so quiet and peaceful. Just to drive there, just the excitement of the drive . . . , up the hill, up mountains and down, descending to elBulli, is very celebrating and beautiful. So that itself is an attraction. Then you get to this temple of gastronomy. It is completely different from everything you have ever seen in your life." (Personal interview, chef and owner of haute cuisine restaurant, United States)
Exclusivity of the restaurant	• "They're open six months during the year, so they'll be open like 100 days or 135 days only. It makes you feel that you need to go there before they close again! . . . When there is a sale at the store and the store is open only for one day, everyone will feel that they need to go." (Personal interview, apprentice at elBulli restaurant)

(*continued*)

- "So few people got to eat there in reality. . . . If they had left it [the restaurant] open [for] lunch and dinner seven days a week, I don't know if they would have been able to keep up with the hype." (Personal interview, chef in haute cuisine restaurant, United States)

Prizes and awards	- "You need to have the reputation, based on Michelin stars or whatever it is, of just being on a different level . . . because you have to play by certain rules." (Personal interview, apprentice at elBulli)
	- "I think they were doing things differently before, but once they had the three stars it may have emboldened them." (Personal interview, chef and owner of restaurant, United States)
Media and press	- "I think the change in media helped because it flattened the world in terms of . . . the idea of a chef becoming a worldwide phenomenon in the way that it is now, is impossible. . . . To me the communication helped to transform them from what could have been isolated to sort of an epidemic." (Personal interview, chef of haute cuisine restaurant, United States)
	- "The more controversial you are, the more famous you get, that's my opinion. I think controversy draws fame." (Personal interview, apprentice at elBulli)
	- "Like in 2001, 2002, the *New York Times* wrote an article about [elBulli]. And if you have the *New York Times* write an article about you, everyone else is gonna write an article about you. And that makes it kind of snowball, that is how the press happens. . . . After that big article in the Sunday *Times*, everyone was talking about [elBulli] in New York." (Personal interview, chef of haute cuisine restaurant, United States)

place and that later expanded demand. On the other hand, the awards and media coverage received by elBulli were in essence recognitions after the fact, that is, post-facto manifestations of the social impact the organization had already acquired. Further, as suggested by one interviewee, the restaurant's exclusive system of reservations may indeed have been a factor that increased the hype about elBulli; yet by itself, again, this constraint emerged as a result of the curiosity that already existed about the elBulli restaurant.

Thus, if our aim is to understand *how* a new universe developed around elBulli's creations, namely *how* old and new "planets" came to be aligned around them, we need to look beyond the factors identified above. We must examine the social practices by which elBulli projected itself into its environment and the effects that those practices had in the consolidation of the organization and its leader's image and identity. This chapter will look at the mechanisms that made it possible for elBulli's creations to become accessible to and expanded upon by a particular thought collective. In doing so, it is important to bear in mind that changes—even revolutionary changes—do not involve absolute shifts in the existing patterns of cooperation, but modifications in the network of interactions and the paradigmatic ways of doing things that shape a field. This chapter examines how elBulli's distinctive approach to cooking was constructed over time and eventually made its way into other kitchens around the world, and the support system generated by the organization to amplify the impact of its creations.

A Context for a New Taste

Innovation happens in context. Our interpretations are necessarily attached to a series of reference points that serve as our basis for interpreting anything new to us. This is especially true in the field of cuisine, given our strong familiarity with food and its preparation. Distinct from other cultural products such as a work of art or an opera, culinary products are necessarily ubiquitous in our ordinary life, and, as such, our previous experiences and preferences inevitably influence our judgments of food. Conveying a new idea of what food can be, therefore, might seem like a quite difficult task, as we all seem to have a fairly concrete idea of what good food tastes like. In short, we all feel like experts when it comes to appreciating food and cooking.

The intrinsically subjective character of taste might lead one to argue that, in theory, there are no constraints to what restaurants can offer. Yet our practical experience shows us the contrary: Depending on what kind of restaurant one chooses to go to, one *expects* to be served a particular kind of food, which consists of a particular set of items, often cooked in quite specific ways. Hence, cooking and serving food at restaurants appears mainly as a negotiation, a game of expectations, in which the chef and the diner engage in a dialogue that determines the kind of culinary products that will be prepared by the chef and craved by the diner. This idea of restaurants as a game of expectations resonates with Mitchell Davis's description of restaurants as fantasies, as places of possibilities, where social identities can be constantly created and reconfigured.[13]

My empirical investigations of elBulli in particular, and my conversations with chefs of other high-end restaurants in general, show that the latitude that is permitted to a chef to innovate does not emerge all of a sudden. Rather, chefs need to build *trust* among their diners so as to be able to express their creativity in ways that can surpass (and sometimes even contradict) the diners' expectations. To do so, a particular *context* needs to be created, a context that allows chefs to attach meaning to their work and consumers to identify the symbolic value of the chef's creations.[14]

Earlier, I considered how an internal framework was developed at elBulli to enable its members to detect and validate the organization's new knowledge. Also, an external context was developed over time by the organization in order to make it possible for external agents—other chefs, gastronomic critics, faculty members of culinary institutes, diners, and interested parties in general—to derive meaning from the elBulli team's work. As referenced by one member of the organization, "If you do not set any limits, your work can be seen as a mere performance, as a show. So one needs to set up a framework of operation." This was ratified by one interviewee who said, "Some dishes I am sure only make sense in that dining room [elBulli's], served by that chef. Once you take it out of that context [that meaning] is lost." This chapter will reveal that radical innovation in any field is made possible by building a distinct basis of knowledge—what Kuhn described as a "paradigm"—against which novelty can be identified and validated by a community.[15] Moreover, as stressed by Latour, it is the continuous movement from the organization's inside to its outside that explains an organization's ability to spread and institutionalize new ideas and practices in the larger system in which it exists.[16]

A New Concept of Fine Dining

The conceptual framework defined by elBulli for the development of a new approach to cooking was demarcated by four parameters. These parameters, which were defined early in the organization's trajectory, determined the kind of pleasure that the restaurant aimed to deliver to its audience: First was the physiological pleasure, corresponding to the basic need that one aims to fulfill when eating. This sort of pleasure is closely associated with the notion of hunger. As Jean A. Brillat-Savarin pointed out in his famous work *The Physiology of Taste*, it refers to the instinctive response of satisfying a necessity.[17] Second was the sensorial pleasure, namely the subjective act of liking or disliking something. This kind of pleasure is attached to our senses and to our individual food preferences. Third was the emotional pleasure attached to a given culinary experience, which is contingent on each situation, based on the company, the scenery, and so on. Last but not least, elBulli positioned the reflective pleasure, which Adrià associated with his notion of a sixth sense, namely the appreciation of culinary creations not through taste buds but according to the underlying ideas and sensations that these creations aim to convey. The diners' appreciation could be more or less emotional or intellectual depending on their prior knowledge, but elBulli would aim for it to always be reflective. One might say that this kind of pleasure is connected with the notion of appetite rather than hunger; it is known only to humans (as opposed to animals) and it involves the incorporation of symbolic social, cultural, and aesthetic values carefully prepared by a creator.

This kind of pleasure also conveys information about the creator and the message that he or she wants to transmit. One member described elBulli's reflective pleasure as follows: "Here is where you can see the footprint of the creator, his wisdom; it is like when you see a movie or [read] a book, and you can recognize the voice of the creator." It is this kind of pleasure that elBulli wanted to stress in developing its "new cuisine," and it was decided that it would do so by developing new concepts and techniques that pushed diners to reconsider their prior notions of what food and cooking can be.

In the mid-1990s, when elBulli started to develop avant garde cuisine primarily through the creation of new concepts and techniques, what members of the organization called the "conceptual approach," it was agreed that the first and second types of pleasure, that is, the gustatory pleasures, could not fail to be present in elBulli's cuisine. However, the fourth type of pleasure was going to be the distinctive feature of elBulli's "magic taste," a term that Adrià and other members of the elBulli team use frequently when talking about their creations, as we might remember from previous chapters. Accordingly, every dish developed at elBulli would include an encrypted message able to be reflectively decoded and consumed by the diner. The emphasis put on each layer of pleasure, one member of elBulli explained, would make it possible for elBulli's creations to reach consumers of the most varied characteristics. First, given that taste is ultimately a physical experience, the consistent presence of the first two forms of pleasure would allow any diner—irrespective of his or her level of gastronomic knowledge—to enjoy a meal at the elBulli restaurant. Second, and most importantly for Adrià, this would also lay the groundwork for those more receptive and curious guests to decipher the message incorporated in each dish, thus entering the game that the elBulli team had carefully prepared for them.

To clarify, back in the 1970s, nouvelle cuisine chefs had also emphasized innovation as a way to move beyond the classical paradigm that governed haute cuisine, but they had done so in a different way. As mentioned previously, while nouvelle cuisine chefs emphasized creativity in their cooking, their creations remained bound to new representations of food. ElBulli's attempt to innovate constituted a departure from this approach insofar as it proposed a shift from producing pleasurable dishes to an emphasis on developing new culinary concepts. The restaurant would build its identity and distinctiveness around this framework, while offering opportunities for anyone to apprehend the meaning of its new cuisine.

The conceptual framework defined early on in elBulli's development, therefore, was aimed at guaranteeing the possibility of providing all consumers with an exceptional dining experience, while at the same time developing gastronomic *inventions* that expressed characteristics that distinguish it from prior culinary developments. Additionally, unlike conventional haute cuisine restaurants, at elBulli chefs would work alongside professionals from other disciplines, such as scientists and designers, in the discovery of conceptual avenues that could offer new ways of delivering pleasure to diners. In short, elBulli would go beyond simply offering a traditional fine dining meal by providing a reflective experience through concepts that would challenge and bewilder diners from start to finish. On a few occasions, Adrià and his team would break out of their own framework to incite new sensations in diners through the presentation of dishes that prioritized reflective pleasure over physical pleasure. Thus, contrary to Proust's famous madeleine episode, where the act of tasting madeleines dipped in tea brings Proust's narrator back to his childhood memories, the value of elBulli's culinary offerings would be based on its ability to *disconnect* diners from their previous conceptions of food and food preparations.

Similar efforts to suppress existing reality toward the establishment of new criteria of appreciation are present in anti-theater, where the focus is the dialogue itself—aiming to be disconcerting and even uncomfortable—and not a story attached to particular circumstances and characters. An archetypal example of this is Samuel Beckett's antiplay *Waiting for Godot*, in which inaction (rather than action) is accentuated, time and place are irrelevant, and there is no clear connection between events—quite the opposite of what one would expect from a classical Shakespearean play, for instance.[18] Like Beckett's anti-theater, elBulli's experimental approach would focus on the dialogue itself, and not on presenting a logical and familiar story aimed at meeting the audience's prior expectations.

Taste and pleasure within a given artistic domain, however, cannot be determined purely by a framework imposed from above by the individual creator or group of creators. As we know from our experiences at restaurants, taste is also constituted "in the making" by the diner based on his or her own abilities and conceptions.[19] As participants in an ongoing dialogue, diners also determine what is a good taste or a new taste. In this respect, the way in which new culinary creations are transmitted plays a crucial role in rendering their innovative content accessible to others, something especially important when the dish's message is not meant only to be physically appreciated, as at elBulli. Imagine that one presents a seemingly inventive and interesting dish without first building an appropriate context in which others can understand how to derive meaning from it. What is most likely to happen in such a situation is that people will find the dish either delicious, satisfactory, or disgusting, but they will fail to recognize any of the encoded messages included in it. For this kind of dialogue to be meaningful, the dish needs to offer opportunities of translation so that people can relate to it. A food writer from New York City pointed out the importance of this by drawing on an anecdote about one memorable, disastrous meal that he experienced at an experimental high-end restaurant:

> I went to this experimental restaurant called [names a restaurant]. It wasn't enjoyable. I was just confused. I couldn't understand. I just felt it was all completely arbitrary. It was not a pleasurable experience at all!
>
> *They just didn't take the time to explain—even if that explanation would've been that they were trying to do something different, to be experimental with food.* After [the meal], I actually tried to talk to the chef, but he just did not care that I liked or disliked, or understood, his food. He took more of the approach of '*letting the food speak for itself.*'
>
> (Personal interview, gastronomic critic, United States; italics mine)

Most diners, in fact, would not go after the chef trying to find cues to make sense of their meals, but would simply cross the restaurant off their list of places to go back to or to recommend to their contacts. Yet this is not what happened at elBulli. In retrospect, we know that despite the restaurant's eccentric location and culinary offerings, by the late 2000s, elBulli received roughly two million requests for reservations and up to three thousand culinary professionals applied to work in Adrià's kitchen as unpaid interns or stagiaires.[20] How did elBulli's new concept of fine dining come to be recognized by its interested audiences?

The public's interest in elBulli's experimental approach was not easily aroused. In conveying elBulli's conceptual culinary approach, the organization did not "let the food speak for itself," as the gastronomic critic quoted above suggested. Quite the contrary, it took time for the organization to find ways to transmit its new language so that it could be understood and accepted by others, and it took this time to the point of putting at risk the very survival of the restaurant. Over the years, a number of mechanisms were deployed and mobilized by elBulli's team that made it possible to effectively communicate the organization's new ideas and practices throughout its external environment. In fact, some of my interviewees who had the opportunity to eat at elBulli suggested that, by the restaurant's final stages, the dialogue that elBulli had established with the outside world was so consistent and intense that the food did indeed seem to speak to those who agreed to take part in it. As described by one of my informants, who visited the elBulli restaurant during its final season:

> I felt the food was very confident. *The food was saying*, 'I am the best in the world.' The food was made by someone who was very comfortable in this stage of his creative process. I felt the style was very mature. I went pretty late in elBulli's history and it wasn't anything like 'Wow! Pau! Disgusting!' at all!
>
> (Personal interview, food scholar, United States; italics mine)

My interviewees' accounts consistently revealed well-formed opinions about elBulli's culinary approach. The organization and its leader seemed to have caused strongly binary reactions among my informants, including those who notably liked or disliked the organization's take on cuisine. Yet none of them seemed to be indifferent to the organization's work. One way or another, they had all managed to make sense of elBulli's creations and to actively respond to them.

Let's Start Talking

The early manifestations of elBulli's newly conceived conceptual approach to cooking did not take an arbitrary form. Rather, new dishes and recipes were presented within a recognizable context that effectively provided cues for outsiders to recognize and appreciate them. A Spanish gastronomic critic who witnessed this stage at the elBulli restaurant shared an anecdote that illustrates this point. In 1994, Adrià presented a new dish he had created, called Textured Vegetable Panache (#247), to a group of gourmands and professionals at his restaurant. This dish, Adrià indicated, expressed the unique features of elBulli's unique culinary language. Rather than being a random elaboration, the dish combined novelty and conventions in quite particular ways: Using the "words" created at elBulli over the previous years, Adrià had produced a reinterpretation of a dish called Gargouillou, originally made by the famous French chef Michel Bras in 1978. In the original version of the dish, Chef Bras included a wide variety of herbs, vegetables, and flowers that were cooked to perfection and served in an aesthetic and poetic manner. The color profile of the dish resembled that of the natural world, a typical characteristic of Bras's signature cuisine. In contrast, Adrià presented a composition in which each ingredient of the original recipe had been manipulated using a specific technique developed at elBulli, including sorbet, mousse, gelatin, and frappé. Moreover, in Adrià's dish the different elements appeared to have been broken apart, rendering the original dish recognizable only from a gustatory standpoint, a culinary concept which members of elBulli would later denominate "deconstruction."

In presenting a dish that was centered on the use of new culinary concepts and techniques, as opposed to, for instance, flavor combinations or ingredients, Adrià invited his guests to take part in elBulli's distinctive culinary experience. To further clarify this for his visitors, Adrià proposed that they try each different ingredient and guess what it was, an exercise that motivated reflection and provocation—precisely the kind of challenge that elBulli aimed to create for its diners. It was the very contrast between the composition made by Adrià and that of Bras, my informant noted, that allowed the gastronomically acculturated participants in Adrià's "game" to appreciate the authenticity that characterized elBulli's line of work.

Other dishes developed at elBulli during this stage were cultivated following this same approach, such as a dish called Cuban-Style Rice (#292), which had the same ingredients as the traditional Spanish recipe with an identical name (rice, tomato sauce, and a fried egg); yet the elements of elBulli's dish were presented in abstract forms and deconstructed, again revealing the distinctive conceptual features of elBulli's cuisine. In this case too, as we can anticipate, it was the very distinctions from the traditional recipe that provided signals to detect the novelty in elBulli's creation. The presentation of deconstructed dishes in the form of traditional food preparations, therefore, represents one mechanism of translation used by the organization to allow outsiders to recognize the innovative value contained in its creations.

During this stage, the possibility for outsiders to interpret elBulli's innovative attempts was further supported by the fact that rather than being served in a capricious fashion, new dishes at the restaurant were presented within a conventional structure: the à la carte menu, which was the standard for haute cuisine restaurants at that time. Broadly, the à la carte menu, which was French in origin, transitioned from appetizers, to entrées, to cheese trolley, to dessert trolley, and concluded the meal with small desserts called "petit-fours." By combing novelty and tradition both within individual dishes and in sequences of dishes, elBulli increased the chances for outsiders to identify and interpret the new ideas included in its distinctive culinary proposal. Academic studies have shown that this mixture between new and existing knowledge used at elBulli for socializing innovations has proved to be a recipe for high impact in other creative ventures, ranging from Edison's invention of the electric lighting system,[21] to Broadway theatrical shows,[22] to academic articles.[23] Within the realm of haute cuisine specifically, sociologists have found a similar pattern in transitioning from classical dishes to creating nouvelle cuisine dishes, which happened gradually over the course of two decades, from 1970 through the late 1990s.[24] Moreover, in studying the master–apprentice relationship, research has shown that to obtain positive evaluations, chefs need to show both compatibility with their former master's work and degrees of novelty.[25]

Along this line, elBulli could have continued innovating through mixing novelty and tradition to develop new dishes. The evidence that I collected, however, suggests that over the following years the team's relentless search for radical novelty in the form of conceptual innovations led them to deviate more and more from conventional standards both at the level of final products (dishes) and at the level of elBulli's menu structure, which put at risk the maintenance of a coherent dialogue between the organization and its surroundings.

Burning Bridges?

As previously discussed, from 1994 on the growing development of new concepts and techniques at elBulli expanded the team's capacity to elaborate novel recombinations and therefore novel dishes, which were increasingly built on elBulli's own language rather than external references. For instance, in 1995 a new interpretation of elBulli's previously mentioned dish Textured Vegetable Panache was created using techniques that had originally been developed at elBulli in sweet preparations. This new dish was called Sweet Version of Textured Vegetable Panache (#322), signifying its direct association with the organization's own prior creation. As we can see in figure 3.3, whereas the dish created at elBulli in 1994 had been inspired by someone else's work (the famous Chef Bras), the second version of this dish, though supposedly new, was built on elBulli's own basis of knowledge—in other words, by further expanding concepts originally developed within the organization. This transition from outside references to internal references in making new products reveals the importance of generating novel concepts that can multiply an organization's possibilities of creation (as opposed to

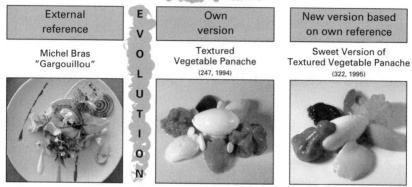

3.3 Evolution of innovations at elBulli.

The diagram depicts the evolution of innovation, taking one of elBulli's dishes as an example. It illustrates the transition from outside references to internal references in making new creations within an organization. From left to right: (i) dish made by Chef Bras in 1978, (ii) elBulli's own interpretation of Bras's dish in 1994, called Textured Vegetable Panache, and (iii) dish made at elBulli in 1995 called Sweet Version of Textured Panache, based on the organization's prior dish. *Sources*: (i) Courtesy of Adam Goldberg, http://www.alifewortheating.com, (ii) and (iii) Courtesy of elBulli. Photograph copyright: Franscesc Guillamet Ferran.

focusing on creating new final products per se). Going back to the example of Apple Inc., the technical and conceptual developments behind the iPhone have enabled the company to develop numerous versions of new final products. The slogan that Apple chose to attract potential buyers to the iPhone 5.0, for instance, "the biggest thing to happen to iPhone since iPhone," manifests the self-referential and generative character of conceptual innovations, as well as the universe of opportunities that they can open to an organization.

There are several other examples of dishes that were created at elBulli during this same period that resulted from synergy within the organization's own creative repertoire. Besides increasingly unique and elBullistic dishes, a new menu structure was developed that deviated from the traditional à la carte menu that had for so long reigned in haute cuisine restaurants. By 1996, elBulli eliminated the cheese trolley—a sacrilege for many gourmands at that time, especially in France—and replaced it with a set of new items invented by members of elBulli's team that expanded prior notions of a fine dining meal, which they labeled "snacks," "tapas," and "avant desserts." Together, these changes introduced a different rhythm to the fine dining experience, which began to be composed of a greater number of increasingly smaller and more provocative courses.

An example of the accumulation of novelty in elBulli's culinary offerings can be identified in the creation of a dish called Smoke Foam (#400) in 1997. This dish consisted of smoky water served in a small glass with a touch of salt and croutons, as described in the recipe presented at the opening of this chapter. This dish was meant to be served at the beginning of the meal, and it was intended to explore the confines of a culinary technique that had recently been created at elBulli, namely "foam." The dish also aimed to provoke diners by literally inviting them to "eat smoke."[26] This dish reveals an important shift in elBulli's attempts to innovate. Rather than representing a combination of old and new knowledge, the dish illustrates the organization's efforts to move beyond a normal science framework by introducing radical inventions through the incorporation of both new concepts *and* new arrangements in the design's components. Yet, however stimulating this culinary creation might be, it raises the question: Why would anyone accept this invitation? More broadly, how did elBulli's increasingly distinctive culinary approach come to be recognized and validated by the interested public? To the eyes of an outsider it would seem as if elBulli was reducing the possibility of maintaining any coherent dialogue with the outside world.

In effect, as was confirmed by members of elBulli and by Adrià himself, during these years several gourmands who in the past had been attracted to elBulli's cuisine were taken aback by the restaurant's newest radical attempts, as they could not make sense of (or simply disliked) whatever it was that Adrià and his team were trying to do. On the Internet, I found a report written by one woman who went to the elBulli restaurant during this stage, and whose testimony about her dining experience largely resembles the confusing and disastrous anecdote described by the American gastronomic critic cited earlier:

> We asked, as it was our custom, for the tasting menu. . . . It was composed by a series of starters. . . . I particularly remember the caramelized quail's egg that consisted of a caramel that when biting it, spread the raw egg in your mouth, and the famous "Smoke foam," for me the most unpleasant of all of what I ate there, given that it had an intense flavor of soap. And I say: What is the importance of getting to this hard technique if the taste is really disgusting?[27]

In spite of this type of unsatisfactory description of elBulli's work, insiders of the organization pointed out that a few enthusiasts remained admirers of Adrià and encouraged elBulli's creative venture. Adrià remembered this as a very hard time during which he took a chance by following a line of work that he truly believed in at the risk of losing it all. However, even during this period, elBulli's bet had gradually started to pay off. In 1995, Gault-Millau, a reputable guide in the gastronomic field, gave elBulli a rating of 19/20. And a year later, the celebrated French Chef Joël Robuchon recognized Adrià as his "heir" and deemed him "the best cook on the planet" on a French television station, an act that had strong resonance throughout the gastronomic landscape. Consequently, elBulli and its leader's notoriety as a groundbreaking restaurant began to surge again.

From this one might conclude that elBulli's cutting-edge creations allowed it to garner the attention of influential intermediaries who, in turn, suddenly boosted the restaurant and its leader's popularity in the culinary avant garde. Although this may be true, it still does not explain how elBulli managed to stay creative in the public eye, nor how the organization's culinary *and* organizational innovations were able to penetrate haute cuisine restaurants around the world in the years to come. If elBulli's recognition had simply been a fortuitous event, it would have died out pretty quickly. But we now know that the public's curiosity only increased during the following years, reaching a peak more than a decade later when Adrià announced the closing of his still-innovative restaurant and its transformation into a whole new organization for innovation, the elBulli Foundation. Thus, there are key pieces of elBulli's story that need to be accounted for to understand the organization's sustained ability to reach and impact its cultural and institutional environment.

First, it is important to remember that by the time elBulli achieved these recognitions, Adrià's professional trajectory and the work developed by the restaurant had largely met the requirements of its institutional field—by systematically building on and expanding the work of its predecessors prior to starting to propose radically new ways of doing things. I have also suggested that elBulli's careful conceptualization of its work through a distinctive "framework of operation" was instrumental in its subsequent recognition. But this is only one step toward achieving legitimacy. For the most part, the validation of elBulli's work derived from the organization's ability to develop *social vehicles* to spread its achievements and to build on and reconfigure an *existing network of interactions* that helped to perpetuate them.

In a similar vein, Becker stated that in the art worlds, innovators who are able to "win organizational victories" are not those whose creations are purely original or aesthetic, but those who succeed in mobilizing a sufficient number of people to expand their ideas. In the case of elBulli, a series of network-building processes were undertaken by the organization to render its new knowledge and practices transportable and accessible to outside parties. These processes were critical in allowing outsiders to appreciate the value contained in elBulli's ever more distinctive creations. Most importantly, these processes prompted the emergence of a group of people who recognized elBulli's work and who were endowed with the talent and skills necessary to extend it in new and unexpected directions.

elBulli News

In a personal conversation at the elBulli workshop, Adrià said to me that dishes are not meant to be understood but simply to motivate feelings and emotions. Yet the act of simply feeding people—irrespective of how good or imaginative the food is—does not offer sufficient evidence to explain how elBulli was able to prompt emotions and expectations in people who had never eaten at the restaurant before and, most likely, never got to. Although it might have seemed as if Adrià and his team were burning bridges by making increasingly unique culinary creations which, in some cases, even contradicted general expectations of good taste, a series of mechanisms were also being mobilized by the organization to disseminate its gastronomic vision, knowledge, and practices beyond the lonely mountains of Cala Montjoi.

While attempts to transmit the organization's developments emerged out of purposeful actions by its members, it initially responded to financial challenges that elBulli needed to overcome. In 1993, to cover the financial loss derived from the off-season of the restaurant in the winter, Adrià and his partner Juli Soler came up with a new idea to generate revenue: They decided to offer a gastronomic course oriented toward culinary professionals and gourmands. They called this course Three Days in Cala Montjoi and issued a bulletin entitled *elBulli News* (the original title was actually in English) that publicized the course among potentially interested parties, high-end restaurants in Spain in particular. Several Spanish chefs whom I interviewed had attended or heard of these classes co-organized by Adrià and Soler in the early 1990s. One chef who participated described how the course was implemented in practice: Classes were taught at the restaurant by Adrià, who used his personal notes to explain the principles that guided elBulli's new cuisine. Among the guidelines proposed by Adrià, the chef remembered the following: "Don't close yourself [off] to any flavor or flavor combination," "don't give preference to your own taste," "learn how to eat," and "know the classic knowledge and techniques." An important part of the course, the chef also noted, included methodologies used at elBulli for developing a signature cuisine, which included "search for local products," "analyze the novel contribution of each dish," "find out how to bewilder your clients," and "do not copy." For this chef, who owned a celebrated avant garde restaurant in Spain at the time of the interview, Adrià's tutelage represented a decisive step in his career. He compared it to such life-altering experiences as the crossing of the Rubicon or a baptism in the River Jordan—a priceless journey into the unknown from which he returned "illuminated":

> . . . Ferran [Adrià] would give us a theoretical course . . . priceless. He would give us a talk, 'here I have my notes' [he would say]. . . . For me this was like a bath in the Jordan River or like crossing the Rubicon . . . it was impressive, a journey of three days, the complexity, the simplicity. It was all so transgressive, so different. When I came out of that trip, it seemed like I had been at a convention for a cult, something from which you come out absolutely inspired, illuminated.
>
> (Interview, chef and owner of haute cuisine restaurant, Spain)

Earlier I tried to show how an important aspect of mobilizing innovation, and especially radical innovation, is generating commitment and validation among a group of followers who can help reinforce and perpetuate a given cause. The workshops created by elBulli revealed the organization's initial efforts to spread its knowledge to external parties. Importantly, the courses were not directed to just any individual but to culinary professionals and gourmands who had the training necessary to recognize the organization's claims. Field studies revealed that similar recruitment practices are employed by religious cults in the mobilization of new systems of beliefs. In *The Making of a Moonie*, for example, Eileen Barker showed how workshops and short courses were a central vehicle used by the Unification Church to transmit the movement's principles and worldview, and to generate successful persuasion among its guests, even if achieving commitment is uncommon.[28]

At elBulli, members explained that due to its success, the Three Days in Cala Montjoi course was offered over a long period, by the end of which a waiting list of interested applicants had mounted. In hindsight, those who participated in the course described it as an opportunity to get a behind-the-scenes look at the elBulli team's experimentations. "We got to be their guinea pigs," and "It was like being at [the] elBulli workshop live," interviewees recalled. Adrià, on the other hand, explained to me that the classes provided an opportunity to reflect on the work performed at elBulli and to try to find ways to explain it to others—as we will see, one of the key practices that describe the work performed at elBulli to this day. As part of the lessons, Adrià showed his students the new dishes that were created at elBulli and got to witness their reactions, something that he would later identify as especially informative in advancing the team's work. After four consecutive years of offering the course and after seeing the value of the interactions that it enabled, attempts to share what was happening inside elBulli expanded further and in increasingly strategic ways.

Staging Culinary Magic

In 1997, as the leader of elBulli, Adrià began to partake in gastronomic conferences that could function as platforms for chefs to meet and discuss their gastronomic ideas and work. Unlike academia, in which this is an accepted practice, conferences were quite uncommon within the world of chefs, as recipes tended to be guarded as precious objects. "We came from an environment of total secrecy," one haute cuisine chef explained when describing his professional trajectory. "The traffic of recipes was brutal. [Recipes] were like tobacco in prison! It was all under cover. One would take notes on recipes on hand-wiping paper because having a notebook [in the kitchen] was not allowed!" In effect, in Spain, the only remnants of social gatherings of chefs had been two so-called "round tables" organized almost two decades earlier by the Basque chefs Juan Mari Arzak and Pedro Subijana during the advancement of their "new Basque cuisine." On that occasion, these chefs had invited the prominent French chef Paul Bocuse to be the guest star. In the late 1990s, when Adrià actively contributed to revitalizing these networking efforts, however, nothing of this kind had ever taken place in Catalonia, nor was it taking place in any other region of Spain. Readers particularly interested in the evolution of gastronomic conferences in Spain can refer to the detailed account written by the journalist Pau Arenos, *La Cocina de los Valientes*.[29]

Working in close collaboration with relevant professionals in the culinary industry at that time (1997), Adrià put together the first conference of cuisine in Catalonia, "The Gastronomic Forum Vic," which offered a specialized platform for chefs to congregate and to share their work. This was the original inspiration for the later creation of several other Spanish conferences that continue to be held today. Among the most renowned are "Madrid Fusion," "The Best of Gastronomy," and "Gastronomika," all of which are organized on an annual basis and are attended by an increasingly wide, international variety of participants. Moreover, from this period until the closing of the elBulli restaurant, Adrià habitually served as a guest star at these conferences.

For elBulli, gastronomic conferences represented both a central outlet to explain and publicize the organization's "good news," and also an opportunity for other culinary professionals to learn from elBulli and others' take on cuisine. The elBulli organization, then, capitalized on a vehicle existing in the context of science to spread its new knowledge and to garner the interest of other producers within its field. The importance of consolidating a peer network relies on the fact that, as argued by White, decisions are made by producers who observe each other in the market, rather than consumers.[30] Given that the final demand for products is unpredictable, producers signal each other about possible combinations of quality and success and make choices based on those signals. The information they collect from these peer interactions, White stated, is critical in determining the actors' relative position and level of centrality in the market. The role that Adrià played as a catalyst of these meetings was central in building his and elBulli's reputation within the existing network of Spanish culinary professionals. A chef who now owns a Spanish restaurant that is rated among the world's best explained elBulli's leader's pivotal role in these gastronomic conferences from the very start:

These [conferences] have been very positive for Spanish cuisine, because they were the first step toward institutionalizing a way of sharing information in a very effective manner. . . . Ferran was the one who started it, this is the story. Maybe you're going to tell him this and he'll say, 'No, no, no, no!'—because the conferences were [formally] organized by other people . . . but Ferran [in fact] was there from the first day.

. . . He [Adrià] was the one doing the big talks: the opening, the closing session, the ones in which the auditorium was packed. He always spoke about interesting and new things; he shared what they had done the previous year at elBulli. He shared everything, he told everything.

This chef then described the repercussions that these spaces for disseminating information had for distributing and monitoring new ideas across the gastronomic community at large:

This was unprecedented. It did not exist in cuisine. One could go to do an internship [at a restaurant] and learn, but standing on a stage and saying, 'We do this like this, this and this . . . do you have any questions?'—this had never been done. And it started here [in Catalonia].

Ferran was not only a participant, he also helped, endorsed, he was like a star. He is the one who has made us cooks into rock stars.

(Personal interview, chef and owner of haute cuisine restaurant, Spain)

Since the late 1990s, gastronomic conferences have become an institutionalized platform for chefs to present their latest work, and the high-end culinary landscape has changed accordingly: A new audience composed of highly specialized professionals emerged out of these social instances that began to operate side by side with the other "tastemakers" in the fine dining segment. From that time onward, my chef interviewees stated, they began to cook not only for diners, gastronomic guides, and critics, but also for a *peer community* which also attributed value to their work. At the turn of the twenty-first century, together, chefs began to actively shape the conception of what is innovative in cuisine, by engaging in a direct or indirect dialogue in this process of interpretation. Gastronomic conferences became central places for showcasing culinary magic or, in the words of another Michelin-star chef, they became the "catwalks" on which chefs validated each other's creations:

> Gastronomic conferences have been like our catwalks, our big showcases. The place where you go and show.... [Now you ask yourself] for whom are you cooking? For the client? For yourself? Or for the next conference?—For the next conference, to present dishes.'
>
> ... Ultimately, there is a lot of vanity in all this. The theater actor or movie actor wants this too. They also aspire to get the applause of the public.
>
> (Interview, chef and owner of haute cuisine restaurant, Spain)

The organization of gastronomic conferences that first occurred in Spain later extended to international settings, including the United States, Europe, and Latin America, and what's most important for purposes of this research, the figure of Adrià as guest star and of elBulli as a central catalyst of an experimental or molecular cuisine transferred as well. A chef working in New York City shared an anecdote with me about the first time he saw Adrià presenting at a conference organized in the United States in the early 2000s. On this occasion, Adrià presented something that later became one of elBulli's most influential conceptual innovations, the culinary technique of spherification. As previously mentioned, this technique involves the creation of edible caviar-like spheres made with alginates that explode in the mouth. In the chef's recollection, he described with excitement how he was chosen by Adrià to show and validate one of elBulli's latest new things:

> We were both doing events and we were introduced to each other and he [Adrià] said: 'Tomorrow I am going to do something special.' It was the day when he announced alginates [spherification].... I was one of the people he [Adrià] chose to come up and taste it. And it was mango alginate!
>
> He said, 'The first people we tell about it are the people in our restaurant, then we tell our country and then we tell the world.' You could hear so much pride [in his voice].
>
> (Personal interview, haute cuisine chef, United States)

The strategy identified by this American chef is, in fact, the same one that elBulli used for spreading information to the outside world: First, the organization circulated and validated new knowledge among its own team; next, elBulli's "news" was spread to culinary professionals in Spain and, after a community had been established, the organization made its knowledge and practices known to the world. Adrià confirmed this by saying: "for a movement to *become a revolution* it needs to gain local strength so that it can later expand to an international level" (emphasis my own). Additional vehicles deployed by the organization to reach an international audience will be examined next.

Another episode that reveals elBulli's sustained presence in these international gastronomic events is Adrià's participation in a conference in Copenhagen which I attended in 2012, called "MAD Symposium." This conference was organized by René Redzepi, the chef whose restaurant was declared number one in the world by the *San Pellegrino* list that year and who is a former apprentice at elBulli. Adrià was invited to give the closing talk at the event. When the time came for Adrià to give his speech and he started walking toward the stage, a storm of cheers and applause filled the auditorium and did not stop until Adrià was ready to start. With the elBulli restaurant having been closed for over a year, Adrià did not speak to his audience about cuisine or food; he explained nothing less than his vision of the current state of haute cuisine and the role of chefs in society. From my observations, Adrià indeed appeared to be a mentor, as he had once been at the Three Days at Cala Montjoi courses. But instead, this time his speech extended beyond representations of food, and was directed at an audience of over 500 culinary professionals from all over the world who gathered at this conference.

The majority of the chefs and food scholars whom I interviewed emphasized that gastronomic conferences had instituted a "before and after" in the history of gastronomy. They stated that these conferences contributed to the establishment of chefs as the most visible and perhaps the most credible actors in the culinary industry, a phenomenon now commonly referred to as "celebrity chefs."[31] During my fieldwork—conducted almost two decades after the first of these conferences was organized in Catalonia—I encountered

3.4 and **3.5** (*top*) MAD Symposium in Copenhagen, July 2012. Picture taken during lunch break. The circus tent was the space where the conference was held. (*bottom*) Adrià as the keynote speaker in the closing session at the conference. Lisa Abend, the journalist who wrote a book about Adrià's apprentices (2011) served as Adrià's translator for the talk. *Source*: M. Pilar Opazo professionals in Spain and in the United States who said that now attendees *expect* to see Adrià at these meetings, sharing elBulli's ideas and vision with the gastronomic community and telling them about the latest news in haute cuisine, regardless of whether they embrace elBulli's experimental approach or not. For those who do follow elBulli's vision and practices, one interviewee noted with amazement, Adrià "is like a God": "[They] need to listen, need to know what he [Adrià] is doing, it doesn't matter what he says; he is the reference, he is like a God . . . in quotation marks," he remarked.

Overall, the role played by Adrià in mobilizing new knowledge very much resembles the figure of a "scientist as an entrepreneur" depicted by Latour.[32] Gastronomic conferences, in this respect, appear as a central medium used by the elBulli organization to maintain its connection with the outside world and to systematically align the interests of other professionals with its own. It is important to note, however, that social phenomena such as celebrity chefs, global gastronomic conferences, or millions of people applying to get a reservation at a restaurant, as happened at elBulli, would not have been possible without two larger central processes that were at play in society: inequality and globalization. Accounting for these social processes is essential in understanding the changes in the culinary landscape during this period, and the role that elBulli played in it.

First, inequality is what makes distinction possible. It enables the existence of a high-end culinary segment, composed of people wanting to go to haute cuisine restaurants, to spend money on costly meals, and to find their way into perhaps very remote locations, with the sole purpose of gaining familiarity with a particular culinary approach. As formulated by Georg Simmel, eating equalizes humans as it is a physiological and fundamental necessity, but dining generates distinction.[33] Meals are a *social ceremony* and as such they affirm class differences and refinement.[34] In short, it is distinction that ultimately motivates people to derive meaning from an eccentric meal, and to later tell others about it, even if a restaurant's offerings might seem unpleasant from the outside, as the elBulli's recipe Smoke Foam clearly illustrates. What's more, the kind of distinction offered by elBulli's dining experience was based on cultural objects that were meant to be appreciated from a conceptual point of view, and thus it invited consumers to become part of a new status group interested in reflectively exploring the confines of fine dining, rather than enjoying it only physically or aesthetically. This is an especially appealing feature in the contemporary information society, in which the production and exploitation of knowledge has become a central quality of social interaction.[35] Food experts whom I interviewed clarified this by saying that in postindustrial society, food has become a key marker of individual and collective identity. Now more than ever, what defines you as a social actor is not how and with whom you eat—that is, your table manners or the people with whom you share a meal—but *what you think* about food and dining.

Further, from the late 1990s to the mid-2000s, globalization surfaced in society, resulting in an increasingly greater access to wider and more diverse information (in the case of restaurants, for instance, to new ingredients, techniques, and equipment). Also, new technologies were created, which made it possible for people to communicate and to participate, either physically or virtually, in events that were happening in locations very distant from their places of origin. Without globalization, and consequently a more interconnected society, none of the changes described above would have been possible in the gastronomic landscape. These changes resonate with the tension between cultural distinction and democratic exclusivity that has been pointed out in culinary discourse: Whereas the former emphasizes that only a few people have the economic resources to access elite restaurants, the latter assumes that in practice, anyone can get a reservation at these restaurants and strive to appreciate a meal's value and significance.[36] Here, therefore, it is important to note that globalization does not eliminate distinction, but helps to reinforce it. A clear example of this in the food world is the spread of sushi from the East to the West that has occurred in the last few decades. Despite (and also because of) its global reach, sushi remains strongly associated with Japanese culture. This explains why restaurants run by Asian-looking professionals appear as a sign of quality to the casual eye; they confirm the cultural origin of sushi and help to renew its Japanese identity, as described by Bestor.[37]

More specifically, the context of Catalonia, where elBulli was located and where Adrià was born, had additional qualities that facilitated the organization's accelerated trajectory of innovation. After the death of the Spanish general and dictator Francisco Franco, Catalonians' strong sense of belonging to the community remained coupled with a high cultural diversity and openness to other countries, due to the region's closeness to the Mediterranean Sea. Hence, central expressions of the Catalonian cultural identity, such as a welcoming spirit to innovation, and a cosmopolitan yet closely controlled model of organization, were also at the heart of elBulli's endeavors.

What is most relevant to notice here, however, is *the ability of the organization*, elBulli, to link to these processes occurring in society at large and to leverage them for the accomplishment of the organization's own vision and goals. In the organizational literature, the ability of organizations to recognize the value of external information and to incorporate it into their own functioning has been denominated "absorptive capacities."[38] These capacities have been said to be a function of the organization's prior knowledge, which is necessary to recognize the new. As we know, elBulli built a self-referential platform to identify, assimilate, and analyze anything new to the organization, which, I found, played a decisive role in enhancing the organization's ability to exploit the knowledge and changes that were happening in its surroundings.

From the evidence presented above, it is possible to conclude that the same dynamics that existed *within* elBulli with respect to distributing the organization's knowledge were enacted by the organization in exploiting its relationship with its environment: ElBulli was continuously sharing information with the outside world, quite consciously, trying to find ways to communicate the organization's latest ideas—especially conceptual innovations—to potentially interested parties, often shortly after they had been generated.

I think what is so special about elBulli is how much they want to share with the world or how much they give of themselves to the industry. They could easily have kept everything under wraps and just stayed ahead of the curve.

But instead they reached out a kind of helping hand and shared all the knowledge that they worked so hard to generate. . . .

(Personal interview, haute cuisine chef, United States)

Although the above quotation suggests that elBulli could have kept its ideas hidden and still "stayed ahead of the curve," this is in fact very unlikely. If elBulli had not made its ideas accessible to others, the chance that it would have become the "most influential restaurant in the world"[39] is perhaps as low as the chance of someone being able to get a reservation to dine at the elBulli restaurant during its final years of existence. It is fairly easy to be a lonely creator in the middle of the mountains—examples of this abound, most of which we are not even aware of—but not a globally recognized *innovator*, as elBulli's leader, Adrià, has been claimed to be by highly influential actors in the culinary field.[40] In 2003, for example, the famous Spanish chef Juan Mari Arzak and the French chef Joël Robuchon acclaimed Adrià as "the most imaginative cook in all history" and "the best cook in the world for technique," respectively. It is possible that the very isolated location of the elBulli restaurant might have motivated the organization's members to come down from the mountains of Cala Montjoi to share their knowledge and explain their vision to the world. But the data that I collected point to other reasons that explain why they did so.

Discourse as a Driver of Innovation

A restaurant to me is a story, and when it has a story everything works.

—Personal interview, chef and owner of haute cuisine restaurant, United States

Sociological studies have shown that a "good" or "distinctive" taste is not merely defined by our taste buds; rather, it is constituted by a multiplicity of factors that interact in complex ways.[41] At a macro level, scholars have pointed out the effects of social and cultural forces on shaping tastes, and also stressed the significance of political tensions in determining the salience of particular foods. For instance, in examining the factors that guide culinary differences between France and England, Stephen Mennell identified a number of processes that led to the formation of particular foodways in each country, such as distinct professionalization processes and culinary ideals.[42] More recently, Michaela DeSoucey proposed the term "gastronationalism" to describe the relationship between food and globalization, marked by both standardization and the emergence of new political identities.[43] On a meso level, academic studies have highlighted the role of authoritative institutions—in particular, gastronomic guides such as the Michelin guide—in delineating the high-end restaurant segment.[44] As Warde pointed out, these intermediaries play a fundamental role in building symbolic boundaries, and thus in shaping distinctive culinary genres.[45] Finally, on a micro level, Rozin proposed individuals' cultural background as the main determinant of what they choose to eat.[46] There is yet an additional driver in determining taste that has received less attention in contemporary studies of haute cuisine: the development and diffusion of a culinary discourse, here understood as written texts or documentation.

Madeleine Ferrieres conducted a historical analysis of official documents regarding food fears from the late Middle Ages onward.[47] She finds that these documents were highly influential in defining the kinds of foods that were sold by producers and cooked by consumers across different regions. Studies of the seventeenth and eighteenth centuries also showed that cookbooks describing the food of the courts, and later that of domestic cooks, were central in shaping food practices and in creating national identities.[48] Similar patterns have been found in the consolidation of the modern gastronomic field. In *Accounting for Taste*, Priscilla Ferguson analyzed gastronomy in nineteenth-century France and found that culinary discourses that proliferated during that period—including the treatises of Carême and later Escoffier, the gastronomic journalism of Grimod de la Reynière, the essays of Brillat-Savarin, and the novels of Balzac—played a key role in the construction of a modern culinary field with a particular French character. The formalization of culinary creations into written texts, Ferguson argued, made it possible to turn taste, which is ephemeral in nature, into an *intellectual product* that could be removed from its immediate context of use, allowing for multiple second-order interpretations to arise.[49]

Another study pointing to the significance of culinary texts in a later time period is Rao, Monin, and Durand's analysis of the emergence of the nouvelle cuisine movement in France.[50] According to the authors, magazine articles and reviews that were written during the period of 1970 to 1997 contributed to making a new repertoire of principles and logics understandable and accessible to the gastronomic community and, in so doing, encouraged the gradual abandonment of classical cuisine by elite French chefs in favor of nouvelle cuisine. In short, consuming food is an essentially individualistic experience. Unlike a work of art or literature, it is not possible for two people to experience the same culinary work. Hence, documentation represents a central vehicle in communicating culinary experiences so that they can be collectively appreciated.

Developing a culinary discourse is also critical to understanding an organization's ability to drive innovation in the contemporary gastronomic field. My chef interviewees systematically highlighted that developing a story—that is, a distinct discourse—was key in determining a restaurant's success. Unlike food or taste, stories are durable in time and, as such, they provide a medium for mediators or "tastemakers" to interpret and validate a restaurant's culinary proposal, something that is especially significant when this proposal significantly deviates from the norm. It is the story behind a high-end restaurant, one interviewee argued, that helps chefs to keep the expectations of tastemakers—clients, other chefs, critics, and guides—aligned with the experience they want to transmit. Stories make guests feel at home when visiting a restaurant, and they are more willing to put themselves in the hands of the chef, two basic elements that chefs aim to achieve when developing a signature cuisine.

In the case of elBulli, the organization's members not only actively developed a formal discourse, a story, which carefully described the restaurant's allegedly unique culinary approach, but also systematically disseminated it through documentation that detailed the organization's claims, characterized

by a particular vision, principles, methods, and achievements. As emphasized by one of elBulli's apprentices:

> You cannot discount the fact that they [elBulli's team members] were com-
> pulsive in their documentation, but more importantly they were compulsive
> in their distribution of data.
>
> (Personal interview, apprentice at elBulli, chef and owner of a restaurant)

ElBulli's team appeared to have undertaken the work initiated by their
predecessors, especially of Carême and Escoffier, by methodically turning the
organization's distinctive taste into written texts that could be interpreted and
used by the interested public. As was mentioned in chapter 2, in 1999, under
Adrià's direction, elBulli's members embarked on the task of cataloguing all of
the achievements developed throughout the restaurant's life. These cataloguing
efforts were not limited to food preparations, but also included descriptions of
the vision, methodologies, and codes deployed within the organization. The
completion of this task, as was mentioned, resulted in a comprehensive analysis that articulated elBulli's perceived innovations into definite manuscripts,
which received the name "general catalogues." In addition, from 2002 on—
that is, during elBulli's so-called year of the retrospective—elBulli started to
publish on a regular basis all the information generated in the form of texts
and audiovisual material.

As it did for the organization's insiders, the circulation of elBulli's catalogues offered outsiders a detailed view into every culinary creation developed
within the organization, classified according to the elBulli language or evolutionary map, the rationale and components of which were carefully explained in the manuscripts. ElBulli's publications also included CDs with
explanatory information about the processes that had led to each new idea
and practice. As indicated, unlike the majority of publications in haute cuisine at that time, the content made available by elBulli, first, was not restricted
to final products, but also incorporated methodical descriptions of elBulli's
culinary concepts and techniques. Second, it included the organization's

underlying philosophy, specifically, the conceptual approach that guided the team's creative efforts. And third, it described the organization's internal practices, including the methodologies used to manage time, space, and teams inside the organization for the development of the kind of creativity that they aimed to achieve. As a whole, then, elBulli's publications told the organization's story by identifying the events that had led to the making of a new cuisine. They did so by specifying causal connections between different organizational practices (e.g., the establishment of an R&D workshop, cross-disciplinary collaborations, or gastronomic trips) and the specific gastronomic results obtained from those practices (e.g., ultimate new dishes or recipes, or new concepts or techniques for the making of those novel recipes). As such, the information contained in elBulli's publications offered the necessary rigidity and interpretive flexibility for readers to apply the organization's ideas and practices in the context of their own work.

As shown in figure 3.6, although books that detailed the work done at elBulli, especially Adrià's work, had been published earlier, it was not until 2002 that the organization began to systematically integrate and stress the publication of all its knowledge as part of its normal functioning. A clear manifestation of this was the creation of its own publishing house in the same year, elBullibooks, which became the branch responsible for the production and distribution of the organization's documentation. Moreover, in 2003, elBulli's publications began to be translated into several different languages, from the expected English, French, and Italian to the perhaps more surprising Japanese and German.

While the diffusion of culinary creations has always been part of culinary practice (first through verbal transmission and later through cookbooks), the exhaustive and methodical publication of every creation developed within a restaurant—to an almost obsessive degree—was specific to elBulli by the early 2000s. By making new products and methods available to anyone, the organization worked to undercut the norm of the "secret recipe" that predominated in the culinary field; once again, building on a common practice of normal science—systematically publishing one's

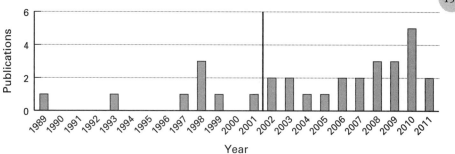

3.6 elBulli's publications (1989–2011).

Number of publications of the elBulli restaurant's work from 1989 to 2011, including books, catalogues, and videos organized by date of publication. The black line, in 2002, marks elBulli's "year of the retrospective" in which Adrià and his team took "a year off from innovating" to recollect and organize the organization's previous knowledge. All books published by elBulli before 1999 are now sold out. *Source*: https://secure.elbulli .com/elbullibooks.

achievements—to promote a distinctive set of ideas and ways of doing things in haute cuisine.

> ElBulli was different not just because of their food.... They were also very open with their recipes. The books each represent an accurate description on how to recreate the dishes—nothing has been left out and an effort has been made to make sure that the technique is accurately described and sometimes video-taped.... As cooks [of elBulli's brigade], we were allowed and expected to track down the recipe for our notebooks, which we always had to have in our pocket.
>
> (Personal interview, apprentice at elBulli, chef and head of R&D
> at haute cuisine restaurant, United States)

It is also important to note that the early diffusion of elBulli's documentation happened at a specific moment in time, that is, when smartphones and social media (e.g., Twitter, Facebook, and others) were not yet prevalent in high-end restaurants. This bolstered the impact that elBulli's documentation had in spreading the organization's work. According to one interviewee:

> This is before the time of Twitter, you know? ElBulli finished before that became a reality. Nobody was tweeting dishes . . . people didn't have their cell phones to take pictures [at restaurants].
>
> (Personal interview, apprentice at elBulli)

In examining the role of "textualization" in the consolidation of culinary identities, Arjun Appadurai pointed out that cookbooks in the contemporary world should not be viewed as neutral objects, but as "revealing artifacts of culture in the making."[51] Following this line of reasoning, my research on el-Bulli reveals culinary texts as political artifacts aimed at expressing a particular worldview, principles and epistemic practices to, hopefully, persuade others of the validity of an organization's claims.

Culinary professionals in Spain and the United States have consistently pointed out that elBulli's publications have been decisive in spreading the word about the restaurant's innovative approach to cooking. Several chef interviewees said they first learned of elBulli's distinctive approach through exposure to one of its books. Irrespective of their own culinary preferences, these interviewees recalled their surprise when they started to flip through the books' pages. One chef in the United States, unconnected to elBulli, indicated:

> Once the books [elBulli's catalogues] started showing up and you turned the pages you were in awe. You couldn't believe that this was going on and this is the type of food that they were making in this little restaurant on the coast. . . . it's just unbelievable. It's like if they were in their own bubble and they were leading the world probably not even realizing it. . . .
>
> (Personal interview, chef at a haute cuisine restaurant, United States)

At that point, this chef noted, he did not have the chance to get to elBulli himself, but the books had given him an "entry ticket" into the creative mind of Adrià and his team. In my research I found that the organizational practice of methodically generating and publishing a discourse played a key role in disseminating and institutionalizing new ideas and practices outside the organization's boundaries. In the case of elBulli, it was possible to identify three main functions that the organization's discourse played in driving innovation within the contemporary gastronomic field: first, conceptualizing innovations; second, socializing innovations; and third, controlling innovations. These functions can also apply to and illuminate the role of discourse in other organizations and industries following creative paths.

Conceptualizing innovations

In a personal conversation with Adrià at the elBulli workshop, he explained to me that "time kills everything" and, for this reason, at elBulli creating has been as important as conceptualizing the organization's work, which they did through written documentation. Adrià emphasized this point by commenting on the work of a chef whom he considered a creative genius, but whose achievements were not well known among culinary professionals. "Well, he hasn't published any books, has he?!" Adrià said to me in his straightforward manner. "How, then, are people supposed to find out what he is up to? [*¡Es que así no te enteras!*]," he stressed.

As has been stated, innovation is not only about having original ideas; it is also about getting ideas recognized by a given community, and such recognition depends critically upon positioning new knowledge within a social and cultural context—whence Adrià's emphasis on the social significance of formalization and publishing:

> Because in the end, everything exists already. . . . So it is a matter of seeing it and conceptualizing it. [One could say that] until 1998 warm jellies did not exist [an innovation incorporated by elBulli in haute cuisine]—this is not true! You could find it [warm jellies] in Chinese cuisine! The fact that in the year

'98 the first warm jelly appeared in [culinary] history is because we conceptualized it.

(Public talk given by Ferran Adrià, as part of the Times Talks, "Food and Wine Festival," October 2011, New York City; author's own translation)

To the extent that formal publications contribute to stabilizing a new discourse within preexisting discourses, they triggered changes in the network of interactions among the participants in a field. This is what happened, for instance, in the case of Pasteur once his inventions spread across his laboratory's external environment. As a result of Pasteur's circulating efforts, his ideas were turned into *inventions* that worked to rebuild the existing network of interactions among farmers, veterinarians, and scientists.[52] Likewise, my interviewees recognized the impact that systematizing and disseminating elBulli's knowledge had on establishing a new reference point in the world of cuisine. They emphasized the effects that this practice had in organizational growth, most notably in positioning Adrià and the restaurant on the culinary map of the twenty-first century.

[ElBulli's team] had a way of owning their content . . . if you look back at maybe French restaurants, years and years ago, you wouldn't see people so much publicizing all their knowledge. At elBulli, I think, they were so intelligent on how they knocked their information out. . . . For me this was such an important part of the elBulli experience. It was not only about the cooking, it also incorporated learning about media. They knew so much about documenting, about content. I really think they were way ahead of the curve in knowing what is good content, and having content keep people captivated. . . . That's why I think they were brilliant.

(Personal interview, apprentice at elBulli, chef and owner of haute cuisine restaurant)

Socializing innovations

By transmitting an innovative discourse in an orderly way, formal documentation also provides an effective medium for rallying allies, an act that has been shown to be decisive for legitimizing fresh ideas within any domain.[53] According to culinary professionals in the United States and in Spain, the amount of content that elBulli was putting out was so exhaustive and detailed that it pushed them to turn their attention to what the elBulli team was cooking up in the now not-so-lonely mountains of Cala Montjoi. Even if one tried to ignore it, one chef remarked, elBulli's work was already "out there," demanding to be considered by the gastronomic community. As Adrià had done at the beginning of his career by purposefully avoiding being influenced by the work of others, once elBulli's publications started to come out, some young chefs explained how they now feared being too much influenced by the work of Adrià and his team:

> You can't ignore it! And it is funny, because for years I actually did purposefully ignore it. There was a period when the primary four volumes [of elBulli's catalogues] came out and for the second one I said: 'I can't look at it, because I will become too influenced by it.' So actually, I did not look at them for a few years . . . because I was actually afraid of that danger of being too influenced by it. Which is odd but true.
>
> (Personal interview, chef at haute cuisine restaurant, United States)

Interviewees also noted how, shortly after their publication, elBulli's materials began to circulate through other channels (such as the Web) and were used for different purposes: for teaching in culinary institutions, to apply specific techniques and concepts in a chef's own work, or simply to gain familiarity with elBulli's distinctive culinary approach. In so doing, culinary professionals around the world fostered the circulation and implementation of elBulli's discourse in new directions.

> What I am doing a lot now is teaching. A lot of people, even though they have access [to elBulli's material], they don't know where to look. . . . [Students] may have seen these techniques but not necessarily seen somebody do them firsthand. . . . So sometimes you need someone to show you how to do it. . . .
>
> (Personal interview, chef at haute cuisine restaurant and faculty member of a culinary institute, United States)

When I first saw Albert Adrià's book [written in 2008 by Ferran Adrià's brother], I thought: 'I could take so much away from this and apply it to what I do.' I mean, just pure presentation-wise. And that shifted [my work].

(Personal interview, chef of haute cuisine restaurant, United States)

ElBulli's publications were also used to prepare for an internship at the restaurant or at other experimental-cuisine restaurants. Just as Adrià once memorized the classics of French cuisine, by the early twenty-first century, elBulli's apprentices described how they memorized elBulli's classics:

Before going to elBulli [as an apprentice] I had already studied the books. Great parts of what they did, I had already learned on my own. In fact, with my fellow stagiaires we had a game of naming a dish [created at elBulli] and others had to guess from which year it was. That tells you that the rest had seen the catalogues of elBulli too.

(Personal interview, apprentice at elBulli, head chef of a restaurant)

Controlling the content of innovations

While the formalization and dissemination of a discourse allows for the sharing of information, it also facilitates the control of content. As we already know, this was a constant fixation of Adrià's in the course of developing a new cuisine. Having control of one's creations is all the more important in an industry like gastronomy, where formal procedures for patenting innovations do not exist. Other examples of this are the fashion industry or the open-source software industry, in which final products are similarly elusive. In music as well, the use of the written note and later of audio recordings to fixate sound facilitated the preservation and expansion of musical genres such as classical music, jazz, and folk.[54]

In all these different contexts, by assigning property rights to discoveries, the socialization of knowledge through formal vehicles functions in a way similar to a patent for an invention. In the case of elBulli, the organization's publications allowed its members to attach creations to an identifiable source and to specify the exact way in which they wanted their achievements to be transmitted.

> They [elBulli's team] are very smart, very smart! Because in a game that's about who can get it out there first, they have been very aggressive about making sure that their materials are out there and accessible.
>
> (Personal interview, chef at haute cuisine restaurant, United States)

By earmarking every creation, systematic publications also contribute to cutting off creativity by redefining the boundaries between inventing and copying someone else's work. In this connection, other culinary professionals pointed out Adrià's ego and how his desire to cultivate a legacy explains elBulli's systematic efforts at diffusion:

> The concept of documenting every single thing that you do, and cataloging, and then sharing it, I realize that is not only altruistic necessarily, but he [Adrià] does want to make sure that, for the people who follow, there is a definitive document. There is no guessing. He does take control of it. He has opened it up to everyone but he controls the ways in which it is presented.
>
> (Personal interview, faculty member of a culinary institute, United States)

> At the end, all this has to do with ego too. Ferran wants to create his brand, he wants elBulli and Ferran Adrià to exist for twenty years more, after he dies, and for this he needs to leave proof. So they have shared all the information of what they have done, but at the same time they're saying: 'this was made by elBulli, this was made by Ferran Adrià.'
>
> (Personal interview, apprentice at elBulli)

It follows that the systematic diffusion of a discourse allowed elBulli to spread its ideas and practices from a local level to an international level and thereby helped the organization to establish a new basis of knowledge in its relevant context of operation. As in normal science, elBulli's manuscripts became textbooks that systematically disclosed the organization's knowledge and achievements in orderly ways.[55] These textbooks contributed to making the organization's claims stronger by synthesizing a new order or paradigm that started to coexist with other culinary developments. Yet it is important to bear in mind that ultimately cuisine is not a discourse but a performative art and, as such, it is necessarily attached to the material and transient nature of food or to the act of cooking.[56] Thus, in understanding elBulli's ability to influence and impact its environment, it is important to account for the group of people who got to learn firsthand from the elBulli team and to try to reproduce the organization's "magic taste" in practice.

Further Recognitions and New Entrants

It immediately comes to mind just the people who have been in that kitchen and then go to do their own thing: the sheer numbers.

—Personal interview, haute cuisine chef, United States

When the elBulli restaurant was awarded a third Michelin star in 1997, only two other restaurants in Spain had achieved such recognition.[57] Obtaining a third Michelin star immediately began to attract cooks from all around the world who wanted to come to the restaurant to work as stagiaires, or unpaid apprentices, a widespread practice in haute cuisine for people who want to learn the tricks of the trade. An owner and chef of a three-starred Michelin restaurant in Spain explained to me how this practice was coordinated on the ground. Usually, he noted, executive chefs call each other on the phone to talk about those members of their staff that they consider skillful and talented and, together, look for ways to place them within their kitchens. "It is a personal exchange," he noted. "Look, I have this guy who is really good but who cannot stay here because I have my staff complete, perhaps you could give him a position? Are you missing someone? Do you know of anyone that might take him?" According to this chef, this social practice, which they informally call *staging*, represents a win-win situation, as it benefits both potential new entrants—allowing them to put the name of another acclaimed restaurant on their résumé—and restaurateurs, by adding more hands and skills for the successful implementation of service.

An executive chef in New York City, who was aiming to obtain a third Michelin star, described the effects of having a group of talented professionals wanting to come to work as apprentices:

> When you have the three Michelin stars you get so much more talented people to come work with you; so, someone who could easily be the [head] chef somewhere else will come and cook the fish for you or make the salad, you know? Do something for you that they view as an opportunity. The most ambitious people are constantly working in the best places because it helps them move their career forward.

> (Personal interview, chef and owner of haute cuisine restaurant, United States)

In 2002, *Restaurant Magazine*, another influential and more recent rating agent in the culinary field, declared elBulli the Best Restaurant in the World (and would do so an unprecedented five times through 2009). About the same time, Adrià began to be featured in influential international media. An article that most American chefs whom I interviewed remembered having seen back then, was a six-page article published in 2003 by the *New York Times Magazine* that offered a detailed view into elBulli's "Laboratory of Taste."[58] At that time, these chefs noted, it was not normal for chefs to be featured so extensively in the press, so after this article was published, "there were chatters in the kitchens" in New York and other cities in the United States talking about the culinary creations made by this "crazy" restaurant in someplace called Cala Montjoi in Spain. Securing the esteem of authoritative gastronomic institutions, together with the elBulli restaurant's greater exposure in the press, exponentially increased the demand worldwide among chefs who wanted to come to elBulli to see Adrià and his team's "culinary magic" performed in practice. As described by an American chef who managed to get a position at elBulli as a stagiaire: "I kept hearing 'number one, number one, number one, number one. . . .' Everyone wanted to go there, so I wanted to go out there!"

The internal composition of elBulli's staff changed significantly as a result of the outside recognition obtained by the restaurant. The graph in figure 3.7 shows the number of culinary professionals who worked alongside elBulli's permanent members from 1997 through 2011. Here I rely on elBulli's taxonomy to classify as stagiaires all those professionals who worked at the elBulli restaurant for one season or more, and "visitors," those who worked there for shorter periods of time (in both cases, these professionals received no monetary compensation for their services, only lodging and food). As depicted in figure 3.7, elBulli's permanent team did not change substantially throughout the period analyzed. The number of external members of the team, on the other hand, notably increased from 1997 on, maxing out at almost twice the number of elBulli's permanent members during the final years of the restaurant's existence. Further, the dotted line indicates the number of different nationalities that were represented among elBulli's staff during each season. While initially the elBulli restaurant's permanent team was composed entirely of Spaniards (primarily Catalonians), by late 2010 the number of people of other nationalities had expanded significantly, ranging from 18 to 20 in all.

This phenomenon is not unique to Adrià or elBulli. Already in the early twentieth century, Escoffier had noted in his memoir that a key driver of the expansion of his modern French cuisine had been the training of thousands of chefs who had implemented his line of work in their kitchens.[59] ElBulli, however, established a system to consistently capitalize on this practice by allowing diverse groups of people to intermingle in its kitchen and, in turn, pave the way for serendipity to emerge, both within the organization and in the apprentices' future work in their new workplaces. In doing so, elBulli equipped itself to deal with the problem of external validation, not only by producing systematic evidence of its accomplishments (in the form of manuscripts), but also by developing a self-generating system that helped to legitimize the new order that the organization aimed to advance.

Chefs whom I interviewed insistently pointed out the large size of the elBulli restaurant's staff and its high internal diversity, in terms of nationality, as a key aspect of the organization. The reasons for a lack of a similar diversity of staff in the restaurants of other chefs varied: Several claimed that it

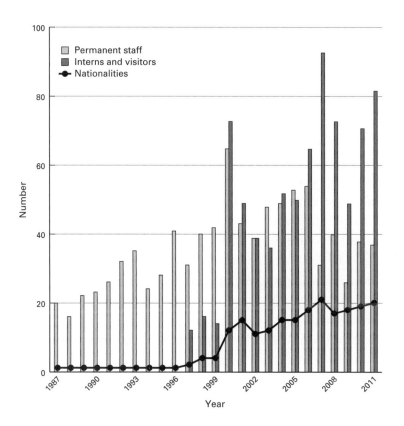

3.7 Evolution of the composition of elBulli's staff.

Information obtained from organizational records of elBulli's historical staff, made available to me in February 2013. Lines with dots indicate the number of different nationalities that were represented at the restaurant from the time Adrià became head chef in 1987 until the closing of the restaurant in 2011.

was due to spatial constraints (especially chefs who worked in New York City) or due to the costs associated with managing such a large team. A few other American chefs asserted that legal constraints made it impossible for them to have so many unpaid interns on their staff. Only those chefs whose restaurants were at the top of the culinary rankings at the time of the interview described themselves as having a staff composition similar to that of elBulli, which ratifies the relevance of securing external recognition in defining the working arrangements within high-end restaurants.

By the time the elBulli restaurant closed its doors in 2011, hundreds of culinary professionals had worked with Adrià and his team as cooks, waiters, or assistant sommeliers, and the restaurant was receiving roughly 3,000 new applications every season. As we will see, the gains that elBulli obtained from the connections with these culinary professionals—as well as the gains obtained by these professionals from elBulli—went far beyond the simple act of adding more hands to the preparation of the restaurant's daily service or adding an extra credit to the résumés of elBulli's apprentices. These connections mobilized a critical mass of people trained to recognize, reproduce, and extend elBulli's distinctive cuisine in new directions. By drawing on existing relations and building new ones, as Becker described, elBulli was able to secure its status in the gastronomic field for years to come.[60]

A Contagious Appetite: Evangelism and Disciples

In an influential study of organizations, Paul DiMaggio and Walter Powell proposed three different mechanisms to explain why organizations come to look alike within an institutional field or, as they put it, how "isomorphic change" occurs.[61] First, they identified coercive isomorphism, which derives from political pressures that lead organizations to be similar to each other; second, mimetic isomorphism is associated with standard responses to external pressures; and third, normative isomorphism defines collective conditions that shape a field. According to these scholars, organizations become more alike in their search for legitimacy, a key ingredient that enables their survival and development. More interesting for our analysis of elBulli, however, is Arthur Stinchcombe's proposal of a fourth mechanism to explain similarities across organizational forms, namely "evangelization," an organization's missionary work.[62] Unlike the other mechanisms, evangelization puts the attention on the focal organization as opposed to external forces in explaining similarities across organizational forms.

In my investigations, I found that evangelization processes enacted by elBulli were—and continue to be—a central factor that explains the organization's sustained influence on its institutional field and also the increasing resemblance of a group of top restaurants in the high-end segment to the elBulli organizational model. It was largely through a community of followers, I argue, that elBulli was able to mobilize a set of new beliefs, knowledge, and practices—both culinary *and* organizational—that were eventually imitated and reproduced by other restaurants and restaurateurs across the culinary field. In so doing, elBulli's "missionary work" enacted changes that contributed to generating a new standard within the high-end restaurant segment— what is now known as the molecular, experimental, or techno-emotional movement in haute cuisine.

Similar to Adrià's closest team, the sheer numbers of culinary professionals who worked at the elBulli restaurant supposedly had the opportunity to be trained by "the hand of the best" and to be initiated, in person, into the organization's creative cause. When one goes to work at one of these "big restaurants," one chef explained to me, one does not merely absorb the recipes that are being cooked there in order to reproduce them later. In brief, it is not only culinary knowledge that chefs look for when staging at these first-class restaurants. Rather, the chef stated, what these restaurants give you "is a defining point, a perspective that is unique and that helps you to form your opinion and, most importantly, to create your standard of what is acceptable and what is not acceptable for you as a chef. The culture of the restaurant leaves a mark on you."

In the same way, having the opportunity to work at elBulli offered culinary professionals a direct look into the organization's vision of innovation and into the methodologies deployed on a daily basis to make their vision a reality. Former apprentices described how, during their internship at elBulli, they gained an awareness of the organization's members' relentless search for novelty via one distinctive path: the generation of new culinary concepts and techniques. As we might recall from chapter 1, Adrià considers this an archetypal form of innovation due to its potential to advance breakthroughs in gastronomy. In the course of spending time at elBulli, therefore, apprentices learned to appreciate the value of perpetual and radical novelty or, as a renowned chef put it, the importance of "creating something different every time"—an appreciation that, as I will show in the next chapter, turned into a double-edged sword, provoking both passion and anguish within the elBulli team. A chef who was an apprentice at the elBulli restaurant at the time of the interview explained:

> The difference between elBulli and any other restaurant in the world is that here, every day, you are learning new techniques and concepts. Other restaurants do not look for techniques, they already have techniques. Those other restaurants search for recipes; they seek out new ingredients and from those ingredients they make a recipe. But not here, here we search for [culinary] techniques and concepts!
>
> (Interview at elBulli restaurant, apprentice, season 2011)

Some culinary professionals pointed out that after having spent some time with Adrià and his team, they quickly realized that they have had this vision for a long time and had built an organizing system that could bring them closer to making it a reality. They figured that for them, it was going to be too difficult to replicate from scratch elBulli's system of working. But what they could do, they said, was to "use their techniques and concepts, their ways of working, their thoughts," in the development of their own work.

A young cook described the moment in which he came to the realization that trying to emulate elBulli's system was not feasible:

> There were moments in which I would try to look for new techniques and in that search I would find a leitmotiv: 'let's see what I can find here!'
>
> ... But [after being at elBulli] I immediately realized that it was impossible for a young cook, from a small town, to discover anything, when there was a restaurant in Girona, with 40 cooks, 10 guys in creativity, a workshop in Barcelona, fully dedicated to this all year: to search, to read ... impossible!

Yet, as mentioned above, this chef did find a way out of this dilemma: to create his own "gustatory universe," building on the new concepts and techniques developed by elBulli.

> ...Whereupon, I decided to take advantage of their techniques and concepts and make them my own. We use spherifications, caviar machines, airs, foams [techniques and methods developed by elBulli], a thousand things that are wonderful and that, taken to our ground, allow us to build a gustatory universe, our own universe.
>
> (Interview, chef and owner of haute cuisine restaurant, Spain)

Another celebrated chef noted that he came to terms with the same dilemma by acknowledging elBulli's creative cause as the flip side to his: Whereas the role of elBulli was to create culinary concepts and techniques, the chef said, his and other culinary professionals' role could be to expand elBulli's inventions into "families." "What we do, what motivates us, is the product, and we study it to see what we can do with it. It is not the culinary technique.... These are two different but complementary paths," the chef clarified. The assessments of these chefs clarify the distinction between final outcomes (culinary products) and conceptual innovations. It also emphasizes the higher potential of the latter to cascade down and impact the work of other actors within a field.

Alternatively, there were those former members of elBulli's staff—often called "Bullinians" by my informants—who did not feel comfortable with elBulli's culinary approach and deliberately decided not to introduce its principles and techniques into their cooking. Yet, even in these cases, these chefs acknowledged having educated themselves about elBulli's techniques and concepts; they tried to do spherifications or foams and tried to understand how to use elBulli's chemical substances in cooking, and they were then able to make an informed decision as to why they were not going to introduce them into their own kitchens. This resonates with Simmel's explanation of obedience *and* rejection as two necessary conditions for fashions to exist.[63] According to Simmel, these dynamics enable the emergence of distinctiveness and exclusivity and, as such, they both constitute signs of imitation of a new trend, just of opposite types.

Chefs connected to the elBulli organization not only reproduced its culinary techniques; they also recreated its organizational practices of documenting and sharing work. Former apprentices noted that after their training at elBulli they started to follow Adrià's working models by aggressively documenting their work; they began to systematically take pictures and keep careful notes on everything that they did. Moreover, they indicated that, instead of keeping their discoveries safe from being copied, they now tried to share them with the whole world, a task that was made significantly easier by the mass use of the Internet and social media.

In this line, one food scholar in the United States suggested that a change appears to have emerged among contemporary haute cuisine chefs who, seemingly following elBulli's path, are publishing their work on a much more regular basis. He emphasized that besides the existing practice of occasionally writing cookbooks, culinary professionals are now publishing their work in highly methodical ways, just like elBulli.

> I met a chef that had everything catalogued, every review, everything. But still he was not publicizing it that much. [But] now, so many chefs are doing that, because he [Adrià] has explained to us why that is important. . . . Ferran has codified the process. He has shown us that you can control creativity. That you should make it a priority.
>
> (Personal interview, food scholar, United States)

One indicator of this in the contemporary gastronomic field can be found, for instance, in a five-volume encyclopedia titled *Modernist Cuisine*. This collection of books was published by the chefs and scientists Nathan Myhrvold, Chris Young, and Maxime Bilet in 2011, the year the elBulli restaurant closed, and Adrià wrote one of the forewords for these publications.[64] Another example is the recent incorporation of haute cuisine chefs as members of editorial boards of international gastronomic magazines and academic journals, a role that was quite rare for haute cuisine chefs even one decade ago.[65]

Spending time at elBulli, therefore, appears to have had "contagious" effects among culinary professionals of several kinds. One chef who confessed to having mixed feelings about "copying" elBulli's work remarked that the efforts made to open up the organization's vision and epistemic practices were the very thing that enabled Adrià and his team to consolidate their legacy. In the chef's words, "The more you share, the more people take your concepts, your ideas and incorporate them into theirs. The more you guarantee your place in history. The more you are never going to be forgotten." In this chef's view, regardless of one's personal preferences in cooking or food, "[Adrià] has to be given credit for what he has done in educating. He is a very smart person." More explicitly, one former member of elBulli pointed out Adrià's deliberate attempts to establish a new order by consolidating a "school of thought," composed of people who believe in elBulli's work and who could later expand it:

> Ferran Adrià has always believed in creating a 'school,' in searching for people to believe in elBulli's cuisine, in the ways we see [the craft of] cooking. This is why in other restaurants in the world you [will] find Bullinian techniques, from manipulating the product to preparations of novel techniques.
>
> (Personal interview, former member of elBulli, chef and owner of
> haute cuisine restaurant, Spain)

Certainly, these network-building efforts are central to the institution of innovation in other fields as well. Fitzgerald, for instance, illustrated how Picasso furthered his standing within the twentieth-century avant garde by fostering interactions with other actors in the art world.[66] These interactions made it possible to connect the work that he conducted in his art studio with the market beyond it. White and White also contended that the acceptance of Impressionism as a new artistic movement was *made possible* not simply by deviating from the norms of the academy, but through the orchestrated efforts of practitioners who supported the new aesthetics and norms that this movement aimed to convey.[67] Later, in the 1960s, Andy Warhol also worked to develop new techniques and aesthetic concepts that could move the advertising world toward becoming a form of art. Yet, for Warhol's work to be recognized as art, he also had to persistently attend public events, carefully separate his commercial work from his artistic work, and actively generate ties with actors and institutions that enabled him to build his image as a new type of artist.[68] Innovation, thus, as pointed out at the beginning of this chapter, requires both embeddedness and institution building within any given social context.

Similar to these efforts, creating a school or thought collective was central in securing the recognition of elBulli's work and to generating a new movement around it. To understand elBulli's ability to educate or evangelize others, then, it is important to look beyond *what* "ex-Bullinians" took from the organization and incorporated into their work, and examine the dynamics that fostered the development of a community of people around the organization. We must also examine the role that this community played in spreading and legitimizing its new ideas and practices in the culinary world.

A Community of Ex-Bullinians

There are many techniques that people don't know and that will become known with the passage of time. The same 'Bullinians' that are traveling around the world will introduce these things.

—Personal interview, apprentice at elBulli restaurant

To reiterate, cuisine is essentially a performative art,[69] and, as such, its diffusion relies essentially upon those who can reproduce it and expand it into new contexts. In the case of elBulli, the organization's vision and inventions traveled in the hands of hundreds of culinary professionals who, after having worked with the elBulli team, moved to widely disparate locations around the world. Interestingly, the organization's reputation seems to have traveled along with them. As a matter of fact, having "elBulli" and "Adrià" on your résumé appears to offer plenty of opportunities for ex-Bullinians to transition into the highest ranks of a restaurant's hierarchy or to start their own businesses, significantly easing the costs associated with being a new entrant into the fine dining market. In the same way that elBulli's core team believed in Adrià's extraordinary capacities, culinary professionals around the world, connected and unconnected to elBulli, believed in (or at least acknowledged) the capacities of those who had been in Adrià's kitchen.

One former apprentice at elBulli, who was a head chef at a renowned high-end restaurant in New York City, described the impact that having worked at the elBulli restaurant had in his professional career:

> The prestige of having elBulli as part your work history is about being more in control of your path. Because when people see that, they automatically believe you. They automatically respect your word and give you the chance to prove your skill. So it makes it easier for finding work, and if you want to do something, say you want to apply for a very ambitious job yourself, you will have the opportunity to do that more so than if you wouldn't have that [experience of working at elBulli] on your résumé.
>
> (Personal interview, apprentice at elBulli, pastry chef of haute cuisine restaurant, United States)

Indeed, network studies have shown that a common benefit that can be obtained from weak ties is improving one's opportunities of finding a job.[70] Accordingly, the richer Adrià became in reputation and fame, the richer those who were connected to him became as well, irrespective of their particular culinary approaches or preferences. In the sociological literature, this dynamic underlying the emergence and consolidation of a network has been denominated the "Matthew Effect," due to its connection with the biblical gospel of Matthew 13:12, which says: "Whoever has will be given more, and they will have an abundance...." Within sociology, this concept was originally used to explain the cumulative recognition acquired by scholars connected to eminent collaborators.[71] In my fieldwork, I found similar network-building processes operating among professionals in the contemporary gastronomic landscape connected to elBulli and Adrià. This might explain why, during my personal conversations, it was common for me to hear my informants

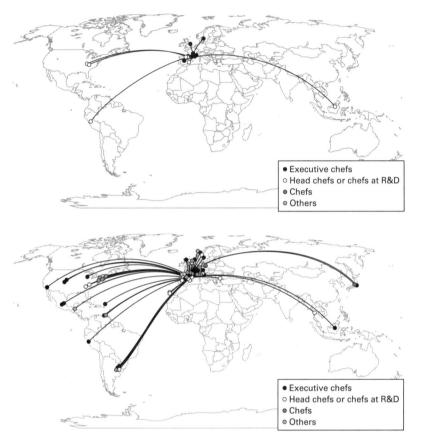

3.8.a–3.8.d elBulli's apprentices around the world (cumulative data from 1997 to 2011).

Workplaces of culinary professionals who worked at the elBulli restaurant from 1997 to 2011 and whose location was accessible by 2013 (N=297). The data is shown cumulatively over the years. *Source:* Own elaboration based on historical records of elBulli made available to the researcher by February 2013. The present location of elBulli's former members, apprentices, and visitors was coded manually by conducting individual searches in public sources (including websites of restaurants, personal websites, and online social networks such as LinkedIn and Chef DB, among others).

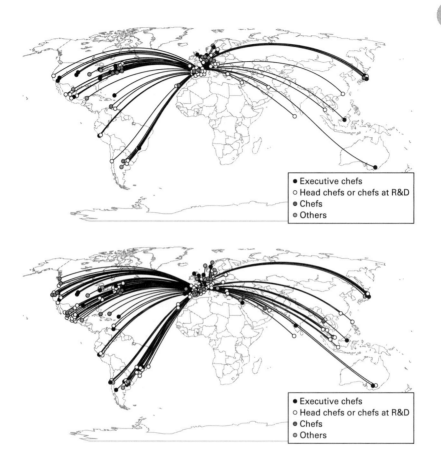

insistently declare that they were "best friends with Adrià," that they "knew him well," that they "had worked with him," or, at minimum, that they "had met him in person." Some of them confirmed their closeness to Adrià by counting the exact degrees of separation that connected them to him. This pattern was most prevalent in the Spanish context, as described by one chef: "I am convinced that every chef in Spain knows a cook that has been at elBulli or knows a cook that knows Ferran." Based on this, the chef concluded that "This spider web that has been created is the most important [aspect] of this revolution."

As a consequence of this virtuous cycle, a community has formed in the high-end restaurant segment that is both benefiting from elBulli and its leader's status and contributing to spread the word and internal *know-hows* of the organization to the most remote places in the world. Figure 3.8 visualizes the "spider web" that formed around elBulli, with the restaurant in Cala Montjoi at the epicenter—a picture that very much resembles the Big Bang metaphor cited at the beginning of this chapter. Quite different from the Big Bang, however, the formation and maintenance of elBulli's spider web did not simply evolve; it was the result of systematic efforts and practices undertaken by the organization that enabled it to enhance its position in its field.

Figure 3.8 illustrates the workplaces of culinary professionals who worked at the elBulli restaurant from 1997 to 2011 and left, and whose location was accessible by public sources in 2013 (N=297). These include former members of elBulli's permanent team and also stagiaires and visitors who worked at elBulli for each period of time, as cooks, assistant sommeliers, or waiters. The data are shown cumulatively over the years and, for purposes of illustration, the four periods shown in the figures were defined according to the changes observed in the data distribution. Although a very raw measure, I propose this as a proxy for the presence and influence of elBulli in the contemporary gastronomic landscape.

The colored dots in the figures illustrate the geographic locations of these ex-Bullinians by 2013, that is, two years after the elBulli restaurant had closed (here it is important to bear in mind that the likelihood of finding the location of professionals whose careers have been more successful is greater than for those whose careers have been less successful; using public sources, for roughly half of these professionals it was possible to find their current location). The black dots indicate those ex-Bullinians who are executive chefs (chefs and owners of restaurants); white dots indicate those who are head chefs at restaurants or members of R&D laboratories at restaurants as of 2013.

As we can see from the figures, the number of culinary professionals connected to elBulli increased consistently over the years. At the end of the period analyzed, these professionals were spread among over 150 different cities around the world, representing a total of thirty-eight different countries across four continents. Moreover, after having worked at elBulli, the vast majority of these professionals appear to occupy strategic positions at their places of work, hence with higher opportunities to introduce their acquired beliefs, knowledge, and skills into their new places of work. It is interesting to note that the majority of ex-Bullinians who, by 2013, were executive chefs of restaurants that were in the top of culinary rankings[72] had worked in elBulli's brigade early in the restaurant's trajectory (i.e., in the 1980s or 1990s) and had left early to create their own businesses. This evidence supports the argument made in chapter 1, which described the process of becoming an innovative and acclaimed restaurant in the gastronomic field as usually a gradual and incremental process, at least in the period analyzed.

The community of culinary professionals that formed around elBulli has been a central agent in mobilizing and legitimizing the organization's work among a wide variety of audiences. For instance, several of my interviewees who never had the opportunity to visit elBulli in person explained how they started to "feed" themselves with information brought back by their colleagues who had spent time with Adrià and his team. Faculty members from important culinary institutions in the United States and in Spain, moreover, acknowledged that while at first they were skeptical of elBulli's work, they later began to understand it better after some of their alumni had worked at elBulli and had explained it to them. In effect, during my fieldwork from 2011 to 2013, all these faculty members confirmed that they had elBulli's publications in their schools' libraries and that sections of elBulli's stock of knowledge had been integrated into their schools' curricula (mainly in elective courses or in master courses, as the core of these schools' training, they all proudly stated, continues to be centered on classical culinary texts, such as *Le Guide Culinaire*, written by Escoffier in 1903).

An additional aspect of elBulli's connections that was revealed during my interviews was the vast amount of energy that Adrià invests in maintaining these connections. In one way or another, the majority of former members of elBulli's core team remain connected with Adrià, as he retains a mentoring role in their lives. They visit Adrià in search of advice, share with him their plans for opening a new restaurant or for changing a menu, and they borrow books from him, books still filled with marginalia, Adrià's own written observations and evaluations. A former member of elBulli's brigade described how these connections that Adrià carefully maintains with ex-Bullinians had later extended among chefs throughout Spain, with Adrià as the primary magnetic force that connected them all:

> Adrià has always been open, generous, and not at all closed to the world. . . . This has generated the possibility for all of us [chefs in Spain] to get along, to help each other. To generate a corporatism well-intended, in the good and positive sense. . . .

He continued by describing the different ways in which these connections were used by chefs in the contemporary culinary landscape: to distribute information on reporters who could write about each other's restaurants or commentators who could evaluate their work, to circulate information about new restaurants and conferences that they should visit, or simply to share the daily anecdotes of service. According to the chef, these interactions contribute to generating a "sentiment of belonging" to the same "revolutionary movement":

> Ferran has always been generous with all of us who are close to him. [He tells us,] 'This journalist is coming [to elBulli], I have told them to come to visit you.' . . .
>
> When we finish the service we call each other to compare things: 'I received a call from X, have you been there? What do you think? Should I go? And how was it? I have been told to go to this conference in Korea, did you go? Is it worthwhile?'
>
> . . . This kind of thing makes you feel that we are all in this together, that you are not alone, we are all here, part of this revolution . . . it generates a sentiment of belonging to a group, to a movement.
>
> (Personal interview, chef and owner of haute cuisine restaurant, Spain)

Not all was smooth sailing, however. Accounts from ex-Bullinians reveal that Adrià and his team were well aware of the value of these connections and that they managed them in strategic ways so as to preserve the organization's status. While maintaining a relationship with elBulli could bring beneficial outcomes to apprentices (such as getting a job or increasing their professional reputation), severing their ties to the organization could risk their chances of finding new opportunities or even jeopardize their social inclusion in the high-end restaurant community.

> They [elBulli team] understood the prestige of having earned a spot at elBulli and became quite upset when someone didn't respect this. . . . One girl [stagiaire], at the end of service, approached X and Y [two members of elBulli team] to say that she wasn't learning enough because she had to spend too much time doing prep work. They immediately released her, it was her last day. Two other cooks felt the same way a week later, so they packed their bags and left in the middle of the night. Ferran sent an e-mail to every three-Michelin-starred chef to explain that they weren't capable of the work in a high-end restaurant, effectively halting their chances to work for another big name chef.
>
> (Personal interview, apprentice at elBulli)

By now, it should come as no surprise that on the last day of the elBulli restaurant's life, Adrià and his team were far from alone. Instead, as I indicated, they were featured in the mass media, surrounded by several of elBulli's disciples, now celebrated chefs, who had traveled all the way up to Cala Montjoi with the sole purpose of helping them prepare the restaurant's "last supper."[73] Unlike in the 1980s segregated world of kitchens described by Fine,[74] I found a community of chefs who regularly circulated their work, participated in the same gastronomic conferences, and actively used their connections to be up to date with the latest news in haute cuisine. Among these chefs, I found that a group of followers had formed around elBulli, with Adrià investing significant effort in maintaining these connections for the institutionalization and expansion of the organization's work.

In order to mobilize revolutionary innovation, a chain of collaboration needs to be developed. While incremental innovations may take off within an existing order, radical innovations require the creation of a new world around them that improves their appreciation and legitimization.[75] As the evidence presented suggests, this does not imply an absolute shift of practitioners toward a new vision, but the commitment of a critical mass of people to a new set of ideas and practices, followed by the rejection of another group so as to generate distinction. As noted by one of elBulli's adherents in the contemporary fine dining industry:

> Behind every cultural movement, a new cultural industry emerges. Before the modernist movement in cuisine, new purveyors, manufacturers, new markets arise, from which all of us have benefited. The fact that elBulli has meant what it has meant has been great for us, because it has pushed all of us forward.
>
> (Field notes, manufacturer of modernist cuisine equipment, Spain)

New networks of collaboration may emerge from peripheral nodes that are able to transmit and spread new ideas from the outside to the inside.[76] Revolutionary innovations may also be mobilized by actors that penetrate the core of a reconfigured network, that is, the new world formed by the introduction of new values and language.[77] This is the kind of dynamic that I saw operating at elBulli. As stated, the organization and its leader had already achieved recognition in its institutional field when it started to promote radical changes in the standard ways of doing things.

The social dynamics behind elBulli's operation explain why the good ideas pioneered by the organization appear to have been more than a short-lived, random fad. It was the reproduction of elBulli's ideas *throughout a community of followers* that made it possible for the organization's vision, knowledge, and practices to consistently trickle down into restaurants around the world and thereby gain the strength of a gastronomic "revolution" that continues still today, at a time when the restaurant has closed its doors and is transitioning into a new organizational form. A chef whose culinary approach he regarded as largely divergent from elBulli's described the changes enacted by the organization in the contemporary gastronomic field as follows:

> I feel that elBulli has drifted into everyone's cooking these days, you know? From the use of sous-vide, bags, and specialized tools in that regard, to things that are more overtly elBulli-inspired, like small caviar of different liquids and things like that. So it's a lot! When foam was very big, that was clearly an influence. The best of everything sort of sticks around and things that don't sort of get lost in time.
>
> (Personal interview, chef and owner of restaurant, United States)

In sum, in my fieldwork I could see how elBulli's culinary vision and methods had spread across the culinary landscape, with an increasing number of restaurants incorporating elements of elBulli's organizational model. The vast majority of my informants were familiar with or "fluent" in elBulli's "language," and many of them had incorporated techniques and concepts pioneered by elBulli into their cooking. Moreover, like elBulli, 60 percent of the haute cuisine restaurants in which my chef interviewees worked were closed for a specific period of time each year and had test kitchens or laboratories of their own (or planned to build them) to fully dedicate the staff's energy to creativity. This practice had become especially prevalent in Spain, where online gastronomic sites announced the collective migration of haute cuisine chefs to "their winter quarters" once a year, in search of "a magic formula" to sustain their creativity.[78] Finally, my chef interviewees, both in Spain and in the United States, also expressed a consistent concern with circulating their work, through participating in conferences, writing books, or posting information on their latest discoveries on the Internet. These dynamics around elBulli indicate the organization's influential role in reshaping the contemporary high-end restaurant segment:

> Now look around: Tell me where the best restaurants in the world are, where they were before, and tell me where they are now. You look at a Michelin

Guide or Relais and Châteaux or anything; and you tell me whether it is Buenos Aires or Tokyo, Paris, London, France, New York, wherever, and they are
cooking the same food up until ten years ago.

   . . . Now, it's hard to give only them [elBulli's team] credit for that, but it
is hard to give credit to anyone else. I mean, you can say a lot of things they
didn't do, but tell me then who did? Tell me where it really came from, if
not there.

(Personal interview, chef and owner of haute cuisine restaurant, United States)

There is still one remaining aspect that is important to account for in understanding the dynamics that support elBulli's spider web: During my interviews,
several chefs said that it was Adrià who had put them and their restaurants on
the culinary map and, as such, they viewed elBulli as an authority from
which many of their reputations were derived. Whether they followed
elBulli's culinary approach or not, almost all asserted that they respected
Adrià and what he has done and considered elBulli as "a key agent in the
contemporary gastronomic concert." In view of this—and faced with the
fairly obvious possibility that the reader may find that more critical opinions
are missing from my analysis—I find it relevant to attest to a social constraint that appeared to be shaping the elBulli's network, at least in the contexts that I studied: It is too difficult and too risky for one's reputation to
deprecate those who occupy influential positions in a field. As one interviewee stated when describing the connections between ex-Bullinians, "Logic-
ally, no one would shoot himself in his own foot, because, in the end, they all
come from the same strain." To explain this social constraint more clearly, I
rephrase a question that one chef, connected to elBulli, posed to me when
talking about the organization and Adrià's standing in the gastronomic
field: "Pilar, would you speak badly about God? . . . If you look back in history, what has happened to those who have dared to do so?"[79]

   Radical innovation does not result simply from connecting otherwise disconnected worlds or from recombining old and new materials. While these
dynamics are certainly at play in the advancement of knowledge, the institutionalization of radical innovation is much more complex. It is an evolving

and self-reproducing process encouraged by an actor's purposeful efforts at establishing a new order, in this case a new cuisine. The elBulli organization did so by building a support system, that is, a machinery of identification and self-referentiality that allows for new ideas and epistemic practices to arise. These are mobilized both by members of the organization and by those connected to the organization from the outside. Internally, elBulli enacts innovation by building a platform for the organization's members to collectively create, document, and expand new ideas. Moreover, the new knowledge generated is methodically evaluated by establishing its similarities and distinctions with existing knowledge, or "old worlds," thereby allowing outsiders to recognize it as well. Externally, elBulli mobilizes revolutionary innovation by consolidating a critical mass of people who recognize—yet do not necessarily approve of—the value of the organization's work. The organization invests great energies in translating new knowledge to outsiders and in cultivating a community of followers who could help validate and perpetuate the creative cause. On the one hand, this community benefits from its connections to the organization; on the other hand, the organization benefits from the growing prestige of its disciples. This dynamic generates a virtuous cycle that stabilizes the organization's authority and secures its status within its field. It is the continuous switching from the organization's inside to its outside, as stated by Latour,[80] that enables elBulli to embed new and arguably crazy ideas into the larger system in which they exist. Finally, the organization systematically amplifies its innovative capacity by building on macro-level changes that are taking place in its surroundings, thereby crystallizing the boundaries of its new order or discipline, elBulli's new cuisine.

Now, Let the Food Speak for Itself

After the elBulli restaurant's closure in 2011, Adrià gave a talk at the headquarters of the Google Company in San Francisco, where he claimed that "Cuisine is a language that everyone speaks and understands." Although this might be generally true, taking all evidence into account, it is possible to illuminate a number of mechanisms that enabled elBulli's unique culinary language to be understood and spoken by others. In developing its vision, elBulli did not "let the food speak for itself," as suggested by the gastronomic critic quoted at the beginning of this chapter in reference to a confusing fine dining experience that he had. In the process of crafting a new language, elBulli's members did not limit themselves only to cooking, nor did they confine their vision only to the organization. On the contrary, specific processes were mobilized *on the ground* by the organization to make its new language accessible to the interested public.

First, a new notion of cuisine was defined, with the potential to appeal to different kinds of addressees, acculturated in haute cuisine or not, yet with distinctive properties that differentiated it from other culinary developments. Second, new stages for the showcasing of elBulli's ideas were assembled, which leveraged the possibilities for the organization to persuade others by offering possibilities to gain familiarity with the organization's knowledge and practices. Third, elBulli's accomplishments were synthesized into definite manuscripts, which told the organization's story in methodical and appealing ways. These texts were later systematically distributed, rendering their content accessible to the interpretation of present and future audiences. Finally, a network of supporters was constituted with the knowledge and skills necessary to incorporate elBulli's new stock of knowledge in kitchens around the world.

The social impact produced by elBulli's work, therefore, was the result of concrete efforts to consolidate an audience that could appreciate their work and contribute to securing its value. To return to a question mentioned earlier in this chapter with reference to the dish Smoke Foam: Why would anyone accept elBulli's invitation to a highly atypical fine dining meal? The answer was clearly stated by a haute cuisine chef in New York City—it was through years of building trust with intended audiences, capturing and sustaining their attention, that elBulli was able to systematically offer an innovative gastronomic taste:

The thing about the *people that went to elBulli is they already knew that they were going for an experience.* He [Adrià] had built that tenure and he had built that loyalty. He'd built that whole aura, that whole essence of what it [the elBulli experience] was about over decades. . . . It is the same for all of us. . . . He [Adrià] had to build a clientele. That's the key of why he could do that. Because if you have people coming to your restaurant who have a completely open mind, then you can start to play with what you want to do—but you have to build it. It is not something that automatically happens. . . . I can't just start cooking and do something crazy if I don't have the loyalty of [people] following. . . .

(Personal interview, chef and owner of haute cuisine restaurant, United States; italics mine)

Let me further explain this argument by using the example of the fine dining meal that the elBulli restaurant offered its clients. Figure 3.9 illustrates the transition of elBulli's culinary offerings, starting from a conventional à la carte menu, French in origin (marked in white, at the left side of the diagram), to the offering of a new tasting menu designed exclusively by elBulli's creative team (marked in gray, on the right side). The figures in the center of the diagram represent those items that over time were either eliminated from or introduced to elBulli's menu, making it increasingly novel and unique (the former marked in white and the latter in light gray). In a nutshell, the diagram illustrates that elBulli's menu by 2002 was indeed quite distinct from a conventional à la carte menu. Yet it also shows that novelty was introduced cumulatively and gradually within elBulli's menu. More precisely, the diagram reveals that the organization's innovative efforts expanded in tandem with the external recognition it obtained from influential gastronomic actors and institutions, like other professionals and the Michelin guide, and its most immediate audience, that is, diners. For instance, only years after the elBulli restaurant was awarded a third Michelin star—and when the level of acceptance of elBulli's customized tasting menu was close to 100 percent—did elBulli venture to completely eliminate the à la carte menu.

The tasting menu that became established at the elBulli restaurant in 2002, and remained fairly stable until the last year of the restaurant's life, therefore, was indeed quite unique and "crazy": Almost all of its items had been created by elBulli's team (e.g., snacks, tapas, avant desserts, morphings, and follies did not exist in haute cuisine); the menu consisted of approximately forty courses, as opposed to the five entrées, cheese trolley, dessert trolley, and petit-fours that characterized a traditional à la carte menu; and the succession of elBulli's courses made it almost impossible for diners to distinguish when the savory/sweet preparations began and ended. In short, by the early 2000s, elBulli's culinary invitation bore little resemblance to the culinary offerings of the type of nouvelle cuisine restaurant it started as. Yet, as the diagram also illustrates, novelty in elBulli's dining experience was not introduced arbitrarily, but through intercalating elements of both normal and revolutionary science—refinement and invention within the same structure. In the case of elBulli, these dynamics were mobilized at different levels—in dishes, the menu, and at the level of the organization itself, as we will see most clearly in chapter 5 and provided signals that enhanced the audience's understanding and acceptance of the organization's proposals for change.

This argument can be confirmed by looking at the culinary offerings served at the restaurants of the chefs whom I interviewed. The proportion of these restaurants that had eliminated the à la carte menu and only offered a tasting menu was roughly 25 percent and consisted of chefs who were at the top of culinary rankings, that is to say, restaurants that had obtained outside recognition by gastronomic authorities (such as the Michelin guide) and/or which have had a relatively long trajectory in the restaurant business. On the other hand, 50 percent of my chef interviewees' restaurants appear to be in a hybrid state with regard to the innovativeness of its mode of culinary offerings, presenting both a customized menu and an à la carte menu for clients to choose from. Although these restaurants had obtained recognition of some sort (e.g., had one or two Michelin stars), they were usually lower in the culinary rankings. Finally, there were those restaurants that only offered an à la carte menu (25 percent). These establishments were usually directed by chefs who had recently started their own businesses or worked at restaurants

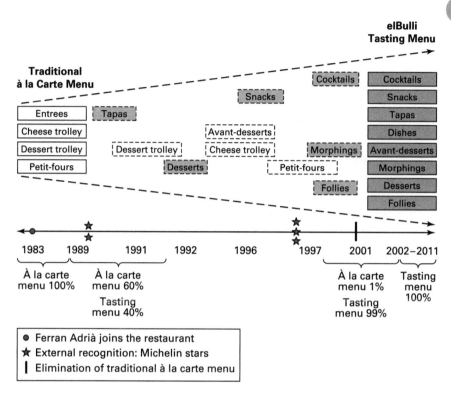

3.9 Process of acceptance and legitimization of the elBulli restaurant's tasting menu (1983–2011).

Evolution of elBulli's menu, from 1993 to 2011. *Source:* Own elaboration based on elBulli's catalogues (1983–2002).

not focused on avant garde cuisine, but rather traditional or mainstream cuisine.

The ability of outsiders to recognize and interpret elBulli's culinary invitation was confirmed by several informants who had the opportunity to eat at the elBulli restaurant. In retrospect, they described elBulli's fine dining experience by using words like "sensory overload," "twilight zone," or "love affair"—words largely associated with excitement and chaos, precisely what recipes like elBulli's Smoke Foam aim to provoke. Yet most of these inter-viewees also claimed to have been able to "read" their meal at elBulli. Most of them had experienced it as a "dialogue," a "questioning process" set by Adrià and his team that called on them to rethink their prior conceptions of food and cooking—to be surprised, to laugh, and to take part in a game for which the instructions were carefully detailed by the waiter. Even those courses that had not matched their taste, many of them asserted, were intel-lectually challenging or interesting in some way. Thus, for the most part, the experience offered at elBulli did not seem to have led diners to confusion. By the time elBulli began to incorporate high levels of novelty into its menu, the majority of diners who came to the restaurant *knew what to expect* when enter-ing elBulli's "game"; they knew how to derive meaning from their meals, how to read between the lines of the elBulli team's "crazy" work—or, at least, and what's ultimately most important, they thought they did. This collective per-ception was reinforced by an interesting dynamic initiated among gastro-nomic critics. Given that elBulli renewed its dish repertoire every year, food writers published reviews of the restaurant every season, in much the same way as is done with dance, music, or theater performances.

Thus, when elBulli's new culinary paradigm began to be known world-wide and the restaurant's recognitions multiplied in the mid-2000s, the elBulli team had already developed a *context* for outsiders to understand and appreciate the novelty of their work, just as they had once created a context *within* elBulli to evaluate their creativity. During the last decade of the res-taurant's life, the large majority of gourmands, critics, and chefs who man-aged to get a reservation at the elBulli restaurant traveled to the mountains of Cala Montjoi *knowing* that they would be putting themselves in the hands of the chef with the intention of *embracing the unexpected*. Whereas in other contexts this attempt might have led to a complete disaster, at elBulli this was precisely what the organization had long aimed for its clientele to expect and desire.

Ultimately, it was specific coordinating mechanisms that made it possible for elBulli's creations to systematically penetrate and impact its environ-ment. Jointly, the extensive content that was made available by elBulli and the establishment of scenarios for peer interactions, as well as the building of a new network and its transformative effects, created a virtuous cycle that helped to consolidate the organization's image and identity as an innovative restaurant and, in so doing, to foster its legitimacy within its field. This explains elBulli's ability to hold the public's attention for so many years, even after the closing of Adrià's acclaimed restaurant—or, as we will see in chapter 4, precisely because of that.

The emergence of a community of people able to understand and "speak" elBulli's "language" played a vital role in forming and preserving a mystical and mythical aura around the organization and its leader. However, like any language, once elBulli's new culinary language became reflexive, it opened up possibilities that had not originally been anticipated by its creators. The next chapter looks into the unintended consequences of elBulli's creative efforts and the bittersweet results of the elBulli team's relentless search for radical—even genuine—novelty.

White Chocolate Water Ice with Mango and Black Olives, #508 1998

© Franscesc Guillamet Ferran

Serves 4 people

To prepare the white chocolate ice slush:

100 g (3.5 oz) of white chocolate
75 g (⅓ cup) of light liquid cream (35% fat)
200 g (1 cup) of water

To prepare the black olive purée:

25 g (1 oz) of black olive purée
25 g (2 Tbsp) of sugar
Water

Other:

125 g (4.5 oz) of mango purée
Maldon salt

Final touches and presentation:

1. Pour one spoonful of mango purée into the glasses.

2. When the dish is about to be served, place 2 spoonfuls of white chocolate ice slush on top, and top it with black olive caramel and 4 crystals of Maldon salt per glass.

(Abbreviated for purposes of illustration.)[1]

4

The Bittersweet Taste
of Relentless Innovation

An Encounter with Ferran Adrià

Once the elBulli restaurant had closed, Adrià and a few other members met
to discuss the design of the new organization, the elBulli Foundation. In
Adrià's words, the foundation was intended to be a creative research center
in which cooks would work alongside professionals from other disciplines
"using cuisine as a common language to create." The meeting was held at the
headquarters of Telefónica R&D,[2] the company that was financially supporting Adrià during the period in which his restaurant was undergoing its
most radical reinvention. Six other employees of Telefónica were included at
the meeting, expecting to witness and perhaps participate in the construction of elBulli's new and, allegedly, once again innovative organization.

The room in which they met offered a full view of the city of Barcelona on
one side and a view of the beach on the other. Adrià arrived at 10 A.M. sharp
and sat in the middle of the room, staring at everyone with his penetrating
gaze. He was wearing black jeans and a long-sleeved black t-shirt, and his
grayish hair was quite messy. From the moment he stepped into the room he
seemed to be fully concentrating on what was about to happen. The conversation started with no formal introductions or greetings of any kind. Within
a few minutes, Adrià was already interjecting clear-cut questions to the
attendees and writing on a paperboard, for everyone to see, the connections

and disconnections between the different topics that were being covered and which, in his view, would contribute to the development of the new organization. For the participants in the meeting—and I was among them—the fast pace of the conversation made it seem as if there was no time to lose or, to put it a different way, as if there was someone standing right outside the door waiting for our conclusions to be delivered, in much the same way as happens in exchanges between cooks and diners.

It was common for Adrià to interrupt speakers before they had finished their sentences with a "No, no, no, no!" followed by a firm restatement of the main objectives that the elBulli Foundation aimed to accomplish. He certainly gave the impression of knowing exactly where he wanted to take the new organization, despite his also explicitly enunciating the uncertainty that surrounded the project at that point in time, and of his ignorance of the best methods to make it work "efficiently and effectively."

When the closing of the elBulli restaurant entered the conversation, Adrià looked at everyone with fire in his eyes and asked:

"Do you know why I closed the elBulli restaurant? Can any of you tell me why?"
"To have less pressure," one man responded, sitting across the table.
"No!" Adrià replied, immediately searching for more answers.
"To have more freedom," someone else said.
"No!" he repeated.

When the participants realized they were not coming up with the right answer, a sudden silence filled the room. Adrià explained:

"We closed because we had turned into an army."

He continued:

"It was what the team wanted. I have the best team in the world. . . . If we hadn't changed, elBulli would have died. We had two options: either we change or we close forever. The easiest way out was to close, because elBulli was already a myth. . . . But we wanted to continue creating."

Thus far, I have examined the workings of the elBulli organization and its infrastructure, designed to produce radical and continuous innovation. Later, I explain how these internal organizational dynamics were combined with practices that encouraged the dissemination and institutionalization of elBulli's new knowledge and practices outside the organization. Like a meal at the restaurant, however, elBulli's organizing system was in fact multidimensional, and as such it inspired mixed feelings and conduct among both the organization's members and those who were part of the organization's universe. In this chapter, I will examine the unintended consequences produced by the interplay between internal and external factors emerging from the workings of the elBulli organization. In doing so, I propose that examining unintended consequences can be just as important, and yield just as much insight, as looking at intended consequences when trying to understand purposeful action,[3] specifically, how innovation is systematically enacted in and by an organization.

From Analogies of Machines to Biological Systems: An Organizing Structure for Mobilizing Change

Analogies have been a common resource used by scholars to explain the workings of organizations, due to their capacity to illuminate common features across seemingly disparate social phenomena. Here, I briefly examine a transition that occurred during the twentieth century in organizational theorizing, namely from the usage of technical analogies to biological analogies. This shift illuminates important aspects of the dilemma faced by contemporary organizations between exploiting and exploring knowledge—or, as I proposed, producing final outcomes and conceptual innovations—so as to encourage the organizations' survival and development.

In the early twentieth century organizational theorizing was filled with analogies to machines as explanations of organizations. From these accounts, an organization's operation was regarded as highly prescriptive and assumed to be oriented toward the pursuit of specific goals in the most efficient way possible. Examples of this abound. Frederick W. Taylor's *Principles of Scientific Management*, for instance, suggested that a machine's performance could be optimized by calibrating the functioning of its individual pieces. An organization's operation, then, could be made most efficient by controlling all of its elements, both social and non-social.[4]

In a similar vein, Max Weber described the bureaucratic organization as consisting of formalized roles and structures that were tightly coupled to each other. According to Weber, the rational side of organizations was so important that the individual worker was condemned to be subordinated to it, in both his material and ideal existence.[5] In his words, "the individual bureaucrat cannot squirm out of the apparatus in which he is harnessed."[6] During the same period, Henri Fayol's administrative theory emphasized hierarchical management—what is now commonly known as the top-down form of administration—and strict obedience to commands made by those higher in the ranks. Not surprisingly, he considered the military to be a suitable representation of the operation of organizations.[7]

What is common among all these analytical approaches? They are all filled with analogies to the working of machines, such as "efficiency," "rationality," "predictability," and "input-output relationships." From these theories, there appears to be no space for uncertainty, exploration, or discovery. Rather, they assume that individuals' behaviors and their social interactions within systems can be prescribed and that they are susceptible to strict manipulation. With regard to mobilizing innovation, these approaches suggest that *exploitation* dynamics may lead organizations to systematically produce new final outputs over and over again. But they leave us in the dark as to how organizations can develop a dynamic structure for the continuous generation and *exploration* of new alternatives.

Starting in the late 1950s, and especially when the external environment of organizations began to be regarded as an essential part of their functioning, more and more biological systems analogies started to permeate organizational theorizing. This gave rise to the study of the adaptive side of organizations and, with it, the role of important social phenomena left unexplored by earlier approaches, such as reflexivity, inventiveness, and dynamism. Well-known conceptions that are representative of this turn include Burns and Stalker's distinction between "mechanistic" and "organic" organizations; the former are more suitable to static external conditions and the latter to changing conditions.[8] They also include March and Simon's theory of "bounded rationality," which emphasized the pursuit of satisfaction rather than optimization within organizations,[9] and, finally, James D. Thompson's use of the biological notions of *homeostasis* and *heterogenesis* to describe the possibility of mutations of organizations (the former corresponding to the system's development via self-stabilization, and the latter to the system's alteration into new forms).[10]

As a result, by the end of the twentieth century, our understanding of what happens in and across organizations became filled with terms such as "sensemaking,"[11] "organizational learning,"[12] or, more recently, "autopoiesis"[13] and "autocatalysis";[14] all of these are also representative of human capacities. Nowadays academics and business professionals alike cite "change" and "resilience" as key factors in explaining an organization's maintenance. In connection with this research, what is important to note here is that in drawing attention to the organic qualities of organizations, these approaches emphasize the organizations' ability to continuously enact change at different levels, as opposed to the production of final outputs only.

How does the modern organization incorporate the properties of both machines and biological systems as essential parts of their functioning? This chapter focuses on the strategies deployed by the elBulli organization to find a way out of this dilemma, and the continuous struggle of the organization to stop reproducing accepted patterns and, instead, keep searching for radical possibilities.

Setting the Standard to Create

Organizations often fall into the trap of assuming that practices and principles which have led to desired ends will continue to do so. As a consequence, those practices that have in the past been associated with successful outcomes tend to be replicated for years on end. In academic literature, this tendency of organizations to reproduce themselves based on previous models of action has been called "organizational or structural inertia" and has been said to put at risk the survival and maintenance of organizations, particularly mature organizations.[15] In the case of elBulli, it was not organizational inertia, but demands for relentless change that caused the organization to fall into a trap of its own.

As has been mentioned, in 1994, after seeing the value of creating new culinary concepts and techniques, the elBulli team declared "conceptual creativity" to be the hallmark of elBulli's cuisine and Adrià placed it at the top of his "creative pyramid." The elBulli team regarded this as a much more significant task than reproducing or recombining knowledge due to its considerably higher potential to leave a mark on the history of gastronomy.

In a book called *The Secrets of elBulli*, published in 1997, Adrià described the importance of conceptual creativity, writing:

> The first premise when creating is setting an objective: Do you want to create only a dish or a new concept? If the cook proposes himself to conceive a *new recipe*, the difficulty can be solved by a dose of taste, imagination, and professionalism. By *combining* a series of ingredients, it is possible to obtain a creation that, while still admitting that it is new, contributes little to the evolution of cuisine.
>
> If, on the contrary, the creator aims to originate *a new concept* and his efforts are successful, a breach can be opened through which new possibilities can be seen. . . . Creating a new concept in cuisine is, in effect, to prompt the emergence of a new route that perhaps will open endless numbers of doors, thus far unsuspected.[16]

This brief extract from Adrià's writings shows that by the late 1990s a specific organizational standard had already crystallized at elBulli: Unlike other high-end restaurants, the main mission of the elBulli restaurant would be to relentlessly generate new concepts and techniques which could produce "true" breakthroughs in gastronomy (and not new dishes, regardless of how imaginative or pleasurable they were). Adrià elaborated on this to me one day at the elBulli workshop, saying that from that period onward, it was decided that elBulli's quest would be to "always go for the top of the pyramid!," regardless of how hard this task might turn out to be. He also firmly asserted that, in doing so, "they would have no compassion for themselves!"

It was these same standards that guided the elBulli team's efforts, that is, their fundamental belief in conceptual creativity, which led the organization to a paradoxical conundrum: Just as the restaurant's reputation seemed to be at its peak, the dynamics that would bring about its termination were unfolding. The elBulli team could have kept the restaurant open year after year by presenting new dishes that built either on their vast knowledge of the work of other chefs or on the vast creative repertoire that they had carefully generated over the years. Yet this was not the task that members of elBulli had set themselves up to accomplish, nor was it the kind of mark that they wanted others to appreciate and remember.

Stop Self-Plagiarism!

The line that separates influence from copying is extremely thin.[17]

An individual's or a group's extraordinary or "magical" abilities depend on the recognition of those subject to their charismatic authority. This applies to all kinds of charismatic identities, ranging from chiefs of corporations, to prophets of religious groups, to political leaders who aim to mobilize change. If the individual or group fails to provide proof of their exceptional qualities, their charismatic authority is likely to fade away.[18] This is especially important in the case of elBulli, considering that the organization and its leader's authority were based on their capacity to produce radical innovation, that is, *inventions* that could offer new ways of conceiving food and fine dining. It has been noted that to sustain commitment, elBulli developed a logic system composed of specific principles, methodologies, and codes that encouraged perpetual validation among its members. Over the years, this system became increasingly strict, allowing the team to systematically see new signs that confirmed whether their efforts were consistent with the organization's final mission. This system also offered proof that contributed to sustaining the members' trust in the magical powers of the organization's leader.

By the late 1990s a new creative principle became enshrined in elBulli's organizing system: honesty. While honesty typically refers to not doing things that are morally wrong or not saying things that aren't true, at elBulli, honesty meant preserving "the dignity of admitting when one is copying." This principle was associated with the challenge that members of elBulli had undertaken back in the 1980s, when deciding to pursue a distinctive line of work in cuisine: They would try not to emulate the work of others, but instead would always search for "the radically new." Interestingly, unlike in other creative fields in which using someone else's work without acknowledging it is formally looked upon as a morally wrong act and considered plagiarism, in gastronomy this practice is not discouraged in any formal way. Thus, by proposing honesty as a creative principle in the organization, members of elBulli were stressing a responsibility that was implicit in their field, namely the need to make explicit reference to the work that inspires one's creativity. To put it in Adrià's terms, "a professional who has achieved the highest level . . . cannot copy and take advantage of the findings obtained by others to move up in the ladder of fame at a velocity that, in reality, does not correspond with his talents."[19] As a result of this, materials published by elBulli from this period on are filled with citations of the original sources that had inspired the work, including the work of other culinary professionals, popular restaurants, food companies, and others. These citations were aimed at providing readers with clear information about the creations that had been originally made by elBulli and those that had not, as analyzed by elBulli's team.

In 2002, nonetheless, when elBulli's members took a sabbatical from innovating in order to compile and analyze all the organization's prior work, elBulli's principle of honesty took an interesting and unexpected turn. If "honesty," as defined at elBulli, meant "to always admit when one is copying," then having full awareness of the organization's knowledge and ideas implied a new responsibility for its members: to always admit when they were copying themselves! Thus, once again, elBulli's system of classification would both constrain and promote the creative work performed within the organization.

Indeed, the recollection of elBulli's work enabled the organization's members to distinguish between those creations that were "truly elBullistic" from those that were not. However, what is most important here is that this recollection also provided evidence for the organization's team to recognize whether they were innovating according to the standards that they had set for themselves—continuously advance revolutionary innovation through new concepts and techniques—or if, instead, they were merely developing new products (i.e., dishes) by *reproducing* or *recombining* their own knowledge in novel ways, a practice considered less original and challenging and, for that reason, lower on Adrià's creative pyramid.

One manifestation of the elBulli members' concern with keeping track of their effectiveness in creating according to their own standards can be seen in an analysis that they performed on an annual basis and included in the organization's catalogues. From 2002 on, this analysis classified every new concept and technique developed at elBulli according to the degree to which it had advanced the organization's culinary knowledge and, by exten-sion, its potential to contribute to gastronomy at large. Three kinds of con-ceptual innovations were identified: "trails," "roads," and "highways"—re-spectively, those that could open minor, medium, and large new avenues of knowledge in cuisine. While trails necessarily designated specific foods and their preparations, highways fostered paths that extended beyond food and that could be applied in a multiplicity of contexts.

Here is an example of how this classification was implemented in practice. As explained by one of elBulli's head chefs, in 1998 the culinary technique of grilling fruits was first developed and used for the creation of several new dishes during that restaurant's season. This new technique, however, repre-sented a "less revolutionary technique," a trail, he indicated, because its ap-plication was subject to a specific kind of product (fruit, such as watermelon or melon) and it represented an extension of an existing popular technique, as opposed to a completely original one. Hence, although this new technique was significant, its contribution was rather limited as its application was inevitably tied to specific foods and their implementation into new dishes. On the other end of the spectrum, the head chef of elBulli explained, there were those "highly revolutionary techniques" ("highways") that could be applied in a wide variety of situations and were able to generate endless avenues for creativity, not only in terms of new dishes, but also in terms of developing new conceptual innovations. He cited foams and spherifications, described previously, as examples of these types of revolutionary creations (for instance, the techniques used to create foams and spherifications were further developed—specifically, into cold and hot foams and "basic" and "reverse" spherification, each of which had different properties and, therefore, countless applications).

According to elBulli's members, these practices of classifying the work done at the organization in increasingly systematic ways was critical to the preservation of elBulli's mission and, in particular, in sustaining the organization's principle of never copying which, as we now know, also included not

4.1 and 4.2 From left to right: dish Watermelon and Beetroot Kebab (#518, 1998), inspired by the technique of grilling fruits, and dish White Bean Foam with Sea Urchins (#240, 1994), representative of the first time foams were served at the elBulli restaurant. *Source*: Courtesy of elBulli. Photograph © *Franscesc Guillamet Ferran*.

emulating their own work. Indeed, classification systems render the work visible, but they also facilitate surveillance.[20] Adrià emphasized this by stating: "Without knowledge and order, one cannot create. Because if you don't have this, many times you are going to end up copying yourself!" Yet despite its obvious importance, Adrià also remarked, the majority of professionals who aim to be innovative do not do this analysis. For some reason, he noted, they do not take the time to rummage over their prior work to see what they find. "Do you know why this is?" Adrià said looking straight at me. "Because it is very hard not to copy, and even harder to realize that you are copying yourself!"

Borhek and Curtis proposed that there are two types of belief systems: those that are highly systematic and empirical, and those that are not systematic and have low empirical relevance.[21] Scientific beliefs and religious or folk beliefs, respectively, are examples of each type. While the clear logic of experimentation and replication of the former makes it possible for these belief systems to be reconstructed over time by any group, the high level of abstraction and interpretation required by the latter allows for new evidence to destroy it if it does not conform to the system's precepts. For this reason, the survival of a nonsystematic belief system usually depends on a charismatic leader who builds a support structure around him. The essentially elusive and subjective character of taste may lead one to think that the belief system formed around elBulli is mainly of a nonsystematic type. Yet the formal procedures and codes developed at the elBulli organization to validate its beliefs reveals the concrete efforts of the organization and its leader to develop a definite structure able to be reproduced by others, just as scientific achievements can be confirmed and perpetuated by a community that may extend well beyond the original creators.

Creative Pressure

People have asked me why I run so much. They think that we are obsessed. But it is not that. . . . This is simply what we do.

—Field notes, Ferran Adrià, at elBulli workshop, Spain

The narratives that I collected reveal that the elBulli team's relentless search for radical novelty, coupled with their incessant evaluation of their achievements, caused both passion and distress in the daily work at the organization. As it turns out, the more new things were developed, the more the appetite for novelty grew inside elBulli and the more difficult it became to fulfill the expectations of the organization's members. As a result of this ever-increasing appetite, the internal pressure associated with having to always generate something radically new increased apace.

Once the practice of creating novel culinary concepts and techniques became established as the organization's primary objective, new rules began to operate in elBulli's daily work. These rules were aimed at pushing the team to continue exploring for newness rather than to keep exploiting results already obtained. For instance, after the first foams were invented in 1994, many dishes that employed this new technique were served at the elBulli restaurant. And the same happened with other "elBullistic" conceptual innovations, such as warm gelatins, caramelization, airs, and the concepts of deconstruction, minimalism, and adaptation. Adrià has stated that continuing to create and refine on the margins is, in fact, a common thing that happens in creative work: "When miniskirts were first invented, catwalks around the world were filled with them," he has repeatedly asserted in public talks. In Adrià's view, this is simply a reflection of a creator's eagerness to show and improve his latest work.[22] But elBulli's working system had faculties that differentiate it from other creative enterprises. The "creative audit" or evaluation that the organization's members performed on a regular basis allowed them to detect *when* and *to what extent* they were repeating their own creations and to look for ways to prevent this from happening. According to one of elBulli's head chefs, they did this by agreeing that "it would be prohibited to re-do our own things!" So, when experimenting at the elBulli workshop, they said, "We could not do liquid spheres, we could not do foams" or whatever it was that they had formerly made. Instead, they needed to start from scratch. This rule, members of the creative team explained, allowed them to "burn their own ships" and thus to keep "throwing themselves into the unknown." Adrià's brother, Albert, stated that this dynamic generated high levels of adrenaline in the work of the creative team; it fostered an excitement that kept them awake all night, eager to start a new day of work to see what they could find:

> It was an excitement that left you sleepless; then you would wake up and start the journey of seven kilometers [to the elBulli restaurant], to put everything in order. Focus on that idea, you saw it so clearly, how is it not going to work?: 'if we do it like this, and then we'll take it out of the mold, and then after it defrosts the center will be liquid! [It has to work!]'
>
> (Personal interview, Albert Adrià, at his restaurant Tickets in Barcelona)

Yet, irrespective of how significant the discoveries or the repercussions that they could have on cuisine at large, elBulli's working system would always prompt the team to continue searching anew for further conceptual innovations. In the words of Albert Adrià, "To understand elBulli, you need to understand that I was part of a football team. I was one piece. My brother was the coach. And I was paid to discover techniques and concepts. Oriol [another head chef] was paid to discover techniques and concepts that could be applied to the restaurant . . . [and in this way of working] there was no limit." Members of elBulli knew that if they continued refining their products on the margins, rather than developing new concepts, they would run the risk of losing their strategic position in their field. Hence, while trying to relentlessly create radical innovations might have indeed generated high levels of excitement, it also required levels of dedication and commitment that were difficult to maintain in practice. Albert Adrià explained how those initial sleepless nights of excitement increasingly turned into nightmares after realizing that there were no limits to elBulli's radical approach to creation:

> The problem with creativity is when it turns into a nightmare. There is no ending, no limit. For me, personally, I realize now that this generated a lot of personal stress. Nobody was telling me: 'You must do this.' We were doing it to ourselves. . . .
>
> Today we have made spherification! And tomorrow we'll make reverse [spherification] and tomorrow. . . .' On the fifth day, you say: 'So now what?!'

Within elBulli, this sentiment was known as "creative pressure" or "creative tension" and was said to have grown "logarithmically" toward the final years of the restaurant's life. This sentiment was further encouraged by changes occurring in the personal lives of team members, which made it increasingly difficult to respond to the organization's exigent goals. Unlike Ferran Adrià, who never had children and still saw elBulli as his "kid," the tightly connected group of cooks who had adopted Adrià's cause as their own now had families who also required their attention and dedication. This situation was summarized by one member of the organization as follows: "It was not easy, we all started to have kids too, so you say, 'Luis [Garcia] has three kids, Mateu [Casañas] has two kids, Oriol [Castro] has two kids, [Eduard] Xatruch has one kid. . . . So there was no longer '*the family.*'" Albert Adrià explained this further by saying that cooking is already a highly demanding profession; cooks usually work until two or three in the morning every day and barely get to see their families. But this was even more the case at elBulli, he stressed, given that apart from the tight schedule there was also the constant pressure to create afresh. In the end, three years before the elBulli restaurant closed, Albert Adrià left the organization during the first years of his child's life and published his dessert book, *Natura*. After leaving elBulli, he opened a new restaurant with a less dramatic approach to cooking, as he noted, which did not require an attempt to generate something conceptually new every time.[23] He described the differences between elBulli's creative approach and that of his own restaurant as follows:

> At elBulli, I always created to be the best. But now I don't. Now, my only aim is to entertain people. There is a huge difference! So huge! Because [at elBulli] it was about inventing the potato omelette [an example of a culinary technique] every day! And on top of that, we were supposed to keep reinventing every time. . . .[24]

But it was not only internal factors that escalated the creative pressure at elBulli. There were also growing expectations in the organization's external environment that needed to be fulfilled and managed. As I suggested, the culinary invitation that the elBulli restaurant proposed to its guests, while it was supposed to be enjoyable in essence, was primarily intended to be *innovative*. It was supposed to be a culinary experience that made guests think differently about what food can be or what cooking can be. In this context, the more the elBulli team propagated their intentions to produce revolutionary innovation and the more they made their latest work available to others, the more they lost control over the effects of their work and of their achievements' ability to continually surprise outsiders.

Prior field studies of high-end cuisine have emphasized the drawbacks associated with being labeled an exceptionally innovative restaurant. According to Parasecoli, haute cuisine chefs try to prevent this from happening because it can be extremely harmful to their businesses.[25] The case of elBulli shows us that the social weight of being marked as a "revolutionary" restaurant indeed reinforced the organization's standard of constantly having to create anew and that this proved too difficult to be sustained.

External Pressures

In 1998, elBulli members made a recipe called Water-Ice of White Chocolate with Mango and Black Olives (#508), at a time when the last version of elBulli's course Three Days in Cala Montjoi was being held during the restaurant's off-season. While some positive creative tension had been mounting during the past years at elBulli, the truth is that this recipe was invented in a moment of "desperation."[26] As described in the organization's records, it was a rainy Sunday afternoon when members of elBulli's brigade were still missing one dessert that was needed for presentation to the class. At the last minute, and without really knowing why, they began to prepare a liquid caramel with black olives and then mixed it with white chocolate. The result was a quite interesting bittersweet sorbet—as bittersweet as the process that had led to its creation—and Adrià proposed to present it to the class, which by now was about to start. To their surprise, when the dessert was served to the students it was one of the most popular recipes during that day's session and, in view of this, the new dessert was later refined by elBulli's team and incorporated into the restaurant's menu.

Unlike the recipes presented at the opening of previous chapters, this dish of elBulli does not include a new concept or technique purposefully implemented by members of the organization; rather, it represents a mere accident. One could argue that any chef, endowed with a solid basis of knowledge and training, has the ability to put things together, evaluate the quality of its taste and generate a final product that can be considered pleasing by diners. In this sense, this recipe denotes incremental or "recombinant innovation" insofar as it combines existing ingredients in novel ways. Similarly, studies of jazz improvisation have suggested that fast tempos are likely to push bands to the limits of their creativity by pressing them to use preexisting, repetitive material.[27] ElBulli, however, was not concerned with the creation of new arbitrary products in the short term, but with the systematic development of conceptual innovations that could open opportunities of discovery in the future. This might explain why the dish aforementioned, Water-Ice of White Chocolate with Mango and Black Olives, although it was included in the organization's records, was not regarded as an iconic recipe of elBulli. While "new" in the eyes of elBulli's team, this dish did not emerge out of the organization's logic system of creation and interpretation, nor did it offer new conceptual avenues that could later be expanded. The dish, then, symbolizes the organization's struggle to cope with external pressures while still continuing to explore for conceptual innovations with the potential to produce breakthroughs in its field.

In any case, social instances like the one described above, in which the elBulli team got to show and explain their latest work to outsiders, were very important in mobilizing elBulli's experimental approach to cooking. These instances also constituted an important source of pressure that further encouraged the team to create anew, especially during the final years of the restaurant's life. While being the first to circulate new ideas enabled elBulli and its leader Adrià to sustain a leading position in the gastronomic avant garde, it also vaporized the newness contained in their ideas. As such, these social instances put further pressure on elBulli's team members to systematically

envision and implement new culinary creations. An additional and more significant example of such instances is the gastronomic conferences that I described in chapter 3. As suggested there, over time these congresses became
larger in number and gathered an increasingly diverse and experienced audience, which incorporated a growing number of people who expected to learn
elBulli's latest news. Former and current members of elBulli described the
pressure exerted by these events, saying:

> Conferences were our Olympic games, where people were waiting for us,
> where we could leave a mark on the field. [Where you could see that] others
> were doing 'this and this' and you could say: 'I already got there.' But then
> conferences began to be conducted all over the world, six, seven congresses a
> year, with massive audiences!
>
> (Personal interview, head chef of elBulli)

> Years ago, chefs had their recipe books and they only looked at them with
> their head chefs. Recipes were hidden. [But later] with showing it all, you
> were forced to reinvent, to do better, to do more [every time].
>
> (Personal interview, former member of elBulli, chef and owner
> of haute cuisine restaurant)

The pressure imposed upon the elBulli team at these conferences was also
recognized by those who attended them. One chef from the United States
pointed out how he perceived the role of elBulli at these events and the growing audience who expected Adrià or other members of the organization to
repeatedly present "culinary magic":

> Imagine every six months the world is looking to you for something new. The
> world is looking to you to reinvent yourself. To give them all new techniques,
> to give them forty new dishes every year. To inspire [them]. . . . It's like, who
> wants the responsibility of having to inspire the world? . . . But with sharing
> comes that responsibility. . . . It's not easy and it just became something that
> was always expected of them.
>
> (Personal interview, haute cuisine chef, United States)

Similar tensions may be found among academics or artists who aim to sustain an influential position in the avant garde of their fields. At elBulli, however, the expectations that built up around the organization's new cuisine included not only other culinary professionals but also a growing number of curious aficionados who wanted to dine at the restaurant, the majority of whom were never chosen to go. As has been mentioned, by 2008 approximately two million people had sent an e-mail to bulli@elbulli.com requesting a reservation every year, hoping to get one out of the 8,000 seats that were assigned by the restaurant's administrative team every season.[28] No wonder people on online gastronomic forums compared the prospects of getting a reservation at elBulli to winning the lottery. The exclusivity of the elBulli restaurant, furthermore, led several of my interviewees to describe it as something different from a restaurant. They noted that regardless of how elevated a restaurant's popularity or status might be, it had never occurred to them that a restaurant could have a waiting list of millions of people, all of them with such a slim chance of getting to dine there in reality. In this respect, other interviewees remarked that at the end "elBulli seemed more like an attraction, a show"—precisely the kind of experience that elBulli's members did not want their culinary invitation to become.

Inside the organization, in turn, the picture also seemed quite complex: It had become increasingly difficult for the team to manage the growing number of requests for reservations and, most importantly, the high expectations of potential guests. These were expectations that they had consciously helped to build in the first place: "Foodies,[29] those thousands and thousands of aficionados, how many of them [actually] came to elBulli?" Adrià said to me in a personal conversation. "Very few, many of them did not come. But among those who did, their levels of exigency were not normal!" Adrià added that in the long run, it would most likely have been impossible to fulfill these expectations.

This challenge becomes especially tricky if we consider that the central message that the elBulli restaurant aimed to transmit to its intended audience was in fact excitement and bewilderment, emotions that tend to dissipate with repetition. At elBulli, as we will see, the efforts of the organization to sustain its charismatic identity were manifested in Adrià's continuous attempts to change the organization's internal structure and procedures so as to enhance the team's creativity, and externally by the constant renovation of the restaurant's menu, the most visible branch of the organization. Yet, despite these efforts, charisma is necessarily unstable in nature and, as such, it is destined to dissipate with the passage of time. My informants who were lucky enough to dine at the elBulli restaurant more than once attested to this by saying that the excitement produced by a first visit to the restaurant was simply unrepeatable. Even if they deliberately tried to be as surprised as they were during their first visit, some informants admitted, this was not possible because they already knew what the core of elBulli's story was about: "Of course, you can still enjoy a magic show if you know how the tricks are done. When something is done well, it is done well," one interviewee affirmed. Yet the original bewilderment they experienced during their first time at elBulli inevitably diminished with subsequent visits. In this connection, another interviewee recognized that he wished he could go "virgin" to elBulli once again, to relive the excitement and perplexity of not knowing what would come next.

In analyzing the external pressures encountered by the elBulli organization, it is important to account for one significant macro-level force that was at play during the restaurant's final years: the mass use of the Internet and social media. Previously, stories about meals at great restaurants traveled mainly by word of mouth or, later, as the case of elBulli suggests, through manuscripts and publications. However, since the mid-2000s, meals at haute cuisine restaurants worldwide, and certainly at elBulli, were increasingly posted on the Web and circulated through online social networks. These reports may well describe every bite experienced at a meal, first via texts and later through photographs and videos. As a result of this, the mystical and mythical aura that surrounded elBulli's unique culinary experience started to take a different form, one that became ever more difficult for the elBulli team to predict, and certainly more difficult to control.

The various internal and external sources of pressure described thus far, and their feedback mechanisms, lead us to one question: How is it possible to fulfill the expectations of an exponentially, or to put it in the words of elBulli's members, "logarithmically" wider and ever-hungrier audience? The solution found at elBulli in trying to achieve this was building mechanisms that could strengthen the control and coordination inside the organization, at least to the extent that still remained within its reach.

Mechanisms of Coordination and Control

During the final decade of the elBulli restaurant's life, a series of procedures began to be introduced in the organization that could further guarantee the delivery of a perfect and innovative service, while still leaving the time that was believed to be necessary to fulfill elBulli's creative mission. The establishment of these procedures was also encouraged by the incorporation of an increasingly larger number of apprentices, which introduced considerably greater complexity to the daily work.

An interesting new method incorporated at the restaurant in the early 2000s was the use of clay molds to simulate, in exact ways, the proportions and forms of each ingredient and preparation that composed the dishes that were being served at the restaurant. Members of elBulli's brigade de cuisine recalled how this simple method solved a significant problem that had started to hamper the work inside the kitchen by making it possible to achieve perfect consistency across every bite of elBulli's customized menu. When the final preparation and presentation of a new dish was determined, a clay prototype of the dish was created by using different colors to indicate the size and shape of each component. Then the clay molds were covered in plastic wrap (for hygienic purposes) and labeled with the name of each ingredient and a corresponding number. This procedure represented a significant improvement in the work inside elBulli's kitchen as it allowed the team to verify the accuracy of every dish, regardless of who was making it.

It is about control. In production, when you are cooking and cutting an asparagus, the asparagus needs to be of the same exact size. What happens?

Preparations that are made at the last minute, when they are plated—a foam, for instance—it can be big or small. So the proportion changes! But since we have the [clay] mold, there is no arguing; one can take out the [clay] mold and put it in front of you. Thus control is guaranteed.

(Field notes, head chef of elBulli)

In the same way that publications made it possible for elBulli to control how the organization's knowledge and practices were distributed to the outside world, this method eliminated the ambiguity in the production of its ultimate products, namely dishes. This was a very demanding task if one accounts for the fact that, from the early 2000s onward, the elBulli restaurant already had over forty cooks in the kitchen, from roughly twenty disparate backgrounds, who needed to instantly coordinate plating for thirty to forty courses that would be served every night to fifty guests in a matter of three to four hours. It is exhausting just to put all of that into one sentence; imagine trying to make it work to perfection in reality!

Not only were individual dishes increasingly controlled; the sequences of dishes that composed elBulli's menu were also ever more strictly regulated. This was a menu that was in continuous renovation, something that by this time was certainly unnecessary from the viewpoint of diners, since the vast majority of them would only go to elBulli once in their lifetime. Moreover, from 2003 onward, Adrià instituted weekly tastings of elBulli's menu that operated as quality controls in the daily workings of the restaurant.[30] These tastings consisted of the following: At least twice a week, Adrià would sit at the wooden table in elBulli's kitchen—a table sometimes used for privileged guests—to evaluate the consistency of the menu that was being served to the customers, right outside the kitchen's door. This practice was described by members of elBulli's brigade as a stressful ritual. Oriol Castro, the director of elBulli's creative team in the restaurant's final years, would bring courses to Adrià and would stand in front of him waiting to see his response. It was not only Castro watching, though, but elBulli's entire brigade as well, who managed to watch Adrià's reactions out of the corner of their eyes while performing their designated tasks.

4.3 and **4.4** From left to right: photograph taken at public exhibition at Museum Palau Robert, Barcelona, 2012. Photograph taken at the elBulli workshop, Oriol Castro, head chef and creative director from 2008 to 2011, July 2012.

> Oriol takes a dish to Ferran. He is trying it and all of what he [Adrià] feels, he transmits in a second, just by eating two bites. All the chemistry, all the stress put into developing that single dish . . . and all of us around him, looking for his approval.
>
> (Interview at elBulli restaurant, apprentice, season 2011)

According to Adrià, these tastings represented an opportunity to "face the truth" by making it possible to assess the consistency and innovativeness within and between each of the culinary creations included in the restaurant's menu:

> We needed to face the truth. It was very hard. [For] many years we knew during the first month [of the restaurant season] that what we were developing

was not as brilliant as it needed to be. I knew it, we knew it. So there was the pressure. But we faced it, I sat through it.

(Field notes, Ferran Adrià at elBulli workshop)

In addition to these weekly tastings, elBulli's members generated production sheets that specified every task that each person needed to accomplish on a weekly and monthly basis, down to the most fundamental tasks, such as sweeping the parking lot or cleaning the rocks at the restaurant's entrance. These sheets also included detailed lists of all the ingredients that needed to be ordered and the exact recipes that would be served at the elBulli staff meal, which they called the "family meal," set out to be served at exactly 6:30 P.M. every day and lasting exactly thirty minutes. From what I was told by my chef interviewees, it is common for cooks to eat on the move or standing up while at work, so the methodical arrangement of elBulli's family meal was something that invariably caught the attention of those who got to work there, some of whom actually tried to replicate this practice at their own places of work after they left.[31]

The list of new procedures incorporated into the daily functioning of the elBulli restaurant does not stop there: Daily meetings of the kitchen staff and wait staff were also established, scheduled to be held at the exact same time every day, before starting the mise en place. In chapter 1, I described my attendance at one of these meetings, explaining how in a matter of ten minutes elBulli's brigade lined up against the kitchen's walls, listening attentively to the head chefs for instructions, with no interruptions of any kind. It was easy to recognize when the meeting had ended, I indicated, because as fast as everyone had assembled in the kitchen, they then spread across the kitchen stations to start working on a specific task. Altogether, the procedures that were implemented to ensure the smooth operation of the elBulli restaurant made its running look very much like a machine that worked with military precision, as Taylor and Fayol emphasized in their conceptualizations of early-twentieth-century organizations.

Adrià explained the objective of introducing increasing order and discipline to the production side of his organization by saying: "[By the end] we had almost attained perfection in production. We wanted to be perfect so we would not have to worry about production [of final outcomes]. It was hard, because it was something so alive, but we did not stop making changes until we reached that goal." However, at elBulli it was not only productive tasks that became increasingly systematized. Creative tasks were also subject to continuous processes of ordering and control. It is possible that, by themselves, none of these processes would have led the elBulli organization to be perceived as an "army," as Adrià himself intimated in the meeting described at the beginning of this chapter. It was rather the combination of all these factors that turned elBulli's working system into a machine whose constitutive elements, both mechanical *and* organic, appear to have fallen into a routine.

Normalizing Innovation

In a study of the Mann Gulch wildfire, a tragedy that took the lives of thirteen smokejumpers in the Helena National Forest in Montana in the United States, the scholar Karl Weick argued that individuals working within the frame of organizational rules are talented at normalizing deviance based on those rules.[32] Weick explained this by showing that it was precisely the act of following established norms (in this case, not dropping their tools) that prevented the smokejumpers from being able to escape calamity. My investigation of elBulli reveals a phenomenon that can be seen as the flip side to the finding proposed by Weick. Similar to Weick's account, the story of elBulli suggests that following the organization's standards led elBulli's members to normalize deviance; yet it was not deviance in a negative sense, such as that associated with disasters. Quite the reverse: What became normalized at elBulli was the production of *innovation*—we might think of it as "positive deviance"[33]—a phenomenon that ultimately led the most visible branch of the organization, Adrià's acclaimed restaurant, to its own end and motivated its reinvention into an entirely new organizational form. While at the outset this might seem like an unfavorable outcome, I argue that this is precisely the kind of path that any organization aiming to take innovation to the extreme should follow.

As we have seen in earlier chapters, various practices were installed over time at elBulli in order to manage creative tasks in more effective and efficient ways. Examples of this are the establishment of an R&D workshop that operated in parallel to the restaurant and the creative team that worked inside the restaurant. Earlier, I tried to show that by decoupling teams, time, and space the organization was able to systematically introduce order *and* dynamism in its structure and thereby deal with the problem of under- and overorganizing.[34] By the final years of the restaurant's life, however, these practices that guaranteed the fluidity of creative endeavors at elBulli had become routine to the eyes of its participants and, as a result, had gradually ceased to motivate the same kind of stimulation necessary for creative sparks to repeatedly occur.

One of the head chefs of elBulli explained how creative processes, and later creativity itself, became more predictable at the organization over the years: "All this turned into a routine, the schedules, the spaces. We knew that we would be six months there [at the restaurant] and six months here [at the workshop] and so on. At the end, it was the routine of closing the restaurant to prepare for the following year and having things that surprised [guests] and that contributed [to elBulli's line of work]." This normalizing pattern had started to manifest itself in the execution of several organizational practices originally associated with creativity, such as in documenting elBulli's work or developing new dishes. A designer who worked with the elBulli team in preparing the organization's yearly catalogues described how this creative process had turned into a routine: While it had started as a spontaneous and fluid process, he noted, it eventually turned into a mechanical task, one which they were already "used" to performing:

> [At first] he [Adrià] did not know how to do it. He just knew that he wanted to have a compilation of all the work that he had done so far, so we started working on the move. . . .
>
> The truth is that at the end we had reached a point in which the rhythm of work was so fast that we could not think. We worked mechanically. One

could put a picture above or below, but the design [of elBulli's catalogues] did not have much further [potential for exploration].

(Interview, collaborator of elBulli)

This pattern also became apparent in the process of developing new dishes, a task that by the last years of the restaurant's life had been optimized up to a point that it resembled the work performed by assembly lines in Ford's production system. As observed by one interviewee: "For Ferran the creativity of generating a new menu annually was routine, it was easy . . . elBulli was like an amazing factory! Do we need to make forty-five dishes, forty-eight new dishes this year? We can make them! And we can make one hundred and forty!" In fact, this was just about the number of dishes that the elBulli team was making during the restaurant's final seasons. By late 2010, therefore, key processes that sustained the elBulli organization's work, including both productive and creative tasks, had become routine to its members. Rather than being a flexible organizing structure, elBulli had started to look a lot like a "factory of creativity" capable of continuously churning out novel outputs (such as dishes or publications of the knowledge generated) at the discretion of its creators.

Considering how long it took the organization to reach this innovative capacity, this could easily have been seen as an opportunity for its members to maintain the status quo in elBulli's operation, or to scale up the business and open several elBullis around the world. After all, the restaurant was still receiving around two million requests for reservations every year, a demand that in theory would have taken centuries to fulfill. Yet rather than being considered an advantage, this situation was regarded as an impasse by the organization's members, who still aimed to take creativity to the extreme. The organization's major goal was to always search for the unknown, to continually generate sparks of novelty by questioning established knowledge and conventions, even its own. In this line, the predictability of elBulli's system of working, its capacity to relentlessly turn the familiar into the unfamiliar, was disheartening to members of the elBulli team. Rather than being innovators, the team had started to think of themselves as cogs harnessed to a

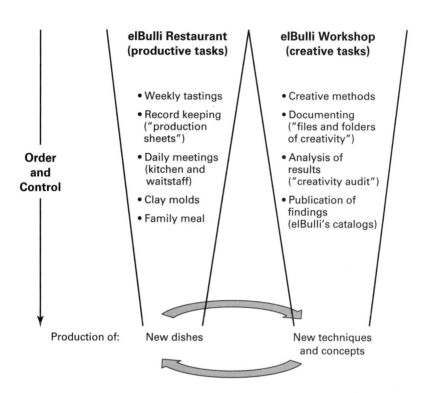

4.5 Mechanisms of order and control implemented at elBulli (1987–2011).

Mechanisms of order and control introduced incrementally within the elBulli organization, aimed at guaranteeing the effective and continuous development of innovation in the form of new dishes (primarily at the elBulli restaurant) and new culinary concepts and techniques, the organization's ultimate mission (primarily at the elBulli workshop). Author's own elaboration.

machine that could not fail, as suggested by Weber in his descriptions of the role of the functionary in a bureaucratic organization. Adrià disclosed this in a meeting held at Telefónica after the elBulli restaurant had closed by saying:

> We knew that we were going to be creative, or more or less creative. . . . We knew that every year we were going to make one hundred and forty dishes

[new final products], one year better, another year worse . . . and this was beginning to generate no adrenaline. . . . We were troublemakers and we had turned into Marines!

(Field notes, Ferran Adrià, meeting at Telefónica, February 2012)

This normalizing pattern is not exclusive to elBulli or to the gastronomic field. Social action in general has a tendency to freeze into ordered patterns that hamper or block fresh action.[35] This is especially true of avant garde organizations or movements whose initial deviant practices and ideals, after being socially accepted, become standards in their own right.[36] Bourdieu suggested that this is what happened, for instance, in the case of the Nouveau Roman and New American Painting, movements that gained recognition because of their divergence from classical approaches to literature and art, but became conventional once their deviations turned into accepted patterns in their fields.[37]

Likewise, behind the monotony that was troubling the elBulli team during the restaurant's final stages resides yet another—and more significant—quandary that can only be recognized by those who are acquainted with the inner motives that guided the organization's innovative efforts. By the restaurant's final years, the elBulli organization was also facing the dilemma of remaining deviant or letting its knowledge and practices become mainstream. Recall that for elBulli, new dishes were only "little contribution" to the future of gastronomy, regardless of how inventive or numerous they were. Hence, the fact that they were able to generate hundreds of new final products every season was not seen as a true accomplishment by the organization's members. The major goal of the organization, as we know, was to continually generate new concepts with the capacity to open novel highways of knowledge in cuisine. Given that this was a much more difficult task to accomplish, this broader mission required the enactment of some kind of mechanism that could sustain the desire for radical novelty inside the organization and that could secure its members' belief and commitment to the organization. The mechanism found at elBulli to accomplish this was the continuous mobilization of change. Like creativity, however, the continuous enactment of change at elBulli proved to have limits, especially when it remained confined within the same organizing structure.

Voraciousness for Change

During my fieldwork, Adrià explained to me the dynamics that, in his view, characterized the development of innovation at elBulli. After a certain period of time, creative sparks seemed to decline at his organization, leading the team to creative "blocks" or "droughts" that needed to be overcome in one way or another. To better explain his argument, Adrià took my notebook, filled with the notes that I had taken throughout that day, and quickly searched for a blank page on which he could visually illustrate his point. He started by drawing a thin line that went up until it reached a threshold, after which it declined. According to Adrià, this trend appears to repeat itself over time: "The passion and excitement goes up; we are creating, we are motivated. But then we find ourselves not coming up with [new] ideas, lacking passion." The trend illustrated by Adrià reflects the development of innovation at his organization only if we look beyond the production of new final products, and instead consider the mode of creativity that "truly" mattered to Adrià and his team: "conceptual innovation." Distinguishing between these two types of innovation—new ultimate products on the one hand and new concepts and techniques on the other—is enlightening, because it allows us to explain how innovation was produced and sustained in practice over the course of the organization's development. This distinction, furthermore, can not only reveal information about the patterns of innovation production at elBulli; it is also instructive about the underlying dynamics that explain an organization's ability to mobilize systematic and radical innovation.

Figure 4.7 is based on information that I collected during my visits to the elBulli workshop; it shows the changes in the development of innovation at the elBulli organization from 1987 to 2011. The number of new dishes (i.e., final products) created over time is marked in gray and the number of new concepts and techniques (which, as we know, was the main focus of the elBulli

4.6 Ferran Adrià and the researcher at the elBulli workshop, Barcelona, January 2013.
Source: M. Pilar Opazo

team's work) in black. The higher level of difficulty of formulating concepts and techniques suggested by members of elBulli can be confirmed by looking at the differences in proportions in the *y*-axes at the left and right sides of the graph: While the total numbers of new dishes produced by the organization varies from zero to over one hundred, the number of new conceptual innovations, as documented by elBulli, varies from zero to twelve. Thus, we can say that it was in fact much harder to come up with an entirely new concept that could itself become the model for successive creations, as affirmed by members of the elBulli. The examples that I have presented throughout this book reveal that this argument applies not only to the elBulli organization or to the gastronomic field, but to other fields such as music, dance, art, technology, and academia as well. To reiterate: Coming up with a new song, painting, dance piece, or academic article is different from developing new conceptual and technical advances that can open new creative avenues for multiple actors in an industry. While interrelated, these are two distinct types of innovation that contribute to the advancement of knowledge within a field.

Returning to the graph, the lack of demarcations for the year 2002 represents the year the elBulli team took off from their regular tasks to revisit the organization's prior work and, in so doing, to try to envision fresh ideas—much as an academic might aspire to accomplish during a long-anticipated sabbatical. An organization's efforts to invest in exploring new opportunities instead of exploiting existing knowledge can also be identified in technology companies such as Google, where engineers can take 20 percent of their time off from their regular tasks to focus solely on innovation (supposedly, innovations such as Gmail and Google News resulted from these time-off periods). Moreover, in the development of business activities, sunk costs are typically assigned to tasks that are not meant to provide favorable returns in the short term but only in the long term.[38]

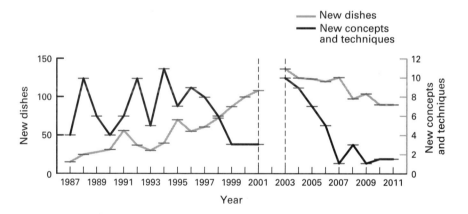

4.7 The evolution of innovation at elBulli (1987–2011).

Total number of new dishes versus new culinary concepts and techniques developed at elBulli from 1987 until 2011, the year of the closing of Adrià's restaurant.
Source: Own elaboration based on information collected at the elBulli workshop.

At first glance, it is possible to see that the graph shows a positive trend in the number of new final products developed at elBulli, especially during the initial period from 1987 to 2001 (when the number of new dishes developed rose from 15 to 108 in total). During the subsequent period, while it is possible to see a slight decrease in the number of new dishes, the average number remained quite high until the closing of the elBulli restaurant in 2011 (126 new dishes on average). In effect, the large number of new dishes developed by the elBulli team during this stage was consistently perceived as an important accomplishment by my interviewees, both in Spain and in the United States, in much the same way as scholarly papers published by an academic are valued within academic circles. The importance of new recipes or dishes in defining a chef's status has also been stressed in sociological studies of haute cuisine, which classify a chef's identity according to his or her signature dishes, as listed in the Michelin guide.[39]

On the other hand, the number of new techniques and concepts developed at elBulli indicates a rather different and more interesting trend. Obviously, it is not possible to estimate causality from this graph in a statistical sense. However, as an ethnographer, I can say that cause and effect relationships can be derived from these data, specifically in regard to interventions or changes implemented at elBulli aimed at fostering conceptual creativity. Broadly, from 1987 to 1997, it is possible to observe an upward trend in the creation of new concepts and techniques, yet it is a trend marked by strong fluctuations—a pattern that looks quite similar to the one depicted by Adrià when he explained to me the development of innovation at his organization. Importantly, these fluctuations appear at moments in which changes were enacted in elBulli. Let us return here to specific examples of changes undergone at the organization during its trajectory to illustrate how this can be so.

In the beginning of the period analyzed, in 1987, Adrià became head chef at the elBulli restaurant and began to drive the organization toward the development of a unique culinary language. After this year, in effect, it is possible to see an increase in the number of conceptual innovations, until a threshold is reached, after which it declined. In 1990, Adrià became co-owner of the elBulli restaurant, an act that significantly expanded his decision-making authority at the organization and, hence, his capacity to guide the team toward the achievement of a shared goal. Once again, after this year, there was a rise in the number of new techniques and concepts that were developed. Later, in 1993, when the number of conceptual innovations had declined again, Adrià implemented several new changes at elBulli, including the inauguration of a fully renovated kitchen (which allowed him to significantly expand the team), and later the establishment of a specialized creative team and a separate space dedicated to creativity in 1994 (the year in which the number of conceptual innovations actually reached its peak). The effect of formal interventions in the development of innovation at elBulli can be observed most clearly in 2003, the year after one of the most important changes in the organization's trajectory had been mobilized: taking a year off to compile and analyze all of the organization's previous work. Here the number of new concepts and techniques escalated to its highest level since the mid-1990s...but it never went up again. After this period the graph shows that there was a sharp decline in the number of conceptual innovations, with slight fluctuations between 2007 and 2009, which were, once again, years in which Adrià enacted changes in the workings of elBulli with the explicit purpose of encouraging the team to continue creating new concepts and techniques. These changes included the establishment of a new schedule (ten days of work with four free days), dividing the creative team into two groups that could compete with each other and generate creative friction, and, finally, changing the restaurant's season (from the traditional summer–spring to autumn–winter), a shift that was aimed at opening opportunities for elBulli's creative team to experiment with products that had not been used at the restaurant (such as wild game meat), thus fostering creative sparks. The potential of this analytical distinction between ultimate outputs and conceptual innovations to illuminate future research into innovation and organizations in general will be discussed in the concluding section.

The connection that I suggest exists between mobilizing change and Adrià's attempts to foster the elBulli team's "appetite for radical novelty" can be clarified by revisiting the notion of charisma as proposed by Weber.[40]

As mentioned earlier, a leader's failure to constantly revolutionize the conditions of production may lead charisma to fall into routine and, consequently, to its demise. This dynamic was at play at elBulli. Within the organization, Adrià was systematically questioning the structures and processes that sustained the daily work, an effort that not only stopped the team from resting on its laurels, as intimated by members of elBulli; it also enabled Adrià to sustain the members' belief in the organization and in its leader's extraordinary capacities. In short, by repeatedly deconstructing the conditions of work, Adrià demonstrated to his team that at elBulli and under his tutelage they were able to perpetually create anew.

This dynamic, I suggest, also operated in the organization's relationship with its external environment. By engaging in a constant reassessment of the collective conditions and standards that shaped its institutional field, elBulli and its leader were able to systematically win adherents and, in so doing, maintain an influential position in the gastronomic avant garde. Preserving change, then, was the strategy used by the organization to remain valid, and to uphold the commitment of its members and its authority within its field. Adrià hinted at this one day at the elBulli workshop, stating that "monotony is the worst enemy of creativity" and citing elBulli's ability to enact change as the main asset of the organization—and, for that matter, of any organization aiming to mobilize perpetual innovation:

> All the stages [of elBulli], the different scenarios, were aimed at [allowing us to] continue creating, to keep moving. After twenty-five years, year after year, change was something that we needed in order to continue creating as we had been [creating].
>
> (Field notes, Ferran Adrià, at elBulli workshop)

It is possible that the elBulli restaurant precipitated its own demise because it turned into an "army," as Adrià himself suggested. But my data show that there is much more to elBulli's story. As the restaurant became popular, it became more and more difficult for it to remain heterodox, at least in the way the organization aimed to deviate from other restaurants within its field. When the elBulli restaurant shut its doors, Adrià and his team were indeed generating new final products over and over again—but they were not significantly expanding the concepts that enabled them to renew elBulli's "vocabulary." As intimated by one member of elBulli, "We knew that we were not creating a sufficient amount [of new concepts] anymore. By the last years, I had told him [Adrià] that we were not creating at the same pace we used to." The organization, therefore, got to a point when it was too difficult to show proof of its exceptional qualities, thus risking its members' belief in the organization's mission and in Adrià as its charismatic leader. Externally, this situation also endangered the maintenance of the organization's status as a revolutionary restaurant, the essential quality around which elBulli had built its identity and gained social recognition. Constantly drawing on its own repertoire of knowledge came at the risk of losing the restaurant's strategic position in the market.[41]

It was easy to say 'this has ended.' I won't create anything new anymore and I am only going to reproduce. And I will make the best menus in the world. But for the people that were going to live this experience, it would become a mere reproduction, like going to a musical. . . .

The thousands of foodies that came [to the elBulli restaurant] were starting to get tired. We needed a cleaning, an obligatory rupture. But a kind and nice rupture, because people did not get to say 'hey, they are not so creative anymore.'

(Field notes, Ferran Adrià, at elBulli workshop)

Indeed, the authority of any corpus of knowledge depends on its ability to continuously renew itself. The authority of science, for example, relies on its capacity to repeatedly refresh the "ingredients" that compose the whole.[42] In art as well, practitioners who are able to leave a mark on their field are those who are able to continuously reinvent their artistic repertory, Picasso being an archetypical example of this.

Earlier I mentioned the study of the Mann Gulch tragedy, which describes how following an organization's rules kept its members from recognizing opportunities to escape from calamity. This study also reveals another phenomenon that contributes to illuminating the story of elBulli: A subset of the group of smokejumpers *was* able to escape from misfortune by *reassembling the organization's rules in innovative ways*. Their actions were, in fact, quite similar to the path followed by Adrià and his team in their attempt to keep the elBulli organization and its spirit alive. By 2011, the elBulli restaurant could have closed, never to reopen again; in fact Adrià saw this as the "the easiest way out," as he pointed out in the meeting described at the opening of this chapter. But what Adrià wanted most was for "elBulli's spirit to never die" and also for the organization's work to keep on living beyond him and his team. To accomplish this, members of elBulli realized that they would need to break out of the organizing structure through which they had created new ideas and epistemic practices and build a new structure that could promote new ones. Rather than waiting for destiny or fortune to do its job, once again elBulli mobilized change. This time, however, the change would require the transformation of the entire organization into a new form, and with it, the generation of a completely new universe of creation.

Taming the Beast

A monster was created, which, in the end, we decided not to kill but to tame and transform into the elBulli Foundation.

—Ferran Adrià[43]

By the final years of the restaurant's life, elBulli's members were developing an average of 126 new dishes every season, many of which incorporated entirely original culinary techniques and concepts that were later spread across the gastronomic landscape. Thus, from the perspective of outsiders, by the time it closed, Adrià's famous restaurant could indeed have been considered at the peak of its game, as was widely suggested by the media after elBulli's "last supper" had taken place. However, the organization's insiders' accounts reveal a different story when explaining the closing of the restaurant, a story that suggests that the organization, in its current form was reaching a point of no return.

Exploiting synergies between the organization's prior knowledge might have allowed the elBulli restaurant to endure for some years and, perhaps, to be successful by general standards. But to elBulli's members, and especially to Adrià, this would have implied the abandonment of the organization's true mission. Indeed, figure 4.7, presented earlier, shows that by the end of the restaurant's life, elBulli was producing markedly lower numbers of new concepts and techniques (decreasing to one or two in the final period analyzed). As noted, this was a fact that the elBulli team was fully aware of, thanks to the system of evaluation they had developed precisely for this purpose. Hence, by 2011, members of elBulli had slowly come to the realization that they were reaching the limits of conceptual creativity, the mode of creation that supported their commitment to the organization as well as the organization's standing in its field. As Adrià said, they had noted that the spirit of elBulli and its ability to relentlessly enact radical change was "falling asleep":

> [We thought,] after all that we have done, what can we do next? We can evolve in the results [new dishes] a 0, 2, or 5 percent, but in the spirit of elBulli, this will make us fall asleep. We need to search for new challenges.
>
> (Field notes, Ferran Adrià, at elBulli workshop)

Another member of the elBulli team explained this quandary as follows: "Perhaps a knowledgeable gourmand could have come [to the elBulli restaurant in the future] and say that he had eaten well . . . but he [Adrià] would *know* that everything came from somewhere [we had previously created] and he would have been disappointed." Analogously, studies of religious movements reveal that the disconfirmation of a cult's beliefs does not necessarily lead to the movement's dissolution. In fact, the most probable outcome that this phenomenon might bring is that, to eliminate the possibility of disconfirmation, the community reinforces its beliefs through advancing a new course of action.[44] This characterizes the process by which the elBulli team dealt with the challenges that it was facing.

Over the course of two decades, elBulli had evolved by proposing ways to think differently about food, about cooking, about service, about the management of restaurants. In the end, elBulli had reached a point at which there were no questions left to be asked, no more structures left to be deconstructed, at least within the frame of a high-end restaurant. For the organization's insiders, the current state of affairs represented a dead-end road that called for a new course of action: "We had taken the model of a restaurant to an extreme," Adrià noted. "We had one of two choices: either we leave [the scene] or we continue, but without deluding ourselves."[45] While elBulli had indeed potentiated innovation to degrees that they had never anticipated, members of the organization acknowledged that it had turned into a "monster," a "beast" that they could no longer control. In their view, the very working system that had for so long sustained the production of innovation at elBulli was now driving the reinvention of the organization itself.

In a memo from a private meeting held after the elBulli restaurant had closed, members of the organization justified this new course of action by stating:

> We had begun to enter routine and monotony. It was hard for us to explore new scenarios. . . .
>
> We can create dishes until the end of our days, but we need to keep asking ourselves: What is cuisine? What is a restaurant? What is the experience of eating? And to do so, we need a new scenario, the elBulli Foundation, a much freer space.
>
> (Memo of private meeting of elBulli's members, June 2012; author's own translation)

To reinvent elBulli and generate a "new" and "freer" scenario to create, the organization took steps similar to those it had undertaken in the past. As when the team had taken a sabbatical to revise all of the organization's achievements, Adrià decreed that they would now take three years off to examine all of the organization's work, culinary and otherwise, to reopen afresh in 2015. It was also agreed on that as the organization changed, so too would the "universe" in which it operated change. Unlike gastronomic restaurants, the workings of the new organization would not be subjected to reservations, waiting lists, or gastronomic rankings of any kind. This new environment would make it possible to "go back to the origins of elBulli," Adrià proposed, a period in which creative processes at the organization were driven mostly by intuition and spontaneity rather than by internal and external pressures. Again, members of elBulli explained this new collective effort by stating that their main purpose would be to explore, once more, whether a new language was possible:

> At the level of cooking, we have been creating a new language for twenty-five years . . . and now we have reached the moment of considering whether another language is possible.
>
> (Memo of private meeting of elBulli's members, June 2012; author's own translation)

In sum, after having attained the goal of institutionalizing a "new cookery," elBulli's members realized their new cuisine was in fact "old." So in order to remain heterodox, they needed to break out of the system that they had generated and build a fresh support structure. Doing so would enable the organization not only to sustain the devotion of its members and of the followers that it had won over the years, but also, as we will see next, to attract new communities that could help the organization carry out its renewed beliefs and claims. In the past, the elBulli team had continuously rebuilt the components that constituted the organization in order for it to remain deviant. Now they could rely on the prestige, resources, and networks that they had gathered over the years to try to continue enacting radical change.

A few months after the elBulli restaurant closed, the conversation in a video of the Adrià brothers was published in an issue of the design magazine *Matador*, which was dedicated exclusively to the figure of Ferran Adrià. This dialogue revealed the main motives behind the closing of the elBulli restaurant and the purposeful actions that drove the organization's reinvention into a new foundation for innovation:

> Ferran Adrià: A monster was created, which, in the end, we decided not to kill but to tame and transform into the elBulli Foundation.

If it had remained a restaurant, elBulli would have died. We simply could not go on as we were—we needed different working hours and more people on our team. Let's see if this project will enable us to continue being creative.

Albert Adrià: Just now, the creative juices have dried up.

Ferran Adrià: Anyway, both physically and mentally it would require too much focus.

Albert Adrià: We need to go back to 1985 [the year Albert joined elBulli restaurant] and go over everything, everything, everything [we have done]! Because there are thousands of things that have been left unsaid!

Ferran Adrià: We need to start all over again![46]

The final chapter represents a journey into the ongoing construction of elBulli's new organization, the elBulli Foundation. I draw on ethnographic accounts collected at the elBulli workshop, the center of operations of elBulli's team after the closure of the restaurant, to explore how an organization is reinvented on the ground. In doing so, I analyze the extent to which a new organizational form emerges as it departs from old organizational structures. I also explore the struggle of Adrià and his team in galvanizing support and impact outside of their field of expertise, the gastronomic field. This last chapter sheds new light on the analysis presented so far by going beyond retrospective accounts and, instead, looking at the ongoing routines, conduct, and beliefs that motivated the elBulli organization's operation at a moment when it was undergoing its most profound transformation.

Peach Melba, #1846

2011

Serves 10 people

© Franscesc Guillamet Ferran

LYO-ALMOND BONES

Ingredients:

LYO-almond bones

Toasted almond milk

▸ EAT THE ALMOND BONE IN TWO BITES

FROZEN MELBA BONES

Ingredients:

Toasted almond milk

Frozen almond bones

Frozen peach bones

100% syrup

Raspberry purée

▸ EAT THE FROZEN BONE IN TWO BITES

MELBA CONE

Ingredients:

Powdered lyophilized raspberry,
and raspberry caramel

Raspberry cones

Vanilla whipped cream

Peach nitro-shots

▸ EAT THE CONE DELICATELY IN FOUR BITES

VANILLA AND RASPBERRY MOCHI

Ingredients:

Sodium alginate base

Spheric-I vanilla mochi base

Powdered lyophilized raspberry

▸ EAT THE MOCHI GENTLY IN ONE BITE

MELBA HERBAL TEA

Ingredients:

Water

Peach leaves

Vanilla pod and seeds

▸ DRINK THE HERBAL TEA IN LITTLE SIPS

FONDUE

Ingredients:

Vanilla seeds, herbal tea, chips,
and whipped cream

CRU peach base

CRU peach wedges

Powdered lyophilized raspberry

Raspberry essence

▸ SOAK EACH INGREDIENT IN THE CREAM BEFORE
EATING

▸ This medley recipe forms a sequence. Each component is served in the order as written.

(Abbreviated for purposes of illustration.)[1]

5

Cooking Up a New Organization

One Day in the Construction of the elBulli Foundation

After the restaurant's closure, the elBulli workshop or *el taller*, as members of elBulli call it, became Adrià and his team's center of operation in the construction of the new organization, the elBulli Foundation. At intervals—basically, during periods when Adrià was not on one of his trips—five to ten members of the elBulli team who would continue to be part of the organization after its transformation traveled to the center of Barcelona, where the elBulli workshop is located, to work alongside Adrià. Rather than experimenting with food, the team gathered to envision and discuss, again and again, the central elements that would constitute the new foundation of creativity.

It is easy to recognize the entrance to the elBulli workshop from the outside, given that the door has a small symbol of a bulldog on the front, just like the restaurant in Cala Montjoi. When I rang the bell that morning, Ferran Adrià was the one who opened the door. "We will be working during the day, so just interrupt us with questions," he said abruptly. "At lunchtime, I'll explain to you where we are at the moment." Before I could reply, Adrià was already walking down the hallway inside the elBulli workshop, dialing some numbers on his mobile phone. I noticed that only the color of his clothes had changed since my last visit: Again, he was wearing a t-shirt, Nike shoes, and black jeans that seemed to be too big for him. It was July 2012. One year had passed since the elBulli restaurant's "last supper" had taken place and since the elBulli team had started to mobilize the entire reinvention of the organization into a new form.

Five other members of elBulli were working at the workshop that day, occupying different locations in the voluminous space. Three of the restaurant's head chefs, Oriol Castro, Mateu Casañas, and Eduard Xatruch, were gathered around the workshop's test kitchen, used in previous years for food experimentation during the restaurant's off-season. This time, however, the kitchen stoves were covered with folders, books, diagrams, and lists of different kinds. The lists contained classifications of different methods, technologies, and creations developed at elBulli. In an open space next to the kitchen was David Lopez, responsible for IT tasks. Like the head chefs, Lopez was working on lists and diagrams, but these were not related to gastronomy. The titles of his diagrams, instead, read as follows: "The Digital World of the elBulli Foundation," "How Technology Can Help Creativity," and "How We Are Going to Communicate and Divulge." As I was looking at the diagrams, I could hear Adrià talking on his mobile phone:

> We are generating the genome of cuisine. This will be amazing! . . . On [indicates a date] I can sit down and explain to you the elBulli Foundation. . . . It will be very exciting as fifty years from now it will still be there! There will be nothing like this in the world!
>
> (Field notes, Ferran Adrià, chef and co-owner of elBulli)

As one can anticipate from the above quotation, just as at the elBulli restaurant, Adrià's strong belief in his own vision of the future will be central in the making of his new organization. Josep Maria Pinto, who had been initially introduced to me as "the theorist of elBulli," was working inside the only closed space of the workshop, usually called "the chapel" by members of the organization, probably due to its stained glass and high, rounded ceiling. According to elBulli's members, this room was used for tasks that required strict solitude, not a common necessity among cooks, who are used to performing the most delicate tasks while surrounded by people and noise. Pinto explained to me that he was working on elBulli's latest catalogues and that by now the manuscripts were close to being ready to be printed.

Just as at the restaurant, the elBulli members did not seem bothered by having someone observing their work or even shadowing them around the workshop all day. As soon as Adrià finished his phone conversation, he called out to the head chefs to show them three diagrams that he had developed and, as he noted, recently presented at an international conference: "The first one contextualizes our cuisine among other cuisines, the second contextualizes research versus creativity, and the third contextualizes avant garde cuisine in the universal history of cooking." He continued to explain each of these diagrams and asked the chefs to develop an improved version of them based on the information that he had just provided. The chefs took extensive notes on what Adrià was saying, as well as photographs of each of the diagrams with their smartphones. They were, in fact, doing something quite similar to what I was doing as a researcher—no wonder my observations at the workshop did not seem to make them uncomfortable. After Adrià had finished his explanations, they all walked toward the kitchen and stood in front of the lists of culinary products, preparations, and technologies that the head chefs had created and later posted on one of the whiteboards that covered the workshop's walls. They started to discuss the information contained in these lists:

Ferran Adrià: Eduard, you need to verify all these products according to the ones that belong to elBulli and [those that could belong] to the elBulli Foundation.

Eduard Xatruch: Like the production sheets [that we did] at the restaurant?

Ferran Adrià: Exactly! ... There is not one official classification. There are classifications of botanical products, or scientific products, but these are different from the ones used in cuisine. So we must explain the 'why' of our [new] classifications!

(Field notes, at elBulli workshop)

Once the head chefs had started to work on this task, Adrià turned to the diagrams that Lopez had developed, aimed at exploring the relationship between creativity and the diffusion of information at the elBulli Foundation. After looking at the diagrams for a few seconds, Adrià asserted: "We need to understand 'how,' 'who,' and 'when.' Organize ourselves! Do you understand? Because if we do not understand it ourselves, we won't be able to explain it to others!" Just as I had seen him do a year ago at his restaurant, Adrià then took a pencil that he had tucked behind his right ear and began to fill the diagrams with notes, arrows, and Post-its that indicated his ideas for rearranging the elements contained in Lopez's diagrams: "this should be here and this there," "this is missing," "this should be smaller, because it is less important," and "this should be connected to this." Adrià's analysis concluded with "Okay, now do them all over again, incorporating these changes." Continuous change was, in fact, the most noticeable pattern that I observed during the construction of the elBulli Foundation.

The whole day went on like this, with elBulli's members developing "maps" of their work and with Adrià supervising every step of the process. The fact that the elBulli members visualized everything that they did and then posted it on the workshop's walls offered external observers the opportunity to see how the work was being done while it was still underway. In fact, at least four different groups of visitors—ranging from journalists to designers to academics—visited the elBulli workshop that day to discuss various projects with Adrià and his team related to the elBulli Foundation. And on each occasion, the organization's members drew on one of the diagrams and lists that they had developed to show evidence of the work they were conducting.

The time did come when Adrià turned to me to explain the current state of their new project: "The elBulli Foundation is an experimental center of creative processes, efficiency, and efficacy, and a model for auditing creativity," he said to me firmly and suddenly. "We are working now to try to understand how in hell we have been able to do what we have done and create all that we have created year after year!" Ultimately, Adrià stressed, the elBulli Foundation is much simpler than it might seem:

> We'll create a large workshop. Less food and more creativity. . . . Our challenge in the future will not be to make new dishes [or new culinary concepts and techniques] that we can later apply to cuisine, but to revolutionize the [organizing] model itself!
>
> (Field notes, Ferran Adrià)

The elBulli Foundation, then, had a key characteristic that distinguished it from the organizational model that preceded it. Unlike the elBulli restaurant, the main expression of the new organization's work would not be culinary creations (regardless of how revolutionary they were), but the production of innovation itself.

To explain to me how elBulli's team would approach this new mission, Adrià took me to one of the desk spaces at the elBulli workshop and sat in front of a computer. He then typed the following words, using only his two index fingers: "origin universe." When the search results came back, he rapidly clicked on a video that appeared at the top of the page. Adrià noted that he had recently presented this video in a talk at a prestigious university in the United States to explain the elBulli Foundation. The video started with a brief description of the Big Bang explosion that happened billions of years ago, followed by the generation of stars and planets, the first glimpses of life on planet Earth, and later the development of the human species—a story with which most of us are familiar. Adrià was noticeably smiling while watching the video, not at all a common expression for him. After it was finished, he turned to me and said:

> Do you know how we are going to start [the elBulli Foundation]? We are going back to the origins. Back to rethinking everything we know. You might say, 'I

think you are crazy!' [But] no, no, no, no, no! . . . We need to know how everything started! I would like to know why men started cooking, when, how!

(Field notes, Ferran Adrià)

Analytically, the organization's reinvention represents a unique opportunity to test and refine the findings presented in previous chapters, by reexamining the practices that operated at elBulli, and discovering new practices that may encourage or hinder an organization's capacity to enact revolutionary change. An analogous research opportunity could have been the replacement of the organization's leader (in this case, of Adrià) while maintaining the same organizational form. Yet, since at elBulli the organizational context had changed, we have a unique view into the team's efforts to institutionalize charisma, that is, to generate a structure that could exist even after the lives of its creators are over and to identify the difficulties associated with this task.

In analyzing elBulli's reinvention, the reader must bear in mind that it is difficult to disentangle the figure of a charismatic leader from the system that he creates. My analysis by no means intends to imply that Adrià's personality played a superficial role in the workings of his organization or that what happened at elBulli could have occurred without him. As a sociologist, however, my focal interest has been to illuminate the relationship between social action and the larger system to which those actions are connected. In this regard, one fruitful avenue of research in the future would be to focus on examining the psychological features of the leader's personality in light of the findings presented in this study.

This final chapter explores the limits of an organization's ability to enact change beyond its field of expertise. The analysis of the construction of the elBulli Foundation will provide new evidence to support the central argument of this book, namely that innovation cannot exist as free-floating, independent materials or actions. In particular, revolutionary innovation (as opposed to incremental or "recombinant" change), must remain linked to a relevant social context and to the actors and institutions that shape this context.

Reconstructing a Mythical Organization

*Fifty years ago, people would have laughed at the possibility of building the
elBulli Foundation. But after all that elBulli has done, people believe in it.*

—Personal interview, food scholar, United States

Over the years, elBulli was innovative in the content of its culinary offerings
by proposing new ways of understanding food and the fine dining experience.
It accomplished this, however, by using an established organizational form
in haute cuisine as its primary locus: a restaurant. Scholarly accounts date the
institution of restaurants in Western society back to the 1760s, characterizing
them as places where food is ordered, prepared by a restaurateur, and served
after the guests' arrival. It is also a place where, having concluded the meal,
guests are charged based on what they have consumed.[2]

By the time elBulli started to propose new ways of doing things in cuisine, restaurants had undergone numerous changes since their foundation
more than two centuries earlier, but they continued to be the organizational
form that predominated in haute cuisine. What is important to note here is
that *only after* elBulli had acquired recognition as an innovative *restaurant*
did the elBulli team begin to mobilize the transformation of the organizational form itself, from a restaurant to a foundation for innovation.
The distinction outlined here between innovation in content versus in the
organizational form is relevant because if, instead, elBulli had started to offer new foods and preparations of food within an unfamiliar context, it is likely
that the impact achieved by the organization would have been significantly less,
potentially even nonexistent. This is because it would have simply been too difficult for outsiders to recognize the novelty contained in elBulli's gastronomic
proposals, and probably would have significantly reduced the number of people
who would have attempted to understand the organization's work.

In my investigations, I found that the same force that supported elBulli's
efforts to innovate in its culinary offerings later appears to have been the
central driver behind the restaurant's transformation into a new form, namely

5.1 and **5.2** (*top*) Ferran Adrià at the elBulli workshop; (*bottom*) the kitchen at the elBulli workshop covered with books and diagrams of the elBulli Foundation, Barcelona, July 2012.

5.3 and 5.4 (*top*) Ferran Adrià, Josep Maria Pinto, and Oriol Castro at "the chapel"; (*bottom*) three of elBulli's head chefs, Oriol Castro, Mateu Casañas, and Eduard Xatruch, and Ferran Adrià at the elBulli workshop, Barcelona, July 2012.

the reputation it had earned from external actors and institutions in the gastronomic field. Much as many of those who religiously applied to get a reservation at the elBulli restaurant, professionals in the contemporary culinary industry (connected and unconnected to elBulli) expressed a common belief that the new foundation would be able to surprise them year after year. They stated that notwithstanding the effects of elBulli's new venture, they considered that "if there is one person who can do this, it's Ferran Adrià." In their view, this was because Adrià has "proved to the world" that he can create enormously and also—and even more significantly—because Adrià has become an icon of innovation and, for this reason, people now believe in his extraordinary capacities. As one interviewee remarked, "He has the luxury of being Ferran Adrià, so people will do things with him and for him [just because of who he is]."

The impact that these beliefs and expectations of elBulli's new organization can have in reality is anything but minimal. As mentioned in previous chapters, people's convictions about positive or negative visions of the future can influence their actual behavior and, consequently, shape the real world. This is what happened, I suggested, at the elBulli restaurant when the vision of one creative mind turned into a collective mission that was undertaken by the organization as a whole and later by those who were connected to it. Based on this finding, at the end of my interviews I asked my informants: Can you visualize the future of elBulli? And if so, how do you see elBulli ten years from now? The answers to these questions offer a peek into the positive feedback between beliefs and actions that supported the emergence of Adrià's new think tank for creativity (see table 5.1). To better illustrate how these beliefs could actually affect reality, on this occasion I have included the names of the interviewees and their specific position in the contemporary gastronomic landscape at the time of the interview. The quotations presented below correspond to selected answers given by recognized professionals in the culinary field, that is, chefs who work at and/or were owners of restaurants that have been awarded Michelin stars or declared among the world's best restaurants.

TABLE 5.1 Visions of elBulli's future by professionals in the gastronomic field

Name of Interviewee	Position and Emblematic Restaurant	Selected Quotations
Joan Roca	Chef and owner, *El Celler de Can Roca* (Three Michelin stars since 2009 and the S. Pellegrino World's Best Restaurant, 2013 and 2015)	"[ElBulli Foundation] will be a neuralgic center of creativity.... Connect all the tools for creativity, like a magnet for the generation of ideas."
Juan Mari Arzak	Chef and owner, *Arzak* (Three Michelin stars, 1989 to present)	"Of course I imagine it [elBulli Foundation], because I am Ferran [Adrià's] friend, he is like a brother to me! ... He will move forward, organizing a center for investigation for all the cooks in the world, for all of us to evolve."
Francis Paniego	Chef and owner, *El Portal Echaurren* (Two Michelin stars, 2014 to present)	"[ElBulli Foundation] will be a place where thousands of new things, thousands of ideas, will emerge and disseminate around the world. Kind of like Apple [Inc.] where new iPhones, new iPads [will be created].... Like a Silicon Valley where people can go to experiment, to see [what's next]."
Wylie Dufresne	Chef and owner, *WD~50* (One Michelin star, 2006 until it closed in late 2014)	"They [the elBulli team] will really expand upon the guild system that has been in place for a long time.... As a cook I go work for 3, 4, 5 different chefs because I want to learn what each of them knows.... And they [the elBulli team] are going to continue that notion.... Creating opportunities for people to get together and share ideas."

(*continued*)

Paco Perez	Chef and owner, *Miramar* (Two Michelin stars, 2010 to present)	"I think that it will be unique in the world; it will be copied all around the world. They will surprise us all with what will happen in Cala Montjoi, like Dalí with Surrealism."
Maxime Bilet	Chef and coauthor of *Modernist Cuisine*	"It's going to become a research center, like a university, and there will be huge ramifications for the world, because each student who goes there will have a different vision, and if they empower them, they will be able to empower others. So it's a great cycle."
Carme Ruscalleda	Chef and owner, *Sant Pau* (Three Michelin stars, 2009 to present)	"[It will be elBulli's] own evolution, of all that they have lived, of all that they have created and served; it will be an evolution toward creativity, shared with the whole world."
Shaun Hergatt	Chef and owner, former *SHO Hergatt* (Two Michelin stars, 2009; 2015 executive chef at Juni)	"He [Adrià] is doing this to educate . . . to try to help people devise, develop, evolve, create and work with what they love to do. . . . Do that on a worldwide basis and educate the planet!"
Jose Andrés	Chef, *FoodThink Group* (Owner of several restaurants including Minibar and Jaleo in Washington, DC)	"He [Adrià] will be the Google and Wikipedia of the food world at once."

The majority of my interviewees expressed a consistent confidence in the distinctiveness of the elBulli Foundation. Yet, instead of comparing Adrià's new organization with a "temple of gastronomy," as they did with the elBulli restaurant, these interviewees depicted its function as analogous to the work of avant garde artists, universities, and high-tech companies, all of which have the advancement of knowledge as their primary goal. While this might suggest that external beliefs are once again aligning with Adrià's "crazy" vision, there are at least two contradictions inherent in elBulli's endeavors that are relevant to point out.

First, by focusing on the process of innovation rather than on food, cooking, or eating, the elBulli Foundation is decoupling from the essential elements that sustained the organization's innovative capacity. Second, and as a result of this, the organization is moving away from the community of practice of culinary professionals that until now had supported its growth and legitimacy, as expressed in the quotations from elite chefs presented in the table. Analyzing elBulli's venture in light of these contradictions will not only tell us about the uncertainty surrounding Adrià's new organization, but also offer insights into relevant issues regarding the production of innovation in general, such as the nature of radical change, the embeddedness and disembeddedness of innovation, and the inevitable decline of revolutionary innovation.

Next, I examine the persistent attempts of elBulli's team to generate a new organizing structure that could secure "elBulli's legacy" and move the organization's innovation more and more into an abstract realm. As a whole, my analysis will show that, due precisely to this extreme conceptual turn, instead of a logical and predictable infrastructure for innovating, what seems to characterize the operation of elBulli's new organization is uncertainty and serendipity.

Connecting the Dots

The total number of dishes ever created at the elBulli restaurant could have been any number. But it wasn't. It was, rather, the number 1,846, which "magically" coincided with the date of birth of Escoffier, one of the fathers of modern French cuisine. As a matter of fact, far from being a coincidence, this number was purposefully selected by elBulli and, specifically, by Adrià. When the last day of the restaurant's life was approaching, the organization's inventory of elBullistic dishes was somewhere between 1,820 and 1,830. Knowing that the counting would soon come to a close, Adrià decided to push his luck by looking for a number that could signify the end of the elBulli restaurant's era. By searching in his books and on the Internet, Adrià discovered that Escoffier was born in 1846, a number that was more or less the total number of dishes that the restaurant was estimated to complete before the shutting of its doors.[3] This number seemed particularly well suited to the circumstance at hand given that, in line with the organization's new mission, Escoffier had not only been the central figure in modernizing classical cuisine—he had also revolutionized the craft of cooking by proposing a new organization of work inside kitchens (the so-called brigades de cuisine) and a new system for codifying cuisine, both of which have been very influential and which also very much represented the focus of elBulli's latest efforts.

To further add to the meaningfulness of the elBulli restaurant's closure, it was also decided that the last dish created at elBulli, number 1,846, would be a new version of one of Escoffier's recipes: the dessert Peach Melba, made with skinned peaches boiled in vanilla-flavored syrup and served on a bed of vanilla ice cream accompanied by raspberry purée.[4] The elBulli restaurant's last creation, therefore, would consist of the following: ElBulli would offer its own interpretation of Escoffier's recipe for Peach Melba by presenting it in a deconstructed form, a culinary concept that had become a hallmark of elBulli's experimental cuisine. As indicated previously, this meant that the original recipe would remain intact from a gustatory standpoint, but its components would appear broken apart, an effect achieved by using different culinary techniques developed at elBulli. What's more, on this occasion the ingredients would be presented in sequence to diners, a new concept that the elBulli team had been exploring recently at the restaurant. This final conceptual touch would introduce additional novelty to Escoffier's recipe by proposing a new rhythm for eating the dish and a new presentation, thus connecting classical knowledge of gastronomy with the organization's own knowledge. To the eyes of elBulli's members, these changes involved a complete transformation of Escoffier's original recipe, turning it into an elBullistic creation. The new dish would follow the organization's technical-conceptual approach by presenting an encrypted message to its audience. And that audience now consisted not only of the diners at the elBulli restaurant, but also of the elite chefs who had joined the team in preparing "elBulli's last supper," as well as the worldwide media that would report on the event.

Let me briefly pause here to examine the significance of elBulli's last dish and its connection with the organization's prior practices. First, *because of* its relation to Escoffier's work, the new recipe Peach Melba offered elBulli an opportunity to close the restaurant by paying homage to the classics of cuisine, namely, what had constituted the starting point for innovation at the organization and the basis of its legitimacy back in the late 1980s. Yet, by deviating from the original recipe, the dish would make it possible to convey the essence that characterized elBulli's "extreme cuisine" while simultaneously offering the necessary cues for outsiders to recognize the novelty contained in it. As such, the dish Peach Melba represents a recombinant innovation strategy by integrating both old and new materials in the production of a new final product. The recombinant character of elBulli's recipes during the restaurant's final stages was confirmed by one of its apprentices:

> A lot of things are said about the crazy, wild, molecular food that they [elBulli's team] made, like N_2 sorbets, caviars, spherifications, foams, or airs. But they also made not-so-technical dishes. A few that come to mind are . . . a drink made from juiced, immature peaches. . . . Lamb tails braised quickly in a pressure cooker, deboned, and seared in a pan. These are the ideas that . . . felt more like a natural extension of normal cuisine than a brand new innovation.
>
> (Personal interview, apprentice at elBulli restaurant's last season)

Moreover, the dish Peach Melba constitutes a micro-representation of the broader project that Adrià's new organization aspired to accomplish: By taking an iconic recipe but presenting it in a completely different form, the organization aimed to move further and further away from the food world. The elBulli Foundation, then, would seek to preserve the organization's spirit of always searching for the new by detaching from food objects and, instead, focusing on developing new methods and structures to create, a unique skill that had differentiated elBulli from other organizations in its field.

One final interesting aspect of elBulli's dish Peach Melba is that it eluci-dates a key ability that the organization had consistently exploited over the years: its storytelling capacities. Like human beings, organizations use narratives to make sense of their world, to develop their identities, and build their relationships with their environments. Just as we select events and characters to construct a coherent story about ourselves, organizations achieve meaning as collective entities by building narratives about their own existence. As indicated by scholars, this process is never ending and constitutes a key aptitude that explains the organizations' survival and development.[5]

As we know, in the case of elBulli, over the course of its trajectory the organization paid great attention to developing a coherent story about it-self, one that could be understood by its members and by potentially inter-ested third parties. During my fieldwork, I was able to appreciate the con-sistency of elBulli's story by looking at the narratives of its current and former members, as they all seemed to rely on the same past events, anec-dotes, and achievements to describe the organization's growth and their specific roles in it. It is likely that elBulli's self-description, manifested in the organization's systematic publications, may have bolstered its members' storytelling abilities. In this sense, the elBullistic recipe Peach Melba represents one final attempt by elBulli to provide internal and external parties with a sensible story that allows them to connect the dots between the organization's past and present and, in so doing, recognize its future possibilities.

From Culinary Innovation to the Innovation of Innovation

Regardless of how "conceptual" elBulli restaurant's culinary approach might have been, it was still grounded in food and the preparation of food. At the new foundation, however, the elBulli team would take the organization's conceptualization efforts to an extreme. A number of developments in Adrià's new organization exemplify this increasing departure from food and cuisine, and thereby from the gastronomic field.

The first project launched by the elBulli Foundation was a "museum center" called ElBulli 1846, a name chosen to commemorate the organization's creative capacity prior to its transformation. This space was going to be located at the original restaurant's installations, with the explicit purpose of sustaining the organization's "mythical aura." Adrià compared it with Dalí's house in Cadaques: "When you go to Dalí's house, you realize that you are not just [visiting] a house! It is where Dalí lived, where he made his paintings!" Similarly, Adrià and his team wanted to convert visitors into participants of elBulli's "myth" by having them visit this branch of the elBulli Foundation, making them characters in the narrative that the organization itself had carefully constructed. As stated by Adrià, "people will be able to see where everything started." "This space will allow the spirit of elBulli to keep on living. This will be our emblematic space."

Instead of the culinary preparations offered at the restaurant, ElBulli 1846 would present the organization's accomplishments through an exhibit curated by elBulli, similar to what artists do to showcase their work. Further, the new space would go beyond topics related to food and dining by including temporary exhibits that explore how creativity is developed across different crafts and the methodologies used in each. It was also originally planned that a new, modernized building would be constructed next to the restaurant's installations, consisting of creative spaces and brainstorming rooms that would emphasize the organization's new focus on innovation, rather than on cooking per se. Yet, even before starting, this project encountered serious limitations. In 2011, a group of ecologists and local citizens of Cala Montjoi collected over 90,000 signatures to stop the construction of elBulli's new building. The groups argued that current regulations do not allow this kind of construction due to the negative effects they can have on the natural environment around elBulli. They also claimed that the protection of the environment must prevail over the interests or vision of any one person, even those who are judged to be extraordinary persons, such as Adrià. In any case, what is important to notice here are the efforts of elBulli's team to build an infrastructure that would no longer be bound to the culinary field. Whereas a restaurant's focus is essentially to feed guests, the main goal of this branch of the elBulli Foundation would be to "feed the elBulli legend" by constantly showing proof of the organization's innovative capacities, culinary or otherwise.

Another initiative that reveals the elBulli Foundation's attempt to move beyond the food world are workshops called Eating Knowledge organized by Adrià in collaboration with Telefónica. As we might remember, in the early 1990s Adrià's workshops at the elBulli restaurant had "illuminated" chefs by offering new conceptions of cooking and fine dining through the presentation of elBulli's unique cuisine. The foundation's workshops, instead, invite professionals outside the realm of gastronomy to open their minds (as opposed to their taste buds) to new ideas and processes to enhance creativity. A "menu" is indeed offered at these meetings, but rather than including elements of a new cuisine it includes both actual and virtual dishes, ranging from the typical bread and butter that is served at the beginning of a meal, to elBulli's anti-food Smoke Foam, to pictures of dishes shown on an iPad, and cards with illustrations of dishes. "This is about knowledge, not about food," Adrià clarifies. "Eating is not enough. If we want to remain in the avant garde, we need to move beyond it."[6] Participants in these meetings are requested to reflect about creativity by eating the bread and butter and reconsidering existing conventions, finding a logical order among the cards with illustrations of dishes, and appreciating the sequence of steps involved in producing a culinary creation, as shown in the videos. While attempting to be innovative, this kind of experience is not a dining experience and not even a culinary experience. Adrià wears a white chef coat at these events, but cooking is a trivial element in it and food is not even present in many of the "dishes." Furthermore, as stated by Priscilla Ferguson, a chef's performance is supposed to be accompanied by "food talk," a dialogue that comments, judges, and criticizes a meal and, in so doing, recognizes the chef as an expert.[7] While this was certainly an essential aspect of the elBulli restaurant, no food talk is involved at the elBulli Foundation's workshops, only commentaries and reflections on creativity and innovation.

In the two examples above, cuisine appears as an analytical tool, as opposed to the substance or medium to innovate. Contrary to predominant trends in contemporary haute cuisine, the experiences proposed by the elBulli Foundation seem to be devoid of common understandings of a meal or the performance of cooking. Against this background, we may ask, will it be possible for elBulli to sustain radical innovation when food is divorced from consumption and from the sensual reality that it necessarily embodies?

A brief description of two tendencies that shape the contemporary gastronomic field might help to illuminate this dilemma. The first trend is characterized by a mixture of sophisticated dining and casual dining, which Christel Lane called the "democratization of fine dining."[8] In *Smart Casual*, Alison Pearlman pointed out that elite chefs are opening more relaxed dining concepts along with conventional restaurants.[9] In New York City, for instance, Chef Daniel Boulud has developed a new type of empire by opening a series of diners and bistros including Bar Boulud, DBGB, and Epicerie Boulud, in parallel to his renowned high-end restaurant Daniel. At Boulud's more casual establishments, guests are able to taste his cuisine while sitting at the bar or even standing up, and as they watch the chefs preparing their meals. Chef David Chang has followed a similar approach with his chain of restaurants called Momofuku, which ranged from Ko, declared among the world's best, to the less formal Ssäm Bar and Noodle Bar, where diners can enjoy Chang's Korean food at affordable prices. Finally, Chef Wylie Dufresne, known for his unusual flavor combinations at the now-closed DW-50, also opened a diner called Alder where experimental concepts and techniques are applied to popular foods, such as donuts or root beer floats.

The second trend in the high-end restaurant sector is a combination of tradition or simplicity and "newness" in the preparation of meals. Whereas the former emphasizes seasonality, the rediscovery of local ingredients, and foraging, the latter seeks to dazzle diners by pairing ingredients that are not normally conceived as compatible, experimenting with new textures, and transforming known foods into new forms. This trend has been pioneered by chefs like René Redzepi in his restaurant Noma in Denmark or Massimo Bottura in Osteria Fransescana, Italy, and is being imitated on a global scale.

Heston Blumenthal's cuisine can also be seen as representative of this approach due to the chef's efforts to take the traditional and present it in new
and analytical forms. Interestingly, like elBulli, these culinary approaches
place a strong emphasis on research, manifested in the construction of "food
labs" that operate alongside high-end restaurants.

Yet, however analytical these chefs' approaches might be, their work is still
grounded in food, cooking, and eating. Unlike the elBulli Foundation, these
chefs' efforts aim to reach *diners* through the presentation of tasty and
thoughtful *culinary preparations*. What's more, chefs in these two gastronomic
trends are not closing their restaurants so as to open new think tanks for innovating. They are, rather, capitalizing on their high-end restaurants' reputation and expertise either to open more casual venues or to build food labs that
could enhance their creative work *within kitchens*. The fact that so many chefs
are doing this is not a coincidence. There are, in fact, significant risks associated with decoupling culinary innovation from food consumption.

According to Pearlman, the blurring of boundaries between sophisticated
and casual dining could have endangered the high status of fine dining.[10]
This has not happened, she explains, because the uniqueness and exclusivity
of fine dining is constantly being reinforced through the culinary preparations offered at high-end restaurants. Thus, it is the very difference between
the chefs' gourmet establishments and their informal counterparts that
secures a basis for the distinction of the fine dining segment and, in so doing,
guarantees its maintenance in the gastronomic field.

By deviating from food and cuisine, however, Adrià and his team seem to
be taking quite a different route. While their efforts might open new and
unpredictable paths for discovery, as envisioned by Adrià, it also puts at risk
the basis of distinction that supported the elBulli organization's credibility.
Would the brand of "Ferran Adrià" or the memory of the elBulli restaurant
be sufficient to generate a new basis of distinction for elBulli's new organization to thrive? Will the elBulli Foundation be able to sustain its credibility
based essentially on conceptual innovation? The side projects of members of
Adrià's team suggest that this might not be the case. In the history of elBulli,
radical innovation worked insofar as it was attached to an actual restaurant

that served food to diners, regardless of how eccentric the food was or how hard it was to get a reservation. The side projects initiated by elBulli's members while the foundation was still under construction reveal that, in fact, it might be too difficult (and perhaps impossible) to maintain the organization's reputation based on abstract notions of innovation and change.

Once the elBulli restaurant closed, the three head chefs of elBulli's brigade, Oriol Castro, Mateu Casañas, and Eduard Xatruch, opened two restaurants, Compartir and Disfrutar (*Share* and *Enjoy*), with a more casual approach to cooking, less exclusivity, and a diverse menu from which guests can choose their meals. In partnership with Ferran Adrià, his brother Albert has also opened a number of casual restaurants that are ingenious in character, including restaurants that serve modern tapas, Mexican cuisine, and Nikkei cuisine, and which seek to offer diners a pleasurable and even entertaining dining experience. What is common to all these enterprises of elBulli's members is that they build on already established culinary styles—and on the reputation acquired from the elBulli restaurant—to open new casual venues. Hence, rather than advancing revolutionary and purely conceptual innovation, Adrià's closest team members seem to be following an already established trend in haute cuisine, just in a different way.[11] A similar pattern can be found in Redzepi's recent plans to close his restaurant Noma and transform it into an urban farm, while opening a more casual restaurant in parallel to this drastic transformation.

Beyond gastronomy, an initiative that can be compared to elBulli's attempts to bring innovation into a purely conceptual realm is Apple University. Prior to his death, Steve Jobs launched this project as a medium to sustain the company's legacy by dissecting the way of doing things at Apple and imparting the organization's *know-hows* to future generations. In courses like What Makes Apple, Apple would instruct employees about the visionary mind of the company's founder and help them internalize the principles and methods that fostered innovation at the organization, such as simplicity, perfectionism, and attention to detail. Unlike the elBulli Foundation, however, Apple is not severing its ties with the technology world or closing the Apple stores so as to focus on the innovation process only. The company's standing, instead, is still based on its ability to produce new technologies that can be used by customers around the world. As in the case of elBulli, even for Apple it would be too difficult to sustain the company's strategic position based essentially on abstract notions of creativity and innovation.

The dynamics analyzed so far reveal the difficulties and limitations of producing radical innovation that is no longer bound to a field. Additional risks can be identified if we look at the elBulli team's attempts to build an increasingly diverse pool of followers, and the organization's progressive decoupling from the community of experts or thought collective that thus far has validated and extended its work.

Building a New Universe

ElBulli tried to open itself to radically new possibilities by blowing up its previous organizing model and constructing a new one. The organization's reinvention, furthermore, was accompanied by the team's efforts to generate a new institutional environment, that is, by connecting the organization with new actors and institutions that could secure recognition of its new vision and goals.

Ever since the restaurant closed, Adrià and his team were constantly initiating projects to publicize the elBulli Foundation and increase the chances of outsiders recognizing the value of their new venture. One of these projects was called "Bullipedia"; it consisted of an online search engine that would compile all of the work done at elBulli, and of other chefs around the world, into a digital format. In doing so, the elBulli team sought to capitalize on a medium that they had not used in the past, but which had become central in distributing data in contemporary society: the Internet and social media. Through Bullipedia, therefore, the organization would try once again to link to the macro-level changes occurring in society by incorporating online tools as its primary weapon.

Readers will not be surprised to learn that the Bullipedia project started by searching for a new classification system, a new language, that would be aligned with the organization's objectives. Bullipedia aimed to be used not only by chefs but also by professionals around the world interested in creativity, and hence it needed to be understood by a wider and more diverse audience. In trying to build a richer and more flexible grammatical structure, members of elBulli gathered at the workshop to develop a new map that could orient users in navigating Bullipedia and that could describe the "most basic elements that constitute the culinary process at large," as members of elBulli said to me. This time, however, the construction of a "map" involved the analysis of information beyond elBulli's work, including ancient and modern cookbooks, gastronomic guides, and data collected from the Internet. In analyzing this information, Adrià and his team seek to understand how culinary professionals organize their work and the processes they deployed in developing their craft, again stressing that process and not culinary production was the main focus of their work.

Moreover, in performing this task, the elBulli team worked in close collaboration with professionals from other industries, including designers, computer scientists, journalists, and philosophers, as this, they thought, would bring them closer to reaching the "new world" that the organization aimed to construct. Let me briefly present a paradigmatic example of one of these interdisciplinary exchanges that took place at the elBulli workshop. On this occasion, Adrià and the scientist Castells were debating how to classify a specific method used to create, the former from a gastronomic standpoint and the latter from a scientific one:

Ferran Adrià: Dry flowers are elaborated products, because they have been dried out. This is a technique for manipulating [food in cuisine]; it is a minimum manifestation, but it is a [culinary] technique.

Pere Castells: But this [dried flower] is not an elaborated product [in science].

Ferran Adrià: No, no, no, no! A dried product is an elaborated product! In cuisine, I'm saying. You are speaking from science. So I don't know. . . .

Adrià made a note on a diagram that was pinned on one of the boards at the elBulli workshop. They all looked at it for a few seconds in silence and continued:

Pere Castells: In botany, a fruit is a fruit, dried or fresh. . . .

Ferran Adrià: Don't you get it?! [Here] fruit is its use, its use in cuisine. [Now] . . . we need to discuss what a fruit is!

Pere Castells: Well, a fruit is something very concrete [in science].

Ferran Adrià: No [it's not]! We need to ask ourselves what it is!

(Field notes, at elBulli workshop, after the restaurant's closure)

The dialogue above shows that, during this stage, uncertainty and confusion dominated the work of the elBulli team. Yet, as had happened at the restaurant, after months of structuring the data collected and developing countless sketches, maps, and graphs, Adrià and his interdisciplinary group of collaborators arrived at a "map" that they considered exhaustive and logical by which to organize the content of Bullipedia. Adrià's eyes lit up when he talked about this project: "Out of everything we are doing, this is the wildest of all!" In his view, Bullipedia—and the map underlying it—would make accessible nothing less than the "genome of the culinary process" and, in so doing, professionals in cuisine and other fields would become participants in the production of knowledge developed in and by the elBulli Foundation.

Aligned with the organization's goal to move beyond cuisine, Bullipedia was first launched in the technology world, specifically, in a cover story on Adrià in the magazine *Wired UK*. In the article, Adrià stressed that Bullipedia was intended to be used "to create," given its potential for amateurs and professionals to find gaps in knowledge that still needed to be explored. This tool, thus, sought to embed elBulli's new organization into a broader network of interactions by building connections with the creative minds of various fields. It would also help build the new foundation's reputation by sharing information for free. As Adrià stated in a public talk in New York City, elBulli Foundation's main concern would not be *who* would participate in it, but giving everyone access to the content developed in and by it. In Adrià's words:

ElBulli has not been closed, it has been transformed. It is a rather strange transformation through which the concept of the restaurant will die. . . . It is a foundation, it is a creative center, there will be no reservations and nobody will pay. So you might ask . . . and who will come?—It doesn't matter.

Imagine you and I want to write a diary, and we want do something different . . . you shouldn't be concerned about who is going to read it. The important thing is that people read it.

(Ferran Adrià, TimesTalks, "Food and Wine Festival," New York City,
October 2011; author's own translation)

Adrià's statement confirms this book's emphasis on innovation as a social
phenomenon and hence needing mobilization. Nonetheless, his statement
also underestimates the importance of embedding radical innovation within
a field of expertise. Haphazardly winning adherents to support a cause may
bring lots of good ideas to the workings of an organization, but these ideas
can easily turn into pure noise if they are not embedded within a coherent
system of collaboration that validates them and helps expand upon them.

New Institutional Ties

In the making of the elBulli Foundation, Adrià and his team were continuously working against the transitory character of charisma by trying to transform it into a permanent structure that could continue existing beyond the
lives of its creators. Although perpetuating charisma might seem an impossible
task, a study by Dan Lainer-Vos and Paolo Parigi proposes that charisma *can*
undergo a process of preservation, but only if the group is able to secure the
recognition of established institutions.[12] The authors show this by using the
case of acolytes of defunct saints in early modern Europe. Their research
showed that the networking efforts of these groups with an established institution (in this case, the Catholic Church) made it possible for acolytes to
carry on "making miracles" even after their leaders' death.

Likewise, in order to preserve the organization's ability to systematically
perform extraordinary acts, elBulli's team was constantly reaching out to institutions from different fields in search of advice and information regarding
their new enterprise. One member of elBulli explained to me the purpose of
mobilizing these connections from the early stages of the elBulli Foundation:

We have asked many people, from the UB [University of Barcelona] to MIT [Massachusetts Institute of Technology] to Telefónica. We have explained the project to them so that it is not something only of our own [creation]. . . . To see if it's viable, if they see it as something strong, at the level of its content and of the technology [used].

(Personal interview, elBulli member)

Little by little, the synergies with these and other institutions extended from informal advice to formal counseling and, in some cases, to official appointments within the elBulli Foundation. For example, in 2014, with the support of Telefónica, elBulli's team built a space called the elBulli Lab, where roughly eighty professionals—not mainly cooks but experts with diverse backgrounds—gathered to generate new ideas and processes that could enhance the foundation's creative work. The projects developed at elBulli Lab ranged from new computational algorithms to search for foods, to databases used to analyze culinary techniques and concepts, to sensors that track the collaborations that lead to new ideas and hence could make them reproducible. Consistent with this kind of task, the motto chosen for the elBulli Lab was "eating knowledge for feeding creativity." A rotating group of culinary professionals would be able to apply to work at this new space, but the elBulli Lab's team would still consist largely of "agitators" from widely disparate disciplines such as science, computation, history, journalism, and design.

Another institution that became a partner of the elBulli Foundation was the University of Barcelona, one of the top universities in Spain. This entity became responsible for managing the knowledge incorporated into Bullipedia. Although the platform or map for organizing the knowledge had originally been developed by Adrià and his group of collaborators, the connection with this academic institution would endow the new tool with credibility by assigning qualified experts who could confirm the quality of the information contained in it, similar to what happens in academia with the content published in peer-reviewed journals. As at the restaurant, Adrià indicated, he expected thousands of people would want to have access to the elBulli Foundation, so they would "have no choice but to select." Pairing up with a university, therefore, would make it possible to establish filters to curate the knowledge produced and implemented at the foundation. These new connections would also strengthen the foundation's access to information and control, two resources that had been central in determining the restaurant's advantageous position within its field.

One final connection that is interesting to point out involves projects launched by the elBulli Foundation with business schools around the world. These consist of formal instances in which MBA students are invited to work side-by-side with Adrià in finding financial and branding solutions for the foundation, and contests that ask students to find new technologies that could boost the distinctiveness of elBulli's new organization.[13] Over the course of several months, Adrià visited a selected group of business schools (including the University of California–Berkeley, Columbia University, Harvard University, London School of Economics, and ESADE) to explain *in person* the underlying vision of the elBulli Foundation and the goals it aimed to accomplish. He presented the new organization as a natural extension of the elBulli restaurant's work, while providing details of the awards and recognitions received by the restaurant and by him as the organization's leader. Active participants in these projects were invited to visit the organization's facilities—the restaurant and *el taller*—to see *in person* how new ideas and practices were generated by Adrià and his team. One student described his visit to the elBulli restaurant as an opportunity to attach reality to Adrià's abstract vision. After being taken to the workshop and faced with the evidence that the organization had produced these achievements, the student explained how his visit helped to confirm his belief in elBulli and Adrià's innovative capacities:

We didn't eat [there], but we got to go all the way over to Cala Montjoi and see the restaurant. It was amazing. It's intact. . . . It is one thing to talk about a foundation as an idea, and then the other thing is when you go there you see the progress, the path a person needs to take, how the space is. . . .

[At the workshop] they had all the archives, all of their books. . . . He [Adrià] has these maps up of the different types of food. . . . How meticulous they work! You sometimes forget it, because you think creative people are just,

'Oh, it just comes out of nowhere.' But no, there is a lot of work and discipline that goes into it, and you can actually see that when you go to the workshop!

(Interview, business school student)

Overall, the elBulli Foundation's ties with external institutions offered Adrià and his team a new and recognized stage from which to publicize their new, innovative mission and to try to align new "planets" around it, which now extended far beyond the culinary industry. In my fieldwork, I noticed how Adrià's discourse changed as the construction of his new organization progressed, systematically incorporating the institutional relationships established over time as a way to endow his claims with legitimacy.

Although one cannot predict the effects that these proselytizing efforts will have on the future of the elBulli Foundation, the data that I gathered reveal an increasing detachment of the organization from actual food, cooking, and the community of practice from which much of elBulli's reputation derived. While rallying allies across weakly connected fields may enable an organization to become a central actor in a newly formed "world," this world might not be cohesive enough to support a new revolution. As previously stated, radical changes succeed when their initiators are able to mobilize a cohesive network of collaboration toward a common goal.[14] Within the frame of the elBulli restaurant, this essential level of cohesiveness was guaranteed by the existence of a group of culinary experts who shared a common basis of knowledge and cognition, and who thus could evaluate and maintain the organization's work. Innovation at the elBulli Foundation, however, seems to lack the unified thought collective necessary to secure a new basis of distinction. The individual contributions and judgments of scientists, designers, artists, philosophers, computer scientists, and cooks might lead to numerous creative sparks inside the elBulli Foundation and in the new universe around it, but not necessarily to paradigms shifts able to revolutionize an industry or to create new industries.

An analogous process of disembeddedness of innovation occurred in the art industry, in particular in Warhol's Factory, which became a temple of pop culture in the 1960s by gathering avant garde professionals from around the world. Like Adrià's restaurant, Warhol's Factory operated at once as a workspace and as a medium for the recruitment of new artists and actors to a new movement. In its origins, the Factory epitomized its leader's vision by imitating the repetitive activities performed by proletarian workers.[15] With Warhol's growing fame, however, the Factory became more and more populated by celebrities as opposed to the art practitioners who helped him maintain and expand the aesthetic values endorsed by the Pop Art movement.[16] By dissociating the work produced from the community of practice from which much of its reputation derived, Warhol's Factory's more and more started to resemble a standard art studio, rather than an avant garde organization. The dynamics behind the elBulli Foundation suggest a similar pattern. Adrià's new organization may well become an eccentric resource used by professionals to incrementally advance knowledge in their respective fields, but perhaps not an organization that systematically produces and institutionalizes revolutionary knowledge itself.

The magic formula of elBulli worked as long as it was applied to the materiality of food and to the sensual reality of the fine dining experience. In this context, the organization used abstract codes and methodologies to make innovation radical and systematic. While the elBulli team is actively trying to apply similar methods to the workings of the new foundation, these efforts are in essence dissociated from the context of food and from the group of experts who maintained and perpetuated the organization's practice. Thus, the evidence that I collected suggests that rather than being a methodical infrastructure for innovating, the functioning of Adrià's new organization is mainly based on serendipity. Quite distinct from the elBulli restaurant—especially during its final stages—anything can happen at the elBulli Foundation.

The Inevitable Decline of Revolutionary Innovation

The dynamics analyzed in this book reveal the intrinsically temporary character of fashions or new orders. While institutionalizing charisma might seem feasible in a field such as religion, which seeks to preserve tradition, the development of the art worlds depends on the mobilization of change. Thus, regardless of how durable a new trend or "order" might be, once it becomes established within a field—say in music, clothing, technology, or gastronomy, as happened with elBulli's new cuisine—its decline is inevitable.

In his classic article "Fashion," Simmel argues that new trends shape every type of social life. They emerge when new elements start being imitated by some and rejected by others. But when a trend reaches a level of acceptance that no longer distinguishes among its participants, then it ceases to exist. This, Simmel states, is not a negative feature of fashions, but the essential element that explains their initial attraction and emergence.[17]

This ever-changing game of tendencies and countertendencies is also present in the culinary field. Precisely due to the transitory nature of fashion, Adrià and elBulli's struggle to perpetually construct (and deconstruct) an infrastructure for radical change is reaching its limits. This does not mean that elBulli's work is going to disappear or that its influence will be forgotten. Most likely, the work of Adrià and elBulli will leave a mark in their field, and their ongoing influence will become part of the textbooks that recapitulate the history of gastronomy. But the organization's pace of innovation, and hence its capacity to exert revolutionary change, is fading away. Accordingly, it is likely that in the future elBulli's radical innovations may come back in recombinant and interesting forms, but, inevitably, they will do so in the context of an already established old order.

In closing this investigation, I hope readers can recognize that besides good ideas, discipline, and the spread of beliefs, mobilizing radical change requires the concrete and often political efforts of a group to garner recognition and to embed innovations within a larger social context. In the conclusion, I explore the opportunities for these findings to be extrapolated to other forms of social life primarily concerned with the development of innovation.

Conclusion

nlike random creative sparks, radical and systematic innovation cannot be explained simply by good fortune, providence, or an individual creator's magical or visionary capacities. Though these elements might help to boost curiosity about a set of creations or lay the groundwork for the institutionalization of innovation to occur, they are only the beginning of an explanation.

Revolutionary innovation involves a series of processes—from envisioning to implementing to socializing to legitimizing—that operate in interactive ways and which jointly bring about something new. Unlike incremental or recombinant innovation, radical innovation requires that ideas be systematically connected to an existing body of knowledge and channeled in interpretive ways so that they can be understood and recognized by a public. Whether elBulli's members were at all times fully conscious of their attempts to consolidate a new basis of knowledge must remain necessarily a subject for discussion. It is possible to say, however, that over the course of more than twenty years, the elBulli organization and especially its leader, Ferran Adrià, was actively involved in a series of actions that *in practice* secured the recognition of a new order or discipline within its field.

As the story of elBulli illustrates, revolutionary innovation was mobilized not only by advancing new ideas, but also by mobilizing a new set of epistemic practices that changed the paradigmatic ways of doing things in cuisine. Rather than limiting their work to serving new presentations of food, elBulli pushed forward a new working system of kitchens as centers of experimentation and research. Teams at elBulli worked as experimental units that pursued knowledge through systematic formulation of problems, data collection, testing, and documenting, resembling the laboratory practices of science. Moreover, while insistently building on the conventional knowledge of gastronomy, elBulli deviated from its predecessors by introducing new instruments as a medium to think differently about food and to generate new expectations about what food can be, rather than merely doing things better or more efficiently. Within the organization, a new technical vocabulary or "language" was established that incorporated elBulli's worldviews and codes, and operated as a source of shared understanding in the creative processes performed within the organization, and in the recognition of elBulli's accomplishments outside the organization. Overall, these practices imbued elBulli's organizational system with sufficient rigidity to connect the members' beliefs and daily actions with the organization's ultimate goals.

Beyond elBulli's "micro-cosmos," the organization proposed changes in the practice of sharing information in gastronomy by defining this as a highly methodical and all-encompassing task. The organization went so far as to establish its own publishing house to distribute all of its creations and methods, an action that was unprecedented for restaurants at that time. Furthermore, an existing practice in gastronomy that the organization amplified was the incorporation of dozens of apprentices and collaborators into elBulli's kitchen. These growing connections systematically linked the organization with the world outside it, and played a crucial role in embedding elBulli's ideas and practices in new contexts, and in enhancing the organization's standing within the culinary field.

Finally, elBulli was also a key mobilizing force behind the institutionalization of new global settings for chefs to stage and circulate their work: gastronomic conferences. Ever since the 1990s, elBulli was behind the organization of these events by persistently showing the organization's work to an increasingly diverse and interconnected community. As a result of these practices, having spent time at elBulli's "laboratory of cuisine" is now conceived as a status symbol among culinary professionals, and it is common to find elBulli's apprentices at the top of culinary rankings, especially those rankings that seek to expose the latest trends in haute cuisine.

Despite the inevitable distinctiveness of my case study, the dynamics observed in this book illuminate patterns of the production of radical innovation in other forms of social life. Like elBulli, there are many collective ventures, mobilized by groups, organizations, or larger collectivities, that emerge from the mind of a charismatic leader and then extend into structures that define and redefine themselves over time. Like elBulli too, these efforts are characterized by the engagement of a group of people, including external actors and institutions, that can help expand and maintain a new cause.

Religious cults, for instance, also seek to promote a set of beliefs and to draw the devotion of followers. They usually involve the presence of a leader who conveys a promising vision of the future, and the development of discourses and practices of their own which may be viewed as inspiring or disturbing to those outside the group. Similar to elBulli's story, these types of ventures need to develop instruments to sustain the devotion of a community so as to allow the cult's beliefs and values to endure, such as texts that codify the cult's worldviews and scenarios to convey and legitimize the cult's claims.[1]

Corporations in which the leader's vision is central to shaping the organization's work follow a similar pattern. In these companies, vehicles are usually designed to effectively disseminate the organization's vision to the outside world, and procedures are defined and redefined over time in order to sustain the company and its leader's charismatic authority.[2] Once again, Apple Inc. appears as a case in point, especially considering the demise of its charismatic CEO, Steve Jobs. As at elBulli, the question in people's minds is whether Apple's major innovations were the result of one individual's talent and visionary capacities (as opposed to simply refining prior achievements in new forms) or if the company will be able to keep producing radical innovations that will continue to revolutionize the technology industry.

Political parties or coalitions often entail the presence of a charismatic leader who is believed to have exceptional qualities and who needs to sustain those beliefs to be able to drive changes in reality. This kind of venture demands sustained effort to persuade people to follow a cause, to garner public attention, and to establish relationships with influential actors and institutions that can endorse the group's proposals for change. If the party or coalition is not able to generate (and constantly regenerate) collective structures that enable it to reproduce itself, and ultimately detach from the original creators, then it is doomed to disappear.

The advancement of new artistic work or movements also involves the enactment of a number of practices aimed at encouraging radical change. As I mentioned in this research, the status achieved by iconic innovators such as Picasso or Warhol did not rely simply on the artists' talent or on the intrinsic originality of their work, but on the mobilization of new patterns of appreciation, techniques, and collaborations that were central to achieving status in their field. It was mentioned that the consolidation of new artistic movements, such as Impressionism or Cubism, follows a similar path by prompting the emergence of new art worlds around them that foster their recognition and validation.[3]

One final and central example presented throughout the book is the construction of scientific facts or, more broadly, the construction of science as a discipline that organizes knowledge according to a particular set of principles. Like advancing a new cuisine, the establishment of science as a discipline required the systematic and practical efforts of practitioners who needed to demarcate what was scientific from what was not, generate arguments that attested to the validity of their claims, and establish new methods that could be replicated and expanded upon by a community.[4]

As at elBulli, the social forces behind these different enterprises actively determine their survival and endurance. If successful, these collective ventures are likely to mobilize a cohesive group of people who recognize and validate their proposal for change, thus contributing to the transformation of what could have remained an idealistic vision into an organized effort that works in reality. Irrespective of whether they exist in the world of cuisine, religion, economy, politics, art, or science, these examples suggest that radical and systematic innovation is neither an accident nor a stroke of genius. Nor does it correspond only to the production of ultimate products or to the disciplined actions that might guide a group's daily work. As is illuminated through elBulli's story, plenty of purposeful action is involved in making radical innovation come true. It was by generating a *structure for mobilizing change* that elBulli was able to navigate its way through the world it was constructing and deconstructing, and in so doing to institutionalize a new order in its field.

The distinction advanced in this book between final products and conceptual innovations also offers opportunities for generalization. Approaching elBulli as a subject of study, one could have looked at the dishes and recipes developed by the organization over time, examining the extent to which they emerged out of recombining knowledge across disparate worlds, such as different culinary styles. Another approach could have been to analyze how different teams' configurations led to new final products. This would have involved examining the different combinations of people (e.g., incumbents and newcomers) who participated in elBulli's brigades over time and the outcomes that emerged from the work of each. While these analytical approaches are highly informative with regard to the structural properties that give rise to new ideas, they are still focused on the production of final outcomes and on the structural properties that lead to those outcomes. Thus, despite the huge contribution these approaches have made, they tend to assume homogeneity across the different types of creations that are integral to producing innovation, and that ultimately enable the consolidation of new genres or paradigms of knowledge within a field.

It is likely that the approaches mentioned would have brought more parsimonious results than the ones I presented here—results that probably would have confirmed existing studies of innovation as *recombination* of new and diverse knowledge across cultures and domains. Nonetheless, much of what explains elBulli's capacity to mobilize radical innovation, if not all, would have been lost in these approximations. The evidence presented in this book suggests that this finding might also apply to the workings of other organizations or industries following creative paths.

The distinction that I proposed between final products and new concepts and techniques has the potential to encourage more nuanced understandings and interpretations of innovation. It can do so by directing our attention to the different dynamics that might contribute to the advancement of knowledge within a field. While this distinction is certainly a simplification of a much more complex social phenomenon, it can provide a basis for the development of a general framework of the different dimensions that are involved in the production of innovation.

How Far Is Too Far? How Far Is Far Enough?

Based on elBulli's case, I have tried to identify analogous patterns in the production of innovation across fields. However, there is an important characteristic of cuisine that distinguishes it from other creative ventures: Cuisine is essentially linked to the material nature of food and to the craft of cooking. In my research I found that, however analytical and abstract, radical innovation at elBulli worked when it was applied to actual food and to the dining experience offered at a restaurant. Once removed from this context, a number of additional difficulties emerged, which threaten the organization's effectiveness in continually mobilizing revolutionary change. By this, I do not mean to suggest that purely conceptual innovation is not valuable or that it is less important. I simply emphasize that, in order to be effective, innovation needs to remain relevant to actual actors and institutions within a given social domain, where it can stimulate changes in the modes of cooperation, language, and work that are produced therein. As I indicated at the beginning of this book, for creative processes to lead to innovations, they must have a social impact and be recognized by a community. The risks of extreme conceptual innovation, therefore, do not derive from its abstract nature, but from the possibility for it to fail to systematically connect—and thereby change—the social context. This is an especially challenging task in a field such as cuisine, given its practical essence and its unavoidable connection with the fragility and physical reality of food.

Thus, when it comes to radical innovation, we might ask: How far is too far? How far is far enough? I hope my analysis of the workings of the elBulli restaurant and the construction of elBulli's new organization has made clear

that, irrespective of the type of innovation or how conceptual it is, both social connectedness *and* differentiation are necessary for paradigm shifts to
take place. On the one hand, if radical innovations are no longer able to galva-
nize the support of a critical mass of people, their development and preservation
is impossible. On the other hand, if everyone follows a revolution, then it
soon becomes the standard pattern of behavior and ceases to exist as such.
These dynamics operate at all levels of social interaction: a talented artist
who never gets to sell his inventive work in life and only gains recognition
once it is placed within a recognized artistic style; a music band that meets
regularly to experiment with new musical techniques and instruments, yet
never reaches an audience; scientists who develop an innovative vaccine and,
after several immunization campaigns and the approval of global health institutions, manage to turn it into a standard medical treatment; or a group of
skilled enthusiasts who devote great effort to building and marketing revolutionary technological designs until they become the classical models for
succeeding designs, thus altering the course of an entire industry or even creating new ones. In all these cases, a sufficient degree of unity *and* distinction
between the innovations produced and the social context in which they are
embedded is missing. Only when a fine balance between these two dynamics
is achieved are new revolutions possible—revolutions that may emerge and
thrive until they become mainstream or fade away, thus paving the way for
this endless cycle to start all over again.

Notes

Introduction

1   The term *field* is mostly associated with Pierre Bourdieu's theory in which conflict and competition appear as the determinants of social relationships. The term *world*, on the other hand, is mostly used to refer to cooperative interactions among actors. Given that both dynamics, competition and co-operation, are present in the gastronomic industry, I use these two terms interchangeably throughout my work.

2   Ferran Adrià, Heston Blumenthal, Thomas Keller, and Harold McGee, "Statement on the 'New Cookery,'" *The Guardian*, December 9, 2006, http://www.theguardian.com/uk/2006/dec/10/foodanddrink.obsfoodmonthly.

3   Ferran Adrià, Albert Adrià, and Juli Soler, *A Day at elBulli* (London: Phaidon Press, 2010).

4   The opening of the elBulli Foundation was initially scheduled by 2014, but then extended into 2015.

5   In *El Viaje de la Innovacion* (Barcelona: Planeta, 2013), a book that was developed in parallel to this investigation, Carlos Domingo establishes a distinction between innovation, creativity, and entrepreneurship, while also adding the term *strategy* (25–27). I found Domingo's analysis particularly interesting given that it considers Ferran Adrià's notion of creativity as the development of new techniques and not only of well-prepared culinary products. Moreover, this analysis goes beyond my distinction by outlining the relationship between strategy and innovation. Specifically, Domingo explains that strategy consists of undertaking different activities than those

assumed by competitors, or in a different way. As a result, Domingo states, strategy can bring a competitive advantage to an innovative enterprise by proposing new ways of doing things.

6 Niklas Luhmann, *Organización y Decisión. Autopoiesis, Acción y Entendimiento Comunicativo* (Barcelona and Mexico City: Anthropos Editorial and Universidad Iberoamericana, 1997), 96.

7 Andrew H. Van de Ven, "Central Problems in the Management of Innovation," *Management Science* 32, no. 5 (1986): 590–607.

8 The tensions between commercial needs and creativity have been pointed out in earlier studies of the high-end restaurant sector. In his contribution to a study of chef-entrepreneurs in New York City, Fabio Parasecoli explained that chefs ensure the financial stability of their restaurants by working with food companies in creating innovative products. Parasecoli, "The Chefs, the Entrepreneurs, and Their Patrons," in *Gastropolis: Food and New York City,* ed. Annie Hauck-Lawson and Jonathan Deutsch (New York: Columbia University Press, 2009). He proposes the cases of Chefs Ferran Adrià and Martin Berasategui in Spain, and Sanchez Romera and David Bouley in the United States, as paradigmatic examples of business models in each country.

1. Context and Vision

1 For complete recipe, please see Juli Soler, Albert Adrià, and Ferran Adrià, *elBulli 1983–1993* (Barcelona: elBullibooks, 2004).

2 Lisa Abend, *The Sorcerer's Apprentices: A Season in the Kitchen at Ferran Adrià's elBulli* (New York: Free Press, 2011).

3 Silviya Svejenova, Marcel Planellas, and Luis Vives, "An Individual Business Model in the Making: A Chef's Quest for Creative Freedom," *Long Range Planning* 43, nos. 2–3 (2010): 408–430.

4 Hayagreeva Rao, Philippe Monin, and Rodolphe Durand, "Institutional Change in Toque Ville: Nouvelle Cuisine as an Identity Movement in French Gastronomy," *American Journal of Sociology* 108, no. 4 (2003): 795–843.

5 James T. Borhek and Richard F. Curtis, *A Sociology of Belief* (New York: John Wiley and Sons, 1975).

6 Ronald S. Burt, "Structural Holes and Good Ideas," *American Journal of Sociology* 110, no. 2 (2004): 349–399; Richard K. Lester and Michael J. Piore, *Innovation: The Missing Dimension* (Cambridge, Mass.: Harvard

University Press, 2004); Monique Girard and David Stark, "Distributing Intelligence and Organizing Diversity in New Media Projects," *Environment and Planning A* 34, no. 11 (2002): 1927–1949; David Stark, *The Sense of Dissonance: Accounts of Worth in Economic Life* (Princeton: Princeton University Press, 2009).

7   In a public talk given by Chef René Redzepi in New York City, for instance, he emphasized that the main goal of his acclaimed restaurant Noma (nominated Best Restaurant in the World in the San Pellegrino list several times) is to provide customers with new flavors and flavor combinations. Redzepi, "A Work in Progress," November 2013.

8   Priscilla P. Ferguson, *Accounting for Taste: The Triumph of French Cuisine* (Chicago: University of Chicago Press, 2004).

9   Robert R. Faulkner and Howard S. Becker, *Do You Know . . . ?* (Chicago: University of Chicago Press, 2009).

10 Public talk by Twyla Tharp at Barnard College, New York City, November 7, 2014.

11 Arthur C. Danto, "The Artworld," *Journal of Philosophy* 61, no. 19 (1964): 571–584.

12 In a statement published by *The Guardian* in 2006 by Chefs Ferran Adrià, Heston Blumenthal, Thomas Keller, and the food expert Harold McGee, however, they explained why they do not identify with the "fashionable term molecular gastronomy." This term, they indicate, refers to the efforts conducted by a workshop of chefs and scientists, originally coordinated by Nicholas Kurti and Herve This, but it does not describe their approach to cooking. Adrià, Blumenthal, Keller, and McGee, "Statement on the 'New Cookery,'" *The Guardian*, December 9, 2006, http://www.theguardian .com/uk/2006/dec/10/foodanddrink.obsfoodmonthly.

13 *New York Times*, July 14, 2011.

14 John F. Padgett and Paul D. McLean, "Organizational Invention and Elite Transformation: The Birth of Partnership Systems in Renaissance Florence," *American Journal of Sociology* 111, no. 5 (2006): 1463–1568.

15 Thomas S. Kuhn, *The Structure of Scientific Revolutions* (Chicago: University of Chicago Press, 1996).

16 ElBulli was founded by Hans and Marketta Schilling. The name *elBulli* derives from the owners' passion for bulldogs.

17 Priscilla P. Ferguson and Sharon Zukin, "The Careers of Chefs," in *Eating Culture,* ed. Ron Scopp and Brian Seitz (New York: State University of New York Press, 1998).

18   Ferran Adrià, quoted in Ferran Adrià, Juli Soler, and Albert Adrià, elBulli, Historia de un Sueño (Cameo Media, S.L.: RTVE, Catalogo Audiovisual 1963–2009, 2009); author's translation.

19   Ferran Adrià, *Los Secretos de elBulli: Recetas, Tecnicas y Reflexiones* (Barcelona: Altaya, 1997).

20   Burt, "Structural Holes and Good Ideas."

21   Ferran Adrià, *elBulli, el Sabor del Mediterráneo*, 1st ed. (Barcelona: Empuries, 1993).

22   Silviya Svejenova, "The Path with the Heart: Creating the Authentic Career," *Journal of Management Studies* 42, no. 5 (2005): 947–974; Svejenova, Planellas, and Vives, "Individual Business Model in the Making."

23   John F. Padgett and Walter W. Powell, "The Problem of Emergence," in *The Emergence of Organizations and Markets*, ed. John F. Padgett and Walter W. Powell (Princeton: Princeton University Press, 2012).

24   Harrison C. White, *Identity and Control: How Social Formations Emerge*, 2nd ed. (Princeton: Princeton University Press, 2008).

25   Mihaly Csikszentmihalyi, *Creativity: Flow and the Psychology of Discovery and Invention* (New York: HarperCollins, 1996).

26   Jorge Fontdevila, M. Pilar Opazo, and Harrison C. White, "Order at the Edge of Chaos: Meanings from Netdom Switchings Across Functional Systems," *Sociological Theory* 29, no. 3 (2011): 178–198.

27   Shona L. Brown and Kathleen M. Eisenhardt, "The Art of Continuous Change: Linking Complexity Theory and Time-Paced Evolution in Relentlessly Shifting Organizations," *Administrative Science Quarterly* 42, no. 1 (1997): 1–34.

28   David Stark, "Recombinant Property in East European Capitalism," *American Journal of Sociology* 101, no. 4 (1996): 993–1027.

2. From Chaos to Order

1   For complete recipe, please see Juli Soler, Albert Adrià, and Ferran Adrià, *elBulli 1983–1993* (Barcelona: elBullibooks, 2004).

2   James G. March, "Exploration and Exploitation in Organizational Learning," *Organization Science* 2, no. 1 (1991): 71–87.

3   Clayton M. Christensen, *The Innovator's Dilemma: When New Technologies Cause Great Firms to Fail* (Cambridge, Mass.: Harvard Business School Press, 1997).

4 In June 2014, an article in the *New Yorker* magazine criticized Christensen's "disruptive theory" by questioning its ability to invariably predict the success or failure of firms and its alleged wide-range applicability across organizations and industries (Jill Lepore, "The Disruption Machine," June 23, 2014). While I agree with this statement, I believe that Christensen's theory does pose an important quandary faced by organizations today, and this is why I decided to incorporate it into my study.

5 Ludwik Fleck, *Genesis and Development of a Scientific Fact* (Chicago: University of Chicago Press, 1979); Bruno Latour, "Give Me a Laboratory and I Will Raise the World," in *Science Observed*, ed. K. D. Knorr-Cetina and M. Mulkay, 141–170 (London: Sage, 1983); Bruno Latour, *The Pasteurization of France* (Cambridge, Mass.: Harvard University Press, 1993).

6 James T. Borhek and Richard F. Curtis, *A Sociology of Belief* (New York: John Wiley and Sons, 1975).

7 Robert K. Merton, *On Social Structure and Science* (Chicago: University of Chicago Press, 1996).

8 Luhmann, *Organización y Decisión: Autopoiesis*, 93.

9 Seymour M. Lipset, *Political Man: The Social Bases of Politics* (Garden City, N.Y.: Doubleday, 1960).

10 Max Weber, *The Theory of Social and Economic Organization* (New York: Free Press, 1947).

11 Erving Goffman, *Asylums: Essays on the Social Situation of Mental Patients and Other Inmates* (New York: Anchor Books / Doubleday, 1961).

12 Philip Selznick, *The Organizational Weapon: A Study of Bolshevik Strategy and Tactics* (New York: Free Press, 1960).

13 The use of the word "family" to refer to a restaurant's staff has been pointed out in other academic studies of the gastronomic field. Gary Fine explains that this metaphor was often used within professional kitchens in an attempt to preserve the workers' loyalty or as an expression of their voluntary commitment to the organization. Fine, *Kitchens: The Culture of Restaurant Work*, 2nd ed. (Berkeley: University of California Press, 2009), 113.

14 Ibid.

15 F. Adrià, A. Adrià, and Soler, *A Day at elBulli*, 39.

16 Jay R. Galbraith, "Designing the Innovating Organization," *Organizational Dynamics* 10, no. 3 (1982): 5–25.

17 Latour, "Give Me a Laboratory"; Latour, *Pasteurization of France*.

18 Anthony Bourdain, television show *No Reservations*, "Decoding Ferran Adrià," 2006.

19 E.g., Brown and Eisenhardt, "Art of Continuous Change"; Kathleen M. Eisenhardt and Shona L. Brown, *Competing on the Edge: Strategy as Structured Chaos* (Boston: Harvard Business School Press, 1998); Gerardo A. Okhuysen and Kathleen M. Eisenhardt, "Integrating Knowledge in Groups: How Formal Interventions Enable Flexibility," *Organization Science* 13, no. 4 (2002): 370–386.

20 Abend, *Sorcerer's Apprentices.*

21 Mary J. Benner and Michael L. Tushman, "Exploitation, Exploration, and Process Management: The Productivity Dilemma Revisited," *Academy of Management Review* 28, no. 2 (2003): 238–256.

22 Frederick W. Taylor, *Principles of Scientific Management* (New York: Harper and Brothers, 1967); M. Weber, *Theory of Social and Economic Organization*; Henri Fayol, *General and Industrial Management*, trans. C. Storrs (London: Sir Isaac Pitman and Sons, 1949).

23 Stark, *Sense of Dissonance*, xvi.

24 Svejenova, Planellas, and Vives, "Individual Business Model in the Making."

25 John Hagel III and Johan S. Brown, "Productive Friction: How Difficult Business Partnerships Can Accelerate Innovation," *Harvard Business Review* 83, no. 2 (2005): 82–91.

26 Steven Weber, *The Success of Open Source* (Cambridge, Mass.: Harvard University Press, 2004).

27 Lewis Carroll, *The Annotated Alice; Alice's Adventures in Wonderland* and *Through the Looking Glass* (New York: Meridian, 1974), 268–269, quoted in Dario Rodriguez and M. Pilar Opazo, *Comunicaciones de la Organización* (Santiago: Ediciones Universidad Católica de Chile, 2007), 77–78; italics mine.

28 John Austin, *Como Hacer Cosas con Palabras; Palabras y Acciones*, 3rd ed. (Barcelona: Phaidon Press, 1990).

29 Rodriguez and Opazo, *Comunicaciones de la Organización.*

30 Carême, *L'Art de la Cuisine Française*, 5 vols. (1833–1834) (Paris: Elibron Classics, 2005); Auguste Escoffier, *Le Guide Culinaire: The Complete Guide to the Art of Modern Cookery*, trans. H. L. Cracknell and R. J. Kaufmann (London: Heinemann, 1979).

31 Andrew Hargadon and Robert I. Sutton, "Technology Brokering and Innovation in a Product Development Firm," *Administrative Science Quarterly* 42, no. 4 (1997): 716–749.

32 Priscilla P. Ferguson, "A Cultural Field in the Making: Gastronomy in 19th-Century France," *American Journal of Sociology* 104, no. 3 (1998): 597–641.

33 Albert Adrià, *Natura* (Barcelona: elBullibooks, 2008).

34 http://www.elbulli.com/cronologia.

35 In my interviews with chefs who worked in or owned haute cuisine restaurants, I would notice that some of them—especially those who had achieved recognition in the gastronomic field—included in their offerings a tasting menu that consisted of dishes made in previous years. Paradigmatic examples of this in Spain and in the United States are the restaurant El Celler de Can Roca, declared Best Restaurant in the World in the 2013 and 2015 San Pellegrino list, and the experimental, now-closed restaurant WD-50, located in the Lower East Side of New York City.

36 F. Adrià, A. Adrià, and J. Soler, *A Day at elBulli*, 115.

37 Geoffrey C. Bowker and Susan L. Star, *Sorting Things Out: Classification and Its Consequences* (Cambridge, Mass.: MIT Press, 1999).

38 White, *Identity and Control*.

39 Charles Kirschbaum, "Jazz: Structural Changes and Identity Creation in Cultural Movements," in *Only Connect: Neat Words, Networks and Identities*, ed. Martin Kornberger and Siegfried Gudergan (Copenhagen: Copenhagen Business School Press, 2006).

40 Howard S. Becker, *Art Worlds* (Berkeley: University of California Press, 2008).

41 Rebecca M. Henderson and Kim B. Clark, "Architectural Innovation: The Reconfiguration of Existing Product Technologies and the Failure of Established Firms," *Administrative Science Quarterly* 35, no. 1 (1990): 9–30.

42 Deborah Dougherty, "Interpretive Barriers to Successful Product Innovation in Large Firms," *Organization Science* 3 (1992): 179–202.

43 James G. March and Herbert A. Simon, *Organizations* (Cambridge: Blackwell, 1993).

44 Stark, *Sense of Dissonance*.

45 March and Simon, *Organizations*, 184.

46 Fine, *Kitchens*.

47 Ibid., 216.

48 Richard L. Daft and Karl E. Weick, "Toward a Model of Organizations as Interpretation Systems," *Academy of Management Review* 9, no. 2 (1984): 284–295.

49 Edwin Hutchins, "How a Cockpit Remembers Its Speeds," *Cognitive Science* 19, no. 3 (1995): 265–288.

50 Public talk Ferran Adrià, as part of the tour "Partners for Transformation" with Telefónica Company, March 2011, New York.

51 Karl E. Weick, "Introductory Essay: Improvisation as a Mindset for Organizational Analysis," *Organization Science* 9, no. 5 (1998): 543–555.

3. Diffusion and Institutionalization of Innovation

1 For complete recipe, please see Ferran Adrià, Juli Soler, and Albert Adrià, *elBulli 1994–1997* (Barcelona: ElBullibooks, 2003).

2 *elBulli's Last Waltz*, documentary aired by the public television of Catalonia.

3 Ibid.

4 Julia Moskin, "After elBulli, Spain looks forward," *New York Times*, June 14, 2011.

5 To name a few examples from mass media in Spain and in the United States: *El Pais*, Spain, July 31, 2011, and *Time World* magazine, August 2, 2011 (http://www.time.com/time/world/article/0,8599,2086363,00.html).

6 Stephen Hawking, *A Brief History of Time*. (New York: Bantam Books, 1998).

7 Fleck, *Genesis and Development of a Scientific Fact*.

8 Becker, *Art Worlds*.

9 Paul M. Hirsch, "Processing Fads and Fashions: An Organization-Set Analysis of Cultural Industry Systems," *American Journal of Sociology* 77, no. 4 (1972): 639–659.

10 Sonia Cowan and Damon Phillips, "Swing: Presentation of Preliminary Findings" (New York: Columbia University, Initiative for the Study and Practice of Creativity and Culture [ISPOCC], March 2015).

11 Mike Barnes, *Captain Beefheart* (London: Quartet Books, 2000).

12 Obituaries in *The Guardian* and the *New York Times*: http://www.theguardian.com/music/2010/dec/21/captain-beefheart-tribute and http://www.nytimes.com/2010/12/18/arts/music/18beefheart.html?_r=0.

13 Mitchell Davis, "Eating out, Eating American," in *Gastropolis: Food and New York City*, ed. Annie Hauck-Lawson and Jonathan Deutsch (New York: Columbia University Press, 2009).

14 Pierre Bourdieu, "The Field of Cultural Production, or: The Economic World Reversed," *Poetics* 12 (1983): 311–356.

15 Kuhn, *Structure of Scientific Revolutions*.

16 Latour, "Give Me a Laboratory"; Latour, *Pasteurization of France*.

17 Jean A. Brillat-Savarin, *The Physiology of Taste* (Seaside, Ore.: Merchant Books, 2009).

18 Ronald Hayman, *Theatre and Anti-Theatre: New Movements Since Beckett* (New York: Oxford University Press, 1979).

19 Antoine Hennion, "Those Things That Hold Us Together: Taste and Sociology," *Cultural Sociology* 1, no. 1 (2007): 109.

20 F. Adrià, A. Adrià, and J. Soler, *A Day at elBulli*.

21 Andrew B. Hargadon and Yellowlees Douglas, "When Innovations Meet Institutions: Edison and the Design of the Electric Light," *Administrative Science Quarterly* 46, no. 476 (2001): 476–501.

22 Brian Uzzi and Jarrett Spiro, "Collaboration and Creativity," *American Journal of Sociology* 111 (2005.): 447–504.

23 Murat Cokol, Raul Rodriguez-Esteban, and Andrey Rzhetsky, "A Recipe for High Impact," *Genome Biology* 8, no. 5 (2007): 406.

24 Rao, Monin, and Durand, "Institutional Change in Toque Ville."

25 Barbara Slavich and Fabrizio Castellucci, "Wishing upon a Star: How Apprentice-Master Similarity, Status and Career Stage Affect Critics' Evaluations of Former Apprentices in the Haute Cuisine Industry," *Organization Studies*, forthcoming.

26 Richard Hamilton and Vicente Todoli, *Food for Thought, Thought for Food* (New York: Actar, 2009), 299.

27 *Ciao!*, Opinions section, http://www.ciao.es/El_Bulli_Roses__Opinion _702792; author's translation.

28 Eileen Barker, *The Making of a Moonie: Choice or Brainwashing?* (Oxford: Basil Blackwell, 1984).

29 Pau Arenos, *La Cocina de los Valientes*, Spanish ed. (Barcelona: Ediciones B, 2012).

30 Eric M. Leifer and Harrison C. White, "A Structural Approach to Markets," in *Intercorporate Relations: The Structural Analysis of Business*, ed. Mark S. Mizruchi and Michael Schwartz (Cambridge: Cambridge University Press, 1987); Harrison C. White, "Where Do Markets Come From?," *American Journal of Sociology* 87, no. 3 (1981): 517–547.

31 José M. Aguilera, *Ingeniería Gastronómica* (Santiago: Ediciones Universidad Católica de Chile, 2011), 269.

32 Latour, *Pasteurization of France*.

33 David Frisby and Mike Featherstone, *Simmel on Culture* (London: Sage, 1998).

34 Pierre Bourdieu, *Distinction: A Social Critique of the Judgement of Taste* (Cambridge, Mass.: Harvard University Press, 1984).

35 Manuel Castells, *The Rise of the Network Society in the Information Age: Economy, Society and Culture*, vol. 1 (Oxford: Blackwell, 2000).

36 Josee Johnston and Shyon Baumann, "Democracy Versus Distinction: A Study of Omnivorousness in Gourmet Food Writing," *American Journal of Sociology* 113, no. 1 (2007): 165–204.

37   Theodore C. Bestor, "How Sushi Went Global," *Foreign Policy* 121 (November–December 2000): 54–63.

38   Wesley M. Cohen and Daniel A. Levinthal, "Absorptive Capacity: A New Perspective on Learning and Innovation," special issue, "Technology, Organizations, and Innovation," *Administrative Science Quarterly* 35, no. 1 (1990): 128–152.

39   Julia Moskin, "After elBulli, Spain looks forward," *New York Times*, June 14, 2011.

40   Arthur Lubow, "A Laboratory of Taste," *New York Times Magazine*, August 10, 2003.

41   Parts of this section have been published in M. Pilar Opazo, "Discourse as a Driver of Innovation: The Case of elBulli Restaurant," *International Journal of Gastronomy and Food Science* 1, no. 2 (2012): 82–89.

42   Stephen Mennell, *All Manners of Food: Eating and Taste in England and France from the Middle Ages to the Present* (New York: Basil Blackwell, 1985).

43   Michaela DeSoucey, "Gastronationalism: Food, Traditions and Authenticity Politics in the European Union," *American Sociological Review* 75, no. 3 (2010): 432–455.

44   E.g., Christel Lane, "The Michelin-Starred Restaurant Sector as a Cultural Industry: A Cross-National Comparison of Restaurants in the UK and Germany," *Food, Culture and Society: An International Journal of Multidisciplinary Research* 13, no. 4 (2010): 493–519; Lane, "Culinary Culture and Globalization: An Analysis of British and German Michelin-Starred Restaurants," *British Journal of Sociology* 62, no. 4 (2011): 696–71; Alan Warde, "Imagining British Cuisine: Representations of Culinary Identity in the Good Food Guide, 1951–2007," *Food, Culture and Society: An International Journal of Multidisciplinary Research* 12, no. 2 (2009): 151–171.

45   Warde, "Imagining British Cuisine."

46   Paul Rozin, "Why We Eat What We Eat, and Why We Worry About It," *Bulletin of the American Academy of Arts and Sciences* 50, no. 55 (1997): 26–48.

47   Madeleine Ferrieres, *Sacred Cow, Mad Cow: A History of Food Fears* (New York: Columbia University Press, 2006).

48   Mennell, *All Manners of Food*.

49   Ferguson, "Cultural Field in the Making"; Ferguson, *Accounting for Taste*.

50   Rao, Monin, and Durand, "Institutional Change in Toque Ville."

51   Arjun Appadurai, "How to Make a National Cuisine: Cookbooks in Contemporary India," *Comparative Studies in Society and History* 30, no. 1 (1988): 22.

52 Latour, *Pasteurization of France.*

53 Fleck, *Genesis and Development of a Scientific Fact*; Kuhn, *Structure of Scientific Revolutions*; Latour, *Pasteurization of France.*

54 Antoine Hennion, "Baroque and Rock: Music, Mediators and Musical Taste," *Poetics* 24 (1997): 415–435.

55 Kuhn, *Structure of Scientific Revolutions.*

56 Ferguson, *Accounting for Taste.*

57 A quantity that doubled by the time I was conducting my fieldwork, fifteen years later.

58 Lubow, "A Laboratory of Taste."

59 Davis, "Eating Out, Eating American"; Auguste Escoffier, *Auguste Escoffier: Memories of My Life* (New York: Van Nostrand Reinhold, 1996).

60 Becker, *Art Worlds.*

61 Paul J. DiMaggio and Walter W. Powell, "The Iron Cage Revisited: Institutional Isomorphism and Collective Rationality in Organizational Fields," *American Sociological Review* 48, no. 2 (1983): 147–160.

62 Arthur L. Stinchcombe, "New Sociological Microfoundations for Organizational Theory: A Postscript," in *Social Structure and Organizations Revisited*, ed. Michael Lounsbury and Marc J. Ventresca (Amsterdam: JAI, 2002), 420–423.

63 Georg Simmel, "Fashion," *American Journal of Sociology* 62, no. 6 (1957): 541–558.

64 Nathan Myhrvold, Chris Young, and Maxime Bilet, *Modernist Cuisine: The Art and Science of Cooking*, 5 vols. (Seattle: Cooking Lab, 2011).

65 Examples of this include the gastronomic magazine *Lucky Peach*, which has celebrity chef David Chang from New York as editor-in-chief. This magazine is published on a quarterly basis by McSweeney Publishing LP. Another example is the academic journal *International Journal of Gastronomy and Food Science*, which includes on its editorial board the chef Andoni Luis Aduriz, whose restaurant Mugaritz is ranked among the world's best restaurants according to the San Pellegrino list.

66 Michael C. Fitzgerald, *Making Modernism: Picasso and the Creation of the Market of Twentieth-Century Art* (New York: Farrar, Straus and Giroux, 1995).

67 Harrison C. White and Cynthia A. White, *Canvases and Careers: Institutional Change in the French Painting World* (Chicago: University of Chicago Press, 1993).

68 Rainer Crone, *Andy Warhol* (New York: Praeger, 1970).

69 Ferguson, "Cultural Field in the Making."

70 Mark S. Granovetter, "The Strength of Weak Ties," *American Journal of Sociology* 78, no. 6 (1973): 1360–1380.

71 Robert K. Merton, "The Thomas Theorem and the Matthew Effect," *Social Forces* 74, no. 2 (1995): 379–424.

72 That is to say, which have been awarded three Michelin stars or are in top positions of the San Pellegrino list.

73 *El Pais*, Spain, July, 31, 2011 (major newspaper in Spain).

74 Fine, *Kitchens*.

75 Becker, *Art Worlds*.

76 Scott A. Boorman and Paul R. Levitt, *The Genetics of Altruism* (New York: Academic Press, 1980).

77 Kirschbaum, *Jazz*.

78 http://www.gastroeconomy.com/2011/12/chefs-en-sus-cuarteles-de-invierno.

79 A note on enemies: There had been, in fact, important controversies around elBulli's approach to cooking. For the purposes of brevity, I do not analyze here a notorious feud between Adrià and the now-deceased Spanish chef Santi Santamaria, both owners of one of the first three-Michelin-starred restaurants in Spain. In my view, this episode only ratifies the arguments I have made so far and, for this reason, I do not include it in my analysis. In a nutshell, the feud consisted of the following: In 2008, Chef Santamaria publicly accused Adrià of introducing dangerous chemical substances into his cooking and claimed that this put the public health at risk. One of my interviewees relied upon the notorious (and apocryphal) story of Wolfgang Amadeus Mozart versus Antonio Salieri to describe this controversy. On this occasion, the networks among Spanish chefs that existed around the figure of Adrià provided significant support in reducing the damage that this feud could have caused to Adrià and elBulli. For interested readers, the specifics of this culinary scandal have been well covered elsewhere. For instance, Chef Santi Santamaria published a book called *La Cocina al Desnudo* (Madrid: Temas de Hoy, 2008) that includes harsh criticism of Adrià's molecular and experimental cuisine. Press articles that reported on this episode include "Spain's Top Chefs Clash over Ingredients and Culinary Innovations" by Victoria Burnett (*New York Times*, June 1, 2008) and "Round Two in the Santamaria vs. Adrià Smackdown" by Lisa Abend (Gourmet.com, November 25, 2008).

80 Latour, "Give Me a Laboratory"; Latour, *Pasteurization of France*.

4. The Bittersweet Taste of Relentless Innovation

1　For complete recipe please see Juli Soler, Albert Adrià, and Ferran Adrià, *elBulli 1998–2002* (Barcelona: elBullibooks, 2002).

2　Telefónica S.A. is a major Spanish telecommunications provider, with a presence in Europe and Latin America, and strategic alliances in Asia. It operates in 24 countries and employs an average of 130,000 professionals (http://www.Telefónica.com).

3　Robert K. Merton, "The Unanticipated Consequences of Purposive Social Action," *American Sociological Review* 1, no. 6 (1936): 894–904.

4　Michael J. Handel, ed., *The Sociology of Organizations: Classic, Contemporary and Critical Readings* (Thousand Oaks, Calif.: Sage, 2003); Taylor, *Principles of Scientific Management.*

5　Max Weber, *The Protestant Ethic and the Spirit of Capitalism*, trans. Talcott Parsons (New York: Dover, 2003).

6　Max Weber, "From Max Weber: Essays in Sociology," in *From Max Weber: Essays in Sociology*, ed. and trans. H. H. Gerth and C. Wright Mills (New York: Oxford University Press, 1946), 228.

7　Fayol, *General and Industrial Management.*

8　Tom Burns and George M. Stalker, *The Management of Innovation* (London: Tavistock, 1961).

9　March and Simon, *Organizations*, 162.

10　James Thompson, *Organizations in Action* (New York: McGraw Hill, 1967).

11　Karl E. Weick, *The Social Psychology of Organizing* (New York: Random House, 1979); Weick, *Sensemaking in Organizations* (Thousand Oaks, Calif.: Sage, 1995).

12　Peter M. Senge, *The Fifth Discipline: The Art and Practice of the Learning Organization* (New York: Doubleday, 1990).

13　Niklas Luhmann, *Organización y Decisión*, Spanish ed., trans. Dario Rodriguez (Mexico City: Herder, 2010).

14　Padgett and Powell, "Problem of Emergence."

15　Michael Hannan and John Freeman, "The Population Ecology of Organizations," *American Journal of Sociology* 82, no. 5 (1977): 929–964.

16　F. Adrià, *Los Secretos de elBulli*, 21–22; author's own translation; italics mine.

17　Ferran Adrià, *Cómo Funciona elBulli: Las Ideas, los Métodos y la Creatividad de Ferran Adrià* (London: Phaidon Press, 2010), 47; author's own translation.

18　M. Weber, *Theory of Social and Economic Organization.*

19 F. Adrià, *Los Secretos de elBulli*, 38; author's own translation.

20 Bowker and Star, *Sorting Things Out*.

21 Borhek and Curtis, *Sociology of Belief*.

22 Examples of these public talks given by Ferran Adrià are: Times Talk, "Food and Wine Festival," New York; and Google company headquarters, San Francisco, both in October 2011.

23 In association with his brother, Ferran Adrià, Albert Adrià opened the restaurants Inopia (2006) and later 41 Degrees and Tickets (2010). The last was ranked No. 42 on the 2015 San Pellegrino list of the World's Best Restaurants and has received the recognition of one Michelin star (since 2013). Since 2014, the Adrià brothers have opened other new restaurants in Barcelona called Bodega 1900 (bar), Pakta (Nikkei cuisine), Hoja Santa, and Niño Viejo (Mexican cuisine).

24 Ferran Adrià, "Ferran Adrià," *Matador* Ñ (March 2012) (issue is dedicated to Adrià; author's own translation).

25 Parasecoli, "The Chefs, the Entrepreneurs, and Their Patrons."

26 Soler, A. Adrià, and F. Adrià, *elBulli 1998–2002*, 195.

27 Weick, "Introductory Essay."

28 F. Adrià, A. Adrià, and J. Soler, *A Day at elBulli*.

29 Given that the term "foodie" tends to have a narrow and pejorative connotation, I only included it when it was explicitly used by my interviewees.

30 Juli Soler, Albert Adrià, and Ferran Adrià, *elBulli 2003–2004* (Barcelona: elBullibooks, 2005).

31 Consistent with the organization's pattern of systematically circulating its work, after the elBulli restaurant had been closed for over a year, the folders that contained the recipes for dishes served at elBulli's staff meal were published as a book (Ferran Adrià, *The Family Meal: Home Cooking with Ferran Adrià* [London: Phaidon Press, 2011]). The book was a bestseller at the time of its publication in Spain in 2012. Almost immediately after its publication the book was translated into English and, furthermore, converted into a software application downloadable for tablets in 2013 by Adrià and his team, with the support of Telefónica.

32 Karl E. Weick, "The Collapse of Sensemaking in Organizations: The Mann Gulch Disaster," *Administrative Science Quarterly* 38, no. 4 (1993): 628–652; Daft and Weick, "Toward a Model of Organizations as Interpretation Systems."

33 Interestingly, Merton (1938) identified innovation as one of the four types of deviant behavior, defined according to the individual's adaptation to the

cultural and institutional patterns of a society (the others being conformity, ritualism, and retreatism).

34   A comprehensive review of the perils of under- and overorganizing can be found in Katherine K. Chen's ethnography *Enabling Creative Chaos: The Organization Behind the Burning Man Event* (Chicago: University of Chicago Press, 2009).

35   White, *Identity and Control.*

36   Becker, *Art Worlds.*

37   Pierre Bourdieu, *The Rules of Art: Genesis and Structure of the Literary Field* (Stanford: Stanford University Press, 1995).

38   Steven Weber, *The Success of Open Source* (Cambridge, Mass.: Harvard University Press, 2004).

39   Rao, Monin, and Durand, "Institutional Change in Toque Ville."

40   M. Weber, *Theory of Social and Economic Organization.*

41   Vanina Leschziner, *At the Chef's Table: Culinary Creativity in Elite Restaurants* (Stanford: Stanford University Press, 2015).

42   Bruno Latour, *Reassembling the Social: An Introduction to Actor-Network-Theory* (New York: Oxford University Press, 2005).

43   F. Adrià, "Ferran Adrià."

44   Leon Festinger, Henry W. Riecken, and Stanley Schachter, *When Prophecy Fails* (New York: Harper and Row, 1956).

45   F. Adrià, "Ferran Adrià."

46   F. Adrià, "Ferran Adrià."

5. Cooking Up a New Organization

1   For complete recipe please see Ferran Adrià, Albert Adrià, and Juli Soler, *elBulli 2005–2011* (New York: Phaidon, 2014).

2   Elliott Shore, "The Development of the Restaurant," in *Food: The History of Taste*, ed. Paul Freedman (Berkeley: University of California Press, 2007). The word *restaurant* to refer to these kinds of establishments was officially included in the dictionary in 1835 (Pitte, 1999).

3   Josep Maria Pinto, "elBulli Cierra sus Puertas," *Anuario 2011* (Barcelona: Editorial Planeta, 2011), 150–151.

4   Escoffier, *Le Guide Culinaire,* 556.

5   Barbara Czarniawska, *A Narrative Approach to Organization Studies* (Thousand Oaks, Calif.: Sage, 1998).

6 Video of the first of these events organized at Telefónica Foundation: http://www.gastronomiaycia.com/2015/02/23/video-del-documental-comer-conocimiento-con-ferran-adria.

7 Priscilla P. Ferguson, *Word of Mouth: What We Talk About When We Talk About Food* (Berkeley: University of California Press, 2014).

8 Christel Lane, *The Cultivation of Taste: Chefs and the Organization of Fine Dining* (Oxford: Oxford University Press, 2014).

9 Alison Pearlman, *Smart Casual: The Transformation of Gourmet Restaurant Style in America* (Chicago: University of Chicago Press, 2013).

10 Ibid.

11 I am particularly thankful to two anonymous reviewers at Columbia University Press for their insightful comments and suggestions in conducting this analysis.

12 Dan Lainer-Vos and Paolo Parigi, "The Miracle Maker, the Acolytes and the Church," *Social Science History* (forthcoming).

13 The MBA course was given at IESE Business School in Barcelona. The contest was called "Ideas for Transformation" and it was designed with the support of Telefónica Company.

14 Becker, *Art Worlds*.

15 Arthur C. Danto, *Andy Warhol* (New Haven: Yale University Press, 2009).

16 Wayne Koestenbaum, *Andy Warhol* (New York: Lipper/Viking, 2001).

17 Simmel, "Fashion."

Conclusion

1 Barker, *Making of a Moonie*; John Lofland, "Becoming a World-Saver Revisited," *American Behavioral Scientist* 20, no. 6 (1977): 805–818; John Lofland and Rodney Stark, "Becoming a World-Saver: A Theory of Conversion to a Deviant Perspective," *American Sociological Review* 30, no. 6 (1965): 862–875.

2 E.g., Jay A. Conger and Rabindra N. Kanungo, "Toward a Behavioral Theory of Charismatic Leadership in Organizational Settings," *Academy of Management Review* 12, no. 4 (1987): 637–647; Daniel Katz and Robert L. Kahn, *The Social Psychology of Organizations* (New York: John Wiley and Sons, 1966).

3 Becker, *Art Worlds*; White and White, Canvases and Careers.

4   E.g., Fleck, *Genesis and Development*; Thomas F. Gieryn, "Boundary-Work and the Demarcation of Science from Non-science: Strains and Interests in Professional Interests of Scientists," *American Sociological Review* 48 (1983): 781–795; Kuhn, *Structure of Scientific Revolutions*; Latour, *Reassembling the Social*.

Appendix

1   Kathleen M. Eisenhardt, "Building Theories from Case Study Research," *Academy of Management Review* 14, no. 4 (1989): 532–550.

2   Dennis A. Gioia, Kevin G. Corley, and Aimee L. Hamilton, "Seeking Qualitative Rigor in Inductive Research: Notes on the Gioia Methodology," *Organizational Research Methods* 16, no. 1 (2012): 15–31.

3   Four interviews conducted with stagiaires of elBulli in the 2011 season were made accessible by Telefónica R&D. I transcribed these interviews and included them as part of the analysis.

4   Kurt H. Wolff, ed., *The Sociology of Georg Simmel* (New York: Free Press, 1964).

References

Abend, Lisa. *The Sorcerer's Apprentices: A Season in the Kitchen at Ferran Adrià's elBulli*. New York: Free Press, 2011.

Adrià, Albert. *Natura*. Barcelona: elBullibooks, 2008.

Adrià, Ferran. *Cómo Funciona elBulli: Las Ideas, los Métodos y la Creatividad de Ferran Adrià*. London: Phaidon Press, 2010.

Adrià, Ferran. *elBulli, el Sabor del Mediterráneo*. 1st ed. Barcelona: Empuries, 1993.

Adrià, Ferran. *The Family Meal: Home Cooking with Ferran Adrià*. London: Phaidon Press, 2011.

Adrià, Ferran. *Los Secretos de elBulli: Recetas, Tecnicas y Reflexiones*. Barcelona: Altaya, 1997.

Adrià, Ferran, Albert Adrià, and Juli Soler. *A Day at elBulli*. London: Phaidon Press, 2010.

Adrià, Ferran, Juli Soler, and Albert Adrià. *elBulli 1983–1993*. Barcelona: elBulli Books, 2004.

Adrià, Ferran, Juli Soler, and Albert Adrià. *elBulli 1994–1997*. Barcelona: elBulli Books, 2003.

Adrià, Ferran, Juli Soler, and Albert Adrià. *elBulli 1998–2002*. Barcelona: elBulli Books, 2002.

Adrià, Ferran, Juli Soler, and Albert Adrià. *elBulli 2003–2004*. Barcelona: RBA Libros, 2005.

Adrià, Ferran, Juli Soler, and Albert Adrià. *elBulli 2005*. Barcelona: RBA Libros, 2006.

Adrià, Ferran, Juli Soler, and Albert Adrià. *elBulli 2005–2011*. New York: Phaidon, 2014.

Adrià, Ferran, Juli Soler, and Albert Adrià. *elBulli, Historia de un Sueño*. N.p.: RTVE, Catalogo Audiovisual 1963–2009, 2009.

Adrià, Ferran, Heston Blumenthal, Thomas Keller, and Harold McGee, "Statement on the 'New Cookery,'" *The Guardian*, December 9, 2006, http://www.theguardian.com/uk/2006/dec/10/foodanddrink.obsfoodmonthly.

Aguilera, José M. *Ingeniería Gastronómica*. Santiago: Ediciones Universidad Católica de Chile, 2011.

Appadurai, Arjun. "How to Make a National Cuisine: Cookbooks in Contemporary India." *Comparative Studies in Society and History* 30, no. 1 (1988): 3–24.

Arenos, Pau. *La Cocina de los Valientes*. Spanish ed. Barcelona: Ediciones B, 2012.

Austin, John. *Como Hacer Cosas con Palabras; Palabras y Acciones*. 3rd ed. Barcelona: Phaidon Press, 1990.

Barker, Eileen. *The Making of a Moonie: Choice or Brainwashing?* Oxford: Basil Blackwell, 1984.

Barnes, Mike. *Captain Beefheart*. London: Quartet Books, 2000.

Becker, Howard S. *Art Worlds*. Berkeley: University of California Press, 2008.

Benner, Mary J., and Michael L. Tushman. "Exploitation, Exploration, and Process Management: The Productivity Dilemma Revisited." *Academy of Management Review* 28, no. 2 (2003): 238–256.

Bestor, Theodore C. "How Sushi Went Global." *Foreign Policy* 121 (November–December 2000): 54–63.

Boorman, Scott A., and Paul R. Levitt. *The Genetics of Altruism*. New York: Academic Press, 1980.

Borhek, James T., and Richard F. Curtis. *A Sociology of Belief*. New York: John Wiley and Sons, 1975.

Bourdieu, Pierre. *Distinction: A Social Critique of the Judgement of Taste*. Cambridge, Mass.: Harvard University Press, 1984.

Bourdieu, Pierre. "The Field of Cultural Production, or: The Economic World Reversed." *Poetics* 12 (1983): 311–356.

Bourdieu, Pierre. *The Rules of Art: Genesis and Structure of the Literary Field*. Stanford: Stanford University Press, 1995.

Bowker, Geoffrey C., and Susan L. Star. *Sorting Things Out: Classification and Its Consequences*. Cambridge, Mass.: MIT Press, 1999.

Brillat-Savarin, Jean A. *The Physiology of Taste*. Seaside, Ore.: Merchant Books, 2009.

Brown, Shona L., and Kathleen M. Eisenhardt. "The Art of Continuous Change: Linking Complexity Theory and Time-Paced Evolution in Relentlessly Shifting Organizations." *Administrative Science Quarterly* 42, no. 1 (1997): 1–34.

Burns, Tom, and George M. Stalker. *The Management of Innovation*. London: Tavistock, 1961.

Burt, Ronald S. "Structural Holes and Good Ideas." *American Journal of Sociology* 110, no. 2 (2004): 349–399.

Carême. *L'Art de la Cuisine Française*. 5 vols. 1833–1834. Paris: Elibron Classics, 2005.

Carroll, Lewis. *The Annotated Alice; Alice's Adventures in Wonderland* and *Through the Looking Glass*. New York: Meridian, 1974.

Castells, Manuel. *The Rise of the Network Society in the Information Age: Economy, Society and Culture*. Vol. 1. Oxford: Blackwell, 2000.

Chen, Katherine K. *Enabling Creative Chaos: The Organization Behind the Burning Man Event*. Chicago: University of Chicago Press, 2009.

Christensen, Clayton M. *The Innovator's Dilemma: When New Technologies Cause Great Firms to Fail*. Cambridge, Mass.: Harvard Business School Press, 1997.

Cohen, Wesley M., and Daniel A. Levinthal. "Absorptive Capacity: A New Perspective on Learning and Innovation." Special issue, "Technology, Organizations, and Innovation," *Administrative Science Quarterly* 35, no. 1 (1990): 128–152.

Cokol, Murat, Raul Rodriguez-Esteban, and Andrey Rzhetsky. "A Recipe for High Impact." *Genome Biology* 8, no. 5 (2007): 406.

Conger, Jay A., and Rabindra N. Kanungo. "Toward a Behavioral Theory of Charismatic Leadership in Organizational Settings." *Academy of Management Review* 12, no. 4 (1987): 637–647.

Cowan, Sonia, and Damon Phillips. "Swing: Presentation of Preliminary Findings." New York: Columbia University, Initiative for the Study and Practice of Creativity and Culture (ISPOCC), March 2015.

Crone, Rainer. *Andy Warhol*. New York: Praeger, 1970.

Csikszentmihalyi, Mihaly. *Creativity: Flow and the Psychology of Discovery and Invention*. New York: HarperCollins, 1996.

Czarniawska, Barbara. *A Narrative Approach to Organization Studies*. Thousand Oaks, Calif.: Sage, 1998.

Daft, Richard L., and Karl E. Weick. "Toward a Model of Organizations as Interpretation Systems." *Academy of Management Review* 9, no. 2 (1984): 284–295.

Danto, Arthur C. *Andy Warhol*. New Haven: Yale University Press, 2009.

Danto, Arthur C. "The Artworld." *Journal of Philosophy* 61, no. 19 (1964): 571–584.

Davis, Mitchell. "Eating Out, Eating American." In *Gastropolis: Food and New York City*, ed. Annie Hauck-Lawson and Jonathan Deutsch. New York: Columbia University Press, 2009.

DeSoucey, Michaela. "Gastronationalism: Food, Traditions and Authenticity Politics in the European Union." *American Sociological Review* 75, no. 3 (2010): 432–455.

DiMaggio, Paul J., and Walter W. Powell. "The Iron Cage Revisited: Institutional Isomorphism and Collective Rationality in Organizational Fields." *American Sociological Review* 48, no. 2 (1983): 147–160.

Domingo, Carlos. *El Viaje de la Innovacion*. Barcelona: Planeta, 2013.

Dougherty, Deborah. "Interpretive Barriers to Successful Product Innovation in Large Firms." *Organization Science* 3 (1992): 179–202.

Eisenhardt, Kathleen M. "Building Theories from Case Study Research." *Academy of Management Review* 14, no. 4 (1989): 532–550.

Eisenhardt, Kathleen M., and Shona L. Brown. *Competing on the Edge: Strategy as Structured Chaos*. Boston: Harvard Business School Press, 1998.

Escoffier, Auguste. *Auguste Escoffier: Memories of My Life*. New York: Van Nostrand Reinhold, 1996.

Escoffier, Auguste. *Le Guide Culinaire: The Complete Guide to the Art of Modern Cookery*. Trans. H. L. Cracknell and R. J. Kaufmann. London: Heinemann, 1979.

Faulkner, Robert R., and Howard S. Becker. *Do You Know . . . ?* Chicago: University of Chicago Press, 2009.

Fayol, Henri. *General and Industrial Management*. Trans. C. Storrs. London: Sir Isaac Pitman and Sons, 1949.

Ferguson, Priscilla P. *Accounting for Taste: The Triumph of French Cuisine*. Chicago: University of Chicago Press, 2004.

Ferguson, Priscilla P. "A Cultural Field in the Making: Gastronomy in 19th-Century France." *American Journal of Sociology* 104, no. 3 (1998): 597–641.

Ferguson, Priscilla P. *Word of Mouth: What We Talk About When We Talk About Food*. Berkeley: University of California Press, 2014.

Ferguson, Priscilla P., and Sharon Zukin. "The Careers of Chefs." In *Eating Culture*, ed. Ron Scopp and Brian Seitz. New York: State University of New York Press, 1998.

Ferran Adrià, and Albert Adrià, *Matador* (March 2012).

Ferrieres, Madeleine. *Sacred Cow, Mad Cow: A History of Food Fears*. New York: Columbia University Press, 2006.

Festinger, Leon, Henry W. Riecken, and Stanley Schachter. *When Prophecy Fails*. New York: Harper and Row, 1956.

Fine, Gary A. *Kitchens: The Culture of Restaurant Work*. 2nd ed. Berkeley: University of California Press, 2009.

Fitzgerald, Michael C. *Making Modernism: Picasso and the Creation of the Market of Twentieth-Century Art*. New York: Farrar, Straus and Giroux, 1995.

Fleck, Ludwik. *Genesis and Development of a Scientific Fact*. Chicago: University of Chicago Press, 1979.

Fontdevila, Jorge, M. Pilar Opazo, and Harrison C. White. "Order at the Edge of Chaos: Meanings from Netdom Switchings Across Functional Systems." *Sociological Theory* 29, no. 3 (2011): 178–198.

Frisby, David, and Mike Featherstone. *Simmel on Culture*. London: Sage, 1998.

Galbraith, Jay R. "Designing the Innovating Organization." *Organizational Dynamics* 10, no. 3 (1982): 5–25.

Gieryn, Thomas F. "Boundary-Work and the Demarcation of Science from Non-science: Strains and Interests in Professional Interests of Scientists." *American Sociological Review* 48 (1983): 781–795.

Gioia, Dennis A., Kevin G. Corley, and Aimee L. Hamilton. "Seeking Qualitative Rigor in Inductive Research: Notes on the Gioia Methodology." *Organizational Research Methods* 16, no. 1 (2012): 15–31.

Girard, Monique, and David Stark. "Distributing Intelligence and Organizing Diversity in New Media Projects." *Environment and Planning A* 34, no. 11 (2002): 1927–1949.

Goffman, Erving. *Asylums: Essays on the Social Situation of Mental Patients and Other Inmates*. New York: Anchor Books / Doubleday, 1961.

Granovetter, Mark S. "The Strength of Weak Ties." *American Journal of Sociology* 78, no. 6 (1973): 1360–1380.

Hagel, John, III, and Johan S. Brown. "Productive Friction: How Difficult Business Partnerships Can Accelerate Innovation." *Harvard Business Review* 83, no. 2 (2005): 82–91.

Hamilton, Richard, and Vicente Todoli. *Food for Thought, Thought for Food*. New York: Actar, 2009.

Handel, Michael J., ed. *The Sociology of Organizations: Classic, Contemporary and Critical Readings*. Thousand Oaks, Calif.: Sage, 2003.

Hannan, Michael, and John Freeman. "The Population Ecology of Organizations." *American Journal of Sociology* 82, no. 5 (1977): 929–964.

Hargadon, Andrew B., and Yellowlees Douglas. "When Innovations Meet Institutions: Edison and the Design of the Electric Light." *Administrative Science Quarterly* 46, no. 476 (2001): 476–501.

Hargadon, Andrew, and Robert I. Sutton. "Technology Brokering and Innovation in a Product Development Firm." *Administrative Science Quarterly* 42, no. 4 (1997): 716–749.

Hawking, Stephen. *A Brief History of Time*. New York: Bantam Books, 1998.

Hayman, Ronald. *Theatre and Anti-Theatre: New Movements Since Beckett*. New York: Oxford University Press, 1979.

Henderson, Rebecca M., and Kim B. Clark. "Architectural Innovation: The Reconfiguration of Existing Product Technologies and the Failure of Established Firms." *Administrative Science Quarterly* 35, no. 1 (1990): 9–30.

Hennion, Antoine. "Baroque and Rock: Music, Mediators and Musical Taste." *Poetics* 24 (1997): 415–435.

Hennion, Antoine. "Those Things That Hold Us Together: Taste and Sociology." *Cultural Sociology* 1, no. 1 (2007): 97–114.

Hirsch, Paul M. "Processing Fads and Fashions: An Organization-Set Analysis of Cultural Industry Systems." *American Journal of Sociology* 77, no. 4 (1972): 639–659.

Hutchins, Edwin. "How a Cockpit Remembers Its Speeds." *Cognitive Science* 19, no. 3 (1995): 265–288.

Johnston, Josee, and Shyon Baumann. "Democracy Versus Distinction: A Study of Omnivorousness in Gourmet Food Writing." *American Journal of Sociology* 113, no. 1 (2007): 165–204.

Katz, Daniel, and Robert L. Kahn. *The Social Psychology of Organizations*. New York: John Wiley and Sons, 1966.

Kirschbaum, Charles. "Jazz: Structural Changes and Identity Creation in Cultural Movements." In *Only Connect: Neat Words, Networks and Identities*, ed. Martin Kornberger and Siegfried Gudergan. Copenhagen: Copenhagen Business School Press, 2006.

Koestenbaum, Wayne. *Andy Warhol*. New York: Lipper/Viking, 2001.

Kuhn, Thomas S. *The Structure of Scientific Revolutions*. Chicago: University of Chicago Press, 1996.

Lainer-Vos, Dan, and Paolo Parigi. "The Miracle Maker, the Acolytes and the Church." *Social Science History* (forthcoming).

Lane, Christel. "Culinary Culture and Globalization: An Analysis of British and German Michelin-Starred Restaurants." *British Journal of Sociology* 62, no. 4 (2011): 696–717.

Lane, Christel. *The Cultivation of Taste: Chefs and the Organization of Fine Dining*. Oxford: Oxford University Press, 2014.

Lane, Christel. "The Michelin-Starred Restaurant Sector as a Cultural Industry: A Cross-National Comparison of Restaurants in the UK and Germany." *Food, Culture and Society: An International Journal of Multidisciplinary Research* 13, no. 4 (2010): 493–519.

Latour, Bruno. "Give Me a Laboratory and I Will Raise the World." In *Science Observed*, ed. K. D. Knorr-Cetina and M. Mulkay, 141–170. London: Sage, 1983.

Latour, Bruno. *The Pasteurization of France*. Cambridge, Mass.: Harvard University Press, 1993.

Latour, Bruno. *Reassembling the Social: An Introduction to Actor-Network-Theory*. New York: Oxford University Press, 2005.

Leifer, Eric M., and Harrison C. White. "A Structural Approach to Markets." In *Intercorporate Relations: The Structural Analysis of Business*, ed. Mark S. Mizruchi and Michael Schwartz. Cambridge: Cambridge University Press, 1987.

Leschziner, Vanina. *At the Chef's Table: Culinary Creativity in Elite Restaurants*. Stanford: Stanford University Press, 2015.

Lester, Richard K., and Michael J. Piore. *Innovation: The Missing Dimension*. Cambridge, Mass.: Harvard University Press, 2004.

Lipset, Seymour M. *Political Man: The Social Bases of Politics*. Garden City, N.Y.: Doubleday, 1960.

Lofland, John. "Becoming a World-Saver Revisited." *American Behavioral Scientist* 20, no. 6 (1977): 805–818.

Lofland, John, and Rodney Stark. "Becoming a World-Saver: A Theory of Conversion to a Deviant Perspective." *American Sociological Review* 30, no. 6 (1965): 862–875.

Luhmann, Niklas. *Organización y Decisión*. Spanish ed. Trans. Dario Rodriguez. Mexico City: Herder, 2010.

Luhmann, Niklas. *Organización y Decisión: Autopoiesis, Acción y Entendimiento Comunicativo*. Barcelona and Mexico City: Anthropos Editorial and Universidad Iberoamericana, 1997.

March, James G. "Exploration and Exploitation in Organizational Learning." *Organization Science* 2, no. 1 (1991): 71–87.

March, James G., and Herbert A. Simon. *Organizations*. Cambridge: Blackwell, 1993.

Mennell, Stephen. *All Manners of Food: Eating and Taste in England and France from the Middle Ages to the Present*. New York: Basil Blackwell, 1985.

Merton, Robert K. *On Social Structure and Science*. Chicago: University of Chicago Press, 1996.

Merton, Robert K. "Social Structure and Anomie." *American Sociological Review* 3, no. 5 (1938): 672–682.

Merton, Robert K. "The Thomas Theorem and the Matthew Effect." *Social Forces* 74, no. 2 (1995): 379–424.

Merton, Robert K. "The Unanticipated Consequences of Purposive Social Action." *American Sociological Review* 1, no. 6 (1936): 894–904.

Myhrvold, Nathan, Chris Young, and Maxime Bilet. *Modernist Cuisine: The Art and Science of Cooking.* 5 vols. Seattle: Cooking Lab, 2011.

Okhuysen, Gerardo A., and Kathleen M. Eisenhardt. "Integrating Knowledge in Groups: How Formal Interventions Enable Flexibility." *Organization Science* 13, no. 4 (2002): 370–386.

Opazo, M. Pilar. "Discourse as a Driver of Innovation: The Case of elBulli Restaurant." *International Journal of Gastronomy and Food Science* 1, no. 2 (2012): 82–89.

Padgett, John F., and Paul D. McLean. "Organizational Invention and Elite Transformation: The Birth of Partnership Systems in Renaissance Florence." *American Journal of Sociology* 111, no. 5 (2006): 1463–1568.

Padgett, John F., and Walter W. Powell. "The Problem of Emergence." In *The Emergence of Organizations and Markets*, ed. John F. Padgett and Walter W. Powell. Princeton: Princeton University Press, 2012.

Parasecoli, Fabio. "The Chefs, the Entrepreneurs, and Their Patrons." In *Gastropolis: Food and New York City*, ed. Annie Hauck-Lawson and Jonathan Deutsch. New York: Columbia University Press, 2009.

Pearlman, Alison. *Smart Casual: The Transformation of Gourmet Restaurant Style in America.* Chicago: University of Chicago Press, 2013.

Pitte, Jean-Robert. "The Rise of the Restaurant." In *Food: A Culinary History from Antiquity to the Present*, ed. Massimo Montanari and Jean Louis Flandrin, trans. Albert Sonnenfeld. New York: Columbia University Press, 1999.

Rao, Hayagreeva, Philippe Monin, and Rodolphe Durand. "Institutional Change in Toque Ville: Nouvelle Cuisine as an Identity Movement in French Gastronomy." *American Journal of Sociology* 108, no. 4 (2003): 795–843.

Rodriguez, Dario, and M. Pilar Opazo. *Comunicaciones de la Organización.* Santiago: Ediciones Universidad Católica de Chile, 2007.

Rozin, Paul. "Why We Eat What We Eat, and Why We Worry About It." *Bulletin of the American Academy of Arts and Sciences* 50, no. 55 (1997): 26–48.

Santamaria, Santi. *La Cocina al Desnudo: Una Vision Renovadora del Mundo de la Gastronomia.* Madrid: Temas de Hoy, 2008.

Schumpeter, Joseph A. *The Theory of Economic Development.* Cambridge, Mass.: Harvard University Press, 1934.

Selznick, Philip. *The Organizational Weapon: A Study of Bolshevik Strategy and Tactics.* New York: Free Press, 1960.

Senge, Peter M. *The Fifth Discipline: The Art and Practice of the Learning Organization.* New York: Doubleday, 1990.

Shore, Elliott. "The Development of the Restaurant." In *Food: The History of Taste,* ed. Paul Freedman. Berkeley: University of California Press, 2007.

Simmel, Georg. "Fashion." *American Journal of Sociology* 62, no. 6 (1957): 541–558.

Slavich, Barbara, and Fabrizio Castellucci. "Wishing upon a Star: How Apprentice-Master Similarity, Status and Career Stage Affect Critics' Evaluations of Former Apprentices in the Haute Cuisine Industry." *Organization Studies,* forthcoming.

Soler, Juli, Albert Adrià, and Ferran Adrià. *elBulli 1998–2002.* Barcelona: elBullibooks, 2002.

Soler, Juli, Albert Adrià, and Ferran Adrià. *elBulli 1983–1993.* Barcelona: elBullibooks, 2004.

Soler, Juli, Albert Adrià, and Ferran Adrià. *elBulli 2003–2004.* Barcelona: elBullibooks, 2005.

Stark, David. "Recombinant Property in East European Capitalism." *American Journal of Sociology* 101, no. 4 (1996): 993–1027.

Stark, David. *The Sense of Dissonance: Accounts of Worth in Economic Life.* Princeton: Princeton University Press, 2009.

Stinchcombe, Arthur L. "New Sociological Microfoundations for Organizational Theory: A Postscript." In *Social Structure and Organizations Revisited,* ed. Michael Lounsbury and Marc J. Ventresca. Amsterdam: JAI, 2002.

Svejenova, Silviya. "The Path with the Heart: Creating the Authentic Career." *Journal of Management Studies* 42, no. 5 (2005): 947–974.

Svejenova, Silviya, Marcel Planellas, and Luis Vives. "An Individual Business Model in the Making: A Chef's Quest for Creative Freedom." *Long Range Planning* 43, nos. 2–3 (2010): 408–430.

Taylor, Frederick W. *Principles of Scientific Management.* New York: Harper and Brothers, 1967.

Thompson, James. *Organizations in Action.* New York: McGraw Hill, 1967.

Uzzi, Brian, and Jarrett Spiro. "Collaboration and Creativity." *American Journal of Sociology* 111 (2005): 447–504.

Van de Ven, Andrew H. "Central Problems in the Management of Innovation." *Management Science* 32, no. 5 (1986): 590–607.

Warde, Alan. "Imagining British Cuisine: Representations of Culinary Identity in the Good Food Guide, 1951–2007." *Food, Culture and Society: An International Journal of Multidisciplinary Research* 12, no. 2 (2009): 151–171.

Weber, Max. *Economy and Society: An Outline of Interpretive Sociology.* Berkeley: University of California Press, 1968.

Weber, Max. "From Max Weber: Essays in Sociology." In *From Max Weber: Essays in Sociology,* ed. and trans. H. H. Gerth and C. Wright Mills. New York: Oxford University Press, 1946.

Weber, Max. *The Protestant Ethic and the Spirit of Capitalism.* Trans. Talcott Parsons. New York: Dover, 2003.

Weber, Max. *The Theory of Social and Economic Organization.* New York: Free Press, 1947.

Weber, Steven. *The Success of Open Source.* Cambridge, Mass.: Harvard University Press, 2004.

Weick, Karl E. "The Collapse of Sensemaking in Organizations: The Mann Gulch Disaster." *Administrative Science Quarterly* 38, no. 4 (1993): 628–652.

Weick, Karl E. "Introductory Essay: Improvisation as a Mindset for Organizational Analysis." *Organization Science* 9, no. 5 (1998): 543–555.

Weick, Karl E. *Sensemaking in Organizations.* Thousand Oaks, Calif.: Sage, 1995.

Weick, Karl E. *The Social Psychology of Organizing.* New York: Random House, 1979.

White, Harrison C. *Identity and Control: How Social Formations Emerge.* 2nd ed. Princeton: Princeton University Press, 2008.

White, Harrison C. "Where Do Markets Come From?" *American Journal of Sociology* 87, no. 3 (1981): 517–547.

White, Harrison C., and Cynthia A. White. *Canvases and Careers: Institutional Change in the French Painting World.* Chicago: University of Chicago Press, 1993.

Wolff, Kurt H., ed. *The Sociology of Georg Simmel.* New York: Free Press, 1964.

Appendix

Research Methods and Data Collection

T hree main different methods were used in this study: in-depth interviews, participant observations, and analysis of archival data. This multi-method approach offered me the possibility of incorporating the considerable amount of information already available about elBulli and also allowed for new patterns to emerge from the triangulation of data.[1] During the process of data collection, I paid special attention to the terms and issues voiced by my informants so as to generate opportunities to discover new concepts, rather than simply confirming existing theories and interpretations.[2] Below I detail each of the methods used and the different kind of information that each provided to my investigation.

In-Depth Interviews

I conducted 95 in-depth interviews with culinary professionals connected and unconnected to elBulli, both in Spain and in the United States. These interviews involved: retrospective accounts of members of elBulli (gathered before the closing of the restaurant and during the organization's transformation), culinary professionals who had worked at elBulli and left, purveyors and collaborators of elBulli, and former apprentices of elBulli restaurant who were working in different parts of the world at the time of the study. Interviews with outsiders of elBulli included: chefs (most of whom worked or owned haute cuisine restaurants at the time of the study), gastronomic critics, faculty members of culinary institutes, and food scholars from widely disparate fields ranging from science, to history, to business and food science. Some individuals were interviewed on repeated occasions, especially those who were current or former members of the elBulli organization. With one exception at the end of the study, I decided not to reveal the identity of my interviewees so as to call attention to the collective patterns that emerge across the individuals' accounts and the social process that they revealed, as opposed to the subjects' personal views and beliefs. In terms of identification, I also decided to use the pronoun *he* to refer to study participants, irrespective of their gender, given the high predominance of men in my research and also in the high-end restaurant sector at large.

Over a period of sixteen months, I spent time in Spain and the United States recruiting and interviewing people. I recruited individuals in person or via e-mail and followed a method of snowball sampling from multiple starts. That is to say, I used diverse sources as starting points to contact potential participants, such as publicly available information on people who had worked at or had written about elBulli. Also, I attended gastronomic events and workshops of various kinds where I could meet chefs or other culinary professionals. Several connections with potential participants happened informally. Many times, after I said a few words about my research, people happened to know someone who had worked at elBulli or had a friend from college who was now a chef at a high-end restaurant. In Barcelona, for instance, when I told my host about my study, she mentioned that her mother had a friend who lived in a small town an hour away from Barcelona, who knew a very famous chef. Perhaps, this Catalonian woman suggested, I would be interested in interviewing her. The chef happened to be Carme Ruscalleda, the female chef with the most Michelin stars in the world. A week later, I was taking a train to her famous restaurant Sant Pau. Many of the connections that I made during my research occurred in a similar manner.

Interviews typically lasted one hour and fifteen minutes; the shortest was thirty minutes and the longest lasted more than three hours. The majority of the interviews were conducted in person. Some, specifically those with individuals who were in a different geographic location than I, were conducted via phone. Three subjects opted for e-mailing answers to me because, as they explained, they did not have time to meet but wanted to contribute to my research.[3] Interviews were conducted in Spanish or in English according to the individuals' preferences.

The questionnaire asked individuals about their professional trajectory and then advanced a series of questions about their experiences and views of the gastronomy field and of elBulli. These questions varied according to the individual's relationship with elBulli or Adrià. I asked chefs about their views on innovation in cuisine and about their ways of approaching creativity in their daily work. At the end of each interview, I delved into the individuals' knowledge and thoughts about Adrià's new organization, the elBulli Foundation, and finished by asking if they could recommend someone else that I could talk to, who might have an opinion similar to or different than theirs. It is important to note that interviews were semi-structured; hence, although a set of predefined questions was established, I was open to new or unforeseen issues emerging during the conversation. For this reason, conversations usually followed different paths according to the individuals' knowledge and experiences. All interviews were recorded and transcribed.

To my surprise, it was not difficult to find individuals who wanted to participate in my study. On the contrary, they seemed curious about my investigation—perhaps the same kind of curiosity that elBulli and Adrià ignites in many people interested in food and fine dining. Chefs especially seemed enthusiastic to talk about their creative processes, and I could see that they enjoyed the exercise of verbalizing how it is that they do what they do. As one interviewee remarked, "It is curious the things that one asks oneself, when being asked." Often they showed me pictures of their work, or the books that inspired them, as a way of illustrating arguments made in the conversation. On a few occasions, chefs asked if I could give them a copy of the recording because they thought that things they said would be useful in their staff meetings or for a conference presentation that they had to prepare. After one interview, for example, one Michelin-starred chef mentioned, "If I would have known that I was going to say something useful for my own work, I would have taken notes of the conversation myself!"

Interviews were conducted at places selected by the individuals. In the case of chefs, we usually met at the restaurants where they worked, most often between shifts or early in the morning. Most of the chefs were wearing their chef coats during our conversations, since they had just come out of the kitchen. Prior to the interview, I was often given a brief guided tour of their restaurants. They showed me the kitchen, indicating where the different kitchen stations were, and explained to me how they organized their work on a daily basis. Then we sat at a table inside the restaurant, usually the one closest to the kitchen or to the restaurant's bar, while other staff members prepared for the next service, performing tasks like sweeping the floor, folding tablecloths, or moving boxes to the kitchen. Other times, they took me to a separate room in the restaurant to talk, often on a second floor, which usually had a table, a few chairs, some cookbooks, and press clippings of recognitions of the chef or the restaurant.

I took extensive notes immediately after each interview, in which I described the setting and the main issues raised in each conversation. In these notes, I tried to carefully distinguish between my personal impressions and thoughts during the interview and what actually happened. At the end of this Appendix, readers will find a list of the people who participated in the interviews for the study.

On a personal note, I find it important to share that, while being a graduate student living on a tight budget, I struggle to sneak into some of the restaurants where my interviewees worked. By taking the guest's perspective, I hoped to experience firsthand how the chef's creative approaches, which they had articulated in words, were manifested in actual dishes and in the dining experience at their restaurants. As a researcher, I believe that complementing the actual products of my interviewee's work with their narratives was an instructive experience. It allowed me to have a different "taste" of my data and to look at it from a new angle.

Participant Observations

Parallel to the interviews, I did participant observations at gastronomic conferences, fairs, and events where culinary professionals gathered. These observations allowed me to see the different scenarios where they meet and the interactions that occurred there, ranging from the chefs' staging of their work, to the purveyors' presentations of their products or services, to culinary competitions in which professionals participate. The scope of these conferences and events varied widely; whereas some were organized almost exclusively for chefs and were relatively small in size (300 to 400 participants), others were open to the public and were visited by thousands of people over a period of a few consecutive days. Broadly, these experiences gave me the opportunity to engage in casual conversations with many culinary professionals and to explore the role that these settings played in their work.

I found that these meetings were not too different from academic conferences; they offered a platform for professionals to meet with colleagues, to present their work, and to be exposed to the work of others. Good food abounded at these meetings, which contributed to a pleasant environment for socializing as well as for unexpected things to occur. Once, for instance, following a casual conversation, I was invited to be part of a jury for a competition on grilled beef. Without having time to ask what this task would require—or certainly to explain that I hardly ever eat red meat—I was taken to a room with sixty other judges who were ready to evaluate ten big pieces of beef (a total of two pounds or so) according to their taste, texture, and cooking time. As a whole, instances like this one provided me with valuable opportunities to understand the social interactions that occurred between chefs and other professionals of the culinary field.

Most interesting for the purposes of my research were the many times when meeting participants would mention elBulli or Ferran Adrià. During these conversations, it was common for people to express their impressions of the organization's work or to share anecdotes of previous meetings where they had seen members of elBulli presenting their work. Adrià also gave formal talks at some of these events, which offered me the opportunity to listen to his views on broad topics such as the state of the art in haute cuisine or the role of chefs in society, as I described in chapter 3. In addition to the intrinsic interest that Adrià's accounts had for my study, it was helpful for me to observe how people reacted to his views and to ask them what their thoughts were after Adrià's talks had taken place.

I also conducted participant observations at different branches of the elBulli organization and at meetings related to elBulli's new organization, the elBulli Foundation. I visited the elBulli restaurant a week before its closure and attended the team's daily meetings, first of the wait staff and then the kitchen staff. After the restaurant closed, I attended meetings and workshops with Adrià and members of Telefónica R&D, which provided insights on different projects of the elBulli Foundation. At intervals, I also did observations at the elBulli workshop, which, as I indicated, was elBulli members' first center of operation during the organization's transformation. My observations at this workshop or *el taller*, offered a window into the dynamics that characterized elBulli team's daily work: how they used the physical space, how tasks were distributed, and how they related to each other, as well as other informal aspects of their work, such as where they go to for lunch or the inside jokes that they regularly make about each other. In gathering these data I paid special attention to the divergences between the actual practices that I observed and what they described in their narratives, as well as to new information or tensions that might emerge.

During the course of a day, I followed elBulli's members around the workshop and occasionally interrupted them with questions. I took detailed notes of every conversation. At the beginning, I wrote down everything that I was seeing and took pictures of the hundreds of diagrams, tables, and lists that were displayed on the large boards that covered every wall of elBulli workshop. Once I had a better sense of how they worked, I developed a series of diagrams, pictures, and conceptual maps of my own, similar to those they developed, and used them to ask questions. This method was very helpful in clarifying information that I collected, and in learning about new aspects of the workings of elBulli and the projects related to the elBulli Foundation that did not easily emerge in formal interviews. I also think that this helped elBulli's members realize that I knew a fair amount about their work and the workings of organizations. Adrià began calling me when something was happening so that I could take notes on it or asking me to work on things that could be useful for them, such as making a list of words that could be included in elBulli Foundation's "new dictionary of creativity" or making diagrams that could be hang on the workshop's walls. One day, based on a conversation we had, Adrià asked me to draw a "map" of elBulli's creative team. After I showed it to him, he said, "Good. Now, let's do another one, but including time in it." And then he added, ". . . one more thing . . . if you are not effective, I'll give you a hard time!" (¡Si no eres efectiva, te dare una bronca!). I only realized that he was joking when I heard him laughing on his way to the office next door. As time passed, I could recognize that some of the ideas that emerged in my conversations with Adrià and his team were included in their conversations, and notes that indicated "Pilar's research" became part of the team's maps.

My study not only created opportunities for them to think differently about their work, but also impacted my own way of working. A few months after I started my fieldwork, I found myself making conceptual maps of my research at my office at Columbia University. I incessantly drew lists and rearranged diagrams to structure my findings and the ways in which they were shaping the story that I was seeing.

Besides the elBulli workshop, I visited other branches of the elBulli organization, such as elBulli Carme, the space dedicated to business activities and the ALICIA foundation, cofounded by Adrià, and known as the "social branch" of elBulli, focused on researching and promoting healthy dietary habits.

Finally, it is worthwhile noting that mine was not an ethnography in which one settles down in a place and follows the subjects in action. It was rather a traveling ethnography, marked by continuous trips back and forth from New York to Barcelona. In this regard, my research mirrored the subjects that I was studying; Adrià himself was constantly traveling, and members of elBulli gathered only intermittently at the elBulli workshop when the construction of the new foundation was taking place. This fact offered an important flavor to my relationship with elBulli's team, one that resonates closely with the figure of the stranger depicted by Simmel.[4] As in Simmel's account, my comings and goings represented constant shifts from intense periods of involvement and closeness—being around Adrià and his team can be nothing but intense—to periods of detachment and disconnection. I believe that this dynamic was vital for developing a critical stance upon my subject of study and also for developing my own picture of the world that I was observing.

Archival Analysis and Other Sources

To enhance my understanding of elBulli's work and historical trajectory, I carefully examined the organization's archives, many of which were presented at a 2012–2013 exhibition at Palau Robert, a public center in Barcelona. These archives contained information about the restaurant since its founding in 1963, including numerous records: Adrià's personal notes on elBulli's cuisine, old menus, pictures, plans, books, and videos of the organization's practices and procedures. During the exhibition, I also had the opportunity to see how visitors made sense of these materials.

For my analysis, I also drew on documentation made available to me by members of elBulli during the organization's reinvention, which included a series of calendars, maps, and memos of meetings mainly related to the elBulli Foundation, as well as other materials written and presented at conferences or courses by the organization's members. Finally, I transcribed and analyzed a number of public talks given by Adrià in different cities around the world, many of which were part of his collaboration with Telefónica Corporation. A list of these events is included at the end of this Appendix.

All the data gathered were coded according to a definite set of categories and principles defined based on both the major terms and concepts raised by informants and those considered relevant by the researcher. The coding of the data was then systematically analyzed using the qualitative software NVivo.

List of Individuals Interviewed

Interviewees who participated in the study

Members of elBulli (mostly repeated interviews): Name of interviewee, Working position

Ferran Adrià, Chef and Owner
Albert Adrià, Former Creative Director (until 2008)
Oriol Castro, Head Chef and Creative Director (2008–2011)
Mateu Casañas, Head Chef Pastry
Eduard Xatruch, Head Chef
David López, Front-of-the-house tasks and IT tasks
Ferran Centelles, Sommelier
Josep María Pinto, Writer and Editor

Albert Raurich, Former Head Chef and part of the creative team
Félix Meana, Formerly, front-of-the-house tasks
Rubén García, Former Head Chef and part of the creative team

*Chefs in the United States: Name of interviewee, Affiliation at interview,
Working position at interview*

Wylie Dufresne, WD~50, Chef and Owner
Maxime Bilet, Author of *Modernist Cuisine*, Chef and Researcher
Johnny Iuzzini, Jean Georges, Executive Pastry Chef
Lee Wolen, Eleven Madison Park, Sous-Chef
Michael Laiskonis, (formerly) Le Bernardin, Executive Pastry
   Chef and Creative Director of Institute of Culinary Education
   (ICE)
Kevin Lasko, Park Avenue, Head Chef
George Mendes, Aldea, Chef and Owner
Jose Andrés, ThinkFoodGroup, Chef and Owner (answered selected
   questions via e-mail)
Brian Sullivan, Ai Fiori, Pastry Chef
David Carmichael, Gilt, Head Pastry Chef
Shaun Hergatt, SHO Shaun Hergatt, Chef and Owner
Harold Moore, Commerce, Chef and Owner
Roger Martinez, Bouley Restaurant, Chef
Dominique Ansel, Dominique Ansel Bakery, Pastry Chef and Owner
   (answered selected questions via e-mail)
Michael Cirino, Arazorashinyknife initiative, Founder and Director

*Chefs in Spain: Name of interviewee, Affiliation at interview,
Working position at interview*

Carme Ruscalleda, Sant Pau, Chef and Owner
Joan Roca, El Celler de Can Roca, Chef and Owner
Juan Mari Arzak, Arzak, Chef and Owner
Martin Berasategui, Berasategui, Chef and Owner
Paco Peréz, Miramar, Chef and Owner
Christián Escribà, Escribà Bakery, Chef and Owner
Diego Guerrero, Club Allard, Head Chef
Francis Paniego, El Portal Echaurren, Chef and Owner
Angel León, Aponiente, Chef and Owner
Carl Borg, Micenplace, Founder and CEO

Stagiaires of elBulli: Name of interviewee, Year at elBulli,
Working position at interview

Will Goldfarb (1999), Ku De Ta, Chef and Owner, Indonesia

Katie Button (2008–2009), Curate, Chef and Owner, Ashville, Tenn.,
USA

Robert Truitt (2007), Altamarea Group, Executive Pastry Chef,
New York, USA

Chad Brauze (2007), Daniel Boulud, R&D Chef, New York, USA

Jeffrey Flinkstein (2008), Hof Kelsten Bakery, Chef and Owner,
Montreal, Canada

Francisco Araya (2008), Spanish Cultural Center, Head Chef, Santiago,
Chile

Julieta Piñon (2008), 81 Restaurant, Tokyo, Japan

Najat Kaanache (2010–2011), elBulli Apprentice final season, 2011

Juan Suarez de Lezo, elBulli Apprentice final season, 2011

Nil Dulcet, elBulli Apprentice, final season 2011

Brandon Difiglio, elBulli Apprentice, final season 2011

Collaborators and purveyors of elBulli: Name of interviewee, affiliation,
Working position at interview

Luki Huber (repeated interviews), Luki Huber, Industrial Designer

Marta Méndez, Self-Employed, Graphic Designer/Pattern Maker

Rosa Mirés, Porto Muiños, Business Owner

Marc Calabuig, International Cooking Concepts (ICC), Founder and
CEO

Annette Abstoss, Abstoss World Gastronomy, Food Connoisseur/Gourmet

Pere Castells, ALICIA Foundation, Head Researcher

Toni Massanes, ALICIA Foundation, Director

Heloise Vilaseca, ALICIA Foundation, Lab Director

Patricia Cabrera, MBA IESE, MBA Student

Scholars: Name of interviewee, Affiliation at interview, Department

Paul Freedman, Yale University, History

Claudi Mans, Universidad de Barcelona, Chemistry

Fabio Parasecoli, New School, Food Studies

Anne McBride, New York University, Food Studies

Cesar Vega, Mars Inc., Food Science

Julián Villanueva, IESE Business School

Faculty members at culinary institutes: Name of interviewee, Affiliation at interview, Working position at interview

Tim Ryan, Culinary Institute of America (CIA), President (New York, USA)

James Briscione, Institute of Culinary Education (ICE), Chef Instructor (New York, USA)

Jordi Butrón, SpaiSucre, Founder and Director (Barcelona, Spain)

Vinyet Capdet, CETT, Studies Coordinator (Barcelona, Spain)

Gastronomic critics/writers: Name of interviewee, Affiliation at interview

Frank Bruni, *The New York Times* (answered selected questions via e-mail)

Paul Adams, *New York Sun* (formerly)

Marta Fernández, *Gastroeconomy*

Xavier Agulló, CookCircus and 7Canibales (repeated interviews)

Pau Arenós (author of *La Cocina de los Valientes*, 2012)

Note: Working position included as stated by individuals at the moment of the interview.

List of Sites of Participant Observations and Other Sites of Data Collection

Visits to branches of elBulli organization, Dates

elBulli Restaurant, July 2011, Girona, Spain

elBulli Carmen, October 2011 and January 2013, Barcelona, Spain

elBulli Workshop, March 2012 to January 2013, Barcelona, Spain

ALICIA Foundation, July 2011, Manresa, Spain

Attendance at public events, Dates

Telefónica y Ferran Adrià, "Partners for Transformation," March 2011, New York, USA

Talk at New Museum, Alice Waters, April 2011, New York, USA

Ferran Adrià, "Ideas for Transformation," Columbia University, Business School, October 2011, New York, USA

Project presentation, "elBulli Foundation," November 2011, Telefónica Digital, Barcelona, Spain

Taste of T, *New York Times* Style Magazine, November 2011, New York, USA

Experimental Cuisine Collective (ECC), eight Monthly Meetings, 2011–2013, New York, USA, including book event, "The Kitchen as Laboratory" with editor Cesar Vega and contributors, February 2012.

Public exhibit "Ferran Adrià and elBulli: Risk, Freedom and Creativity" at Palau Robert, Barcelona, Spain, January 2012.

Talk Show, MACBA, Ferran Adrià and Enric Ruiz Geli, July 2012, Barcelona, Spain

New York Wine and Food Festival, Nathan Myhrvold, October 2012, New York, USA

New York Wine and Food Festival, Daniel Boulud Panel Discussion, October 2013, New York, USA

92y.org, Talk by René Redzepi, "Work in Progress," November 2013, New York, USA

The Drawing Center, Ferran Adrià, "Notes on Creativity," January 2014, New York, USA

Attendance at gastronomic conferences and fairs, Dates

"GastroTech Days" Conference, October 2011, Barcelona, Spain

Gastronomika, November 2011, San Sebastian, Spain

Alimentaria, March 2012, Barcelona, Spain

MAD Symposium, July 2012, Copenhagen, Denmark

Star Chefs, September 2013, New York, USA

Public Talks transcribed of Ferran Adrià, Dates

Madrid Fusión press conference: Ferran Adrià and Juli Soler, March 2010 and 2011, Madrid, Spain

Food and Wine Festival: Ferran Adrià, October 2010, New York, USA

Ferran Adrià and Telefónica: "Partners for Transformation," March 2011, New York, USA

Talk at Business School Columbia University: Ferran Adrià and Telefónica, October 2011, New York, USA

Talk at Google Company: Ferran Adrià., October 2011, San Francisco, California, USA

Talk at Gastrotechdays Conference: Ferran Adrià, October 2011, Telefónica Digital, Barcelona, Spain

Ferran Adrià and Telefónica: "Partners for Transformation," November 2011, Buenos Aires, Argentina

IESE, Global Alumni Reunion 2011: Ferran Adrià, November 2011, Barcelona, Spain

Ferran Adrià and Telefónica: "Partners for Transformation," June 2012, Santiago, Chile

Lecture Series, Harvard Course "Science and Cooking": Ferran Adrià, December 2010, 2011, and 2012, Boston, Massachusetts, USA

Index

Page numbers in *italics* refer to figures and tables.